ADVANCE PRAISE FOR

Literacies, Lies, & Silences

"Heather E. Bruce's compelling and insightful description of the power of writing in a high school women's studies class provides new and important constructions of writing, gender, and the complexities of growing up female in America."

Elizabeth A. Flynn, Professor of Humanities,
Michigan Technological University

"The high school students enrolled in women's studies classes at Aspen Grove are lucky to know Heather E. Bruce, but the readers of this important ethnography are even luckier to hear the record of what these students wrote about—and how they imagined their future selves. Candid, troubling, thoughtful, the stories of these students are at the heart of a book that will sometimes haunt you. This book is a valuable and extensive analysis of how gender is produced in language and how in changing that language we can transform lives. Bruce frames her study with a thoughtful, nuanced discussion of contemporary theories and theorists. By rereading Janet Emig, synthesizing Judith Butler, Lester Faigley, Susan Miller, and others, and returning body, gender, and sexual experiences to a discussion of composing, Bruce offers intelligence and hope to the often fraught discourse between essentialists and social constructionists. She also offers clear suggestions for how we might reconfigure composition pedagogies to better align the feminist and postmodern in today's public classrooms, allowing all students, especially girls and women, to compose lives rich in possibility and reality. I can't wait to order this book for my graduate classes in composition theory and pedagogy."

Sarah Jane Sloane, Associate Professor of English,
Colorado State University

"In *Literacies, Lies, & Silences,* Heather E. Bruce brings together a multidisciplinary body of scholarship on girls' psychosocial development, composition theory, and postmodern feminist theories to illuminate the vital function of writing in students' lives. The young women at Aspen Grove High School, whose women's studies class was the object of study, write to analyze and challenge powerful social ideologies that narrowly construct their lives. As they write, the students reconstruct transformative spaces for growth and agency that are unique to their own lives. Although this book foregrounds writing in a high school women's studies classroom, Bruce presents a compelling and lucid argument for the importance of writing in all disciplines, along with examples to guide teachers in creating empowering opportunities for their own students at all grade levels."

Joy S. Ritchie, Director of Women's Studies,
University of Nebraska-Lincoln

Literacies, Lies, & Silences

AC / SS

Adolescent Cultures, School & Society

Joseph L. DeVitis & Linda Irwin-DeVitis
General Editors

Vol. 20

PETER LANG
New York • Washington, D.C./Baltimore • Bern
Frankfurt am Main • Berlin • Brussels • Vienna • Oxford

Heather E. Bruce

Literacies, Lies, & Silences

Girls Writing Lives in the Classroom

PETER LANG
New York • Washington, D.C./Baltimore • Bern
Frankfurt am Main • Berlin • Brussels • Vienna • Oxford

Library of Congress Cataloging-in-Publication Data

Bruce, Heather E.
Literacies, lies, and silences:
girls writing lives in the classroom / Heather E. Bruce.
p. cm. — (Adolescent cultures, school and society; vol. 20)
Includes bibliographical references and index.
1. English language—Composition and exercises—Study and teaching
(Secondary)—United States—Case studies. 2. Women's studies—
United States—Case studies. 3. Women—Education (Secondary)—
United States—Case studies. 4. Feminism and education.
I. Title. II. Adolescent cultures, school & society; vol. 20.
LB1631 .B77   808′.042′0712—dc21   00-030644
ISBN 0-8204-5042-1
ISSN 1091-1464

Die Deutsche Bibliothek-CIP-Einheitsaufnahme

Bruce, Heather E.:
Literacies, lies, and silences:
girls writing lives in the classroom / Heather E. Bruce.
-New York; Washington, D.C./Baltimore; Bern;
Frankfurt am Main; Berlin; Brussels; Vienna; Oxford: Lang.
(Adolescent cultures, school and society; Vol. 20)
ISBN 0-8204-5042-1

Cover design by Joni Holst
Cover art by Nancy R. McMillan, McMillan Group Westport, CT

The paper in this book meets the guidelines for permanence and durability
of the Committee on Production Guidelines for Book Longevity
of the Council of Library Resources.

© 2003 Peter Lang Publishing, Inc., New York
275 Seventh Avenue, 28th Floor, New York, NY 10001
www.peterlangusa.com

Printed in the United States of America

To the women in my life who made this possible:

Emma Walker and the women's studies students at Aspen Grove High School

and

to the men in my life who have lived undaunted with the women in my life:

Dylan, Justin, and Bruce

Table of Contents

Acknowledgments

This is what you learned in college: A man desires the satisfaction of his desire; a woman desires the condition of desiring.... This is what you learned in graduate school: In every assumption is contained the possibility of its opposite.
—Pam Houston, "How to Talk to a Hunter"

For a project that culminates a decade of work, adequate acknowledgments seem both necessary and impossible. Many, many people have made indelible contributions to the completion of this work. I could not have done this without their support.

No words can convey my depth of gratitude and indebtedness to my dissertation advisor, Donna Deyhle, whose thorough reviews, insistence on excellence, and ongoing friendship helped to shape early drafts of this manuscript. Other members of my dissertation committee were instrumental in helping me design the study. Thomas Huckin suggested I reexamine the work of Janet Emig and introduced me to critical discourse analysis. Andrew Gitlin pushed me to think through the femininity of my teaching. Audrey Thompson directed me to Judith Butler and feminist performance theory. Kathryn Stockton provided an exemplary model of pedagogy and crossed boundaries to introduce me to Emma Walker.

I could have accomplished none of this without the friendship and collegial support of "Emma Walker" and Claudia Wright, who have taught me everything I know about making visible the invisible worlds of adolescent girls. It is on the back of their labor that my work was unburdened. The sentences are mine, but the foundational ideas originated with them.

I also must acknowledge, posthumously, women's studies student Emma Schmidt. Emma helped me most to understand young women's need for the habit of freedom and the courage to write and say exactly what they think; and I acknowledge all the students who elected women's studies at Aspen Grove High School from 1992 to 1996 for inviting me into their lives and telling me their stories. Thanks especially to Solo, JoAnna, Trisha, LeTisha, Sharon, Margaret, Louise, Alisa, Rachel, Kate, and Thomas.

I also am indebted to my writing groups which have worked with me on drafts along the way: Kathryn Fitzgerald and Scott Oates; Suzanne Holland, A. Susan Owen, and Karen Porter. Thanks also to Frank

Margonis, Julian Edgoose, and Laura Doctor Thornburg whose brilliant insights have always been exact and illuminating. Nancy Bristow and Sarah J. Sloane at the University of Puget Sound and G. G. Weix and Dawn Walsh at the University of Montana provided opportunities for me to get important feedback on the work. Christine Kline and Janet Emig welcomed me into their professional circles and gave generously of their support and time. My colleagues in the Department of English at the University of Montana have been enthusiastic supporters. Thanks especially to Jill Bergman, Casey Charles, Debra Magpie Earling, Katie Kane, and Mark Medvetz—wonderful friends and co-workers all.

My dear friend Nancy Rankin McMillan of the McMillan Group in Westport, CT, read the manuscript in order to illustrate the cover. The illustrations she developed visually depicted the nuanced complexities in the text and for those visions and her efforts I am grateful.

I also thank the members of the Steffensen Cannon family for their generous contribution in support of my graduate work at the University of Utah. Some revisions to the manuscript were made possible by a Martin Nelson junior sabbatical at the University of Puget Sound.

Joe and Linda Irwin DeVitis, Erik Fritz, Tatiana Bissell, Doug Goertzen and Jacqueline Pavlovic are to be commended for their help in shaping the final manuscript.

I am without question always and ever grateful to my sons, Dylan and Justin Brunjes, whose presence in my life gives meaning to everything I do. You shared your mother during the years of your adolescence so that she might do what was needed. Thank you both for continually showing me the way home and invariably reminding me about the need to laugh and to listen to the music. You have grown into manhood in most honorable ways. Finally, thanks to my husband, Bruce Adams, for the distractions, the reminders, and the questions that have pushed me toward completion of the project. Thanks for keeping me close to the heart of things and for teaching me that "Eventually all things merge into one, and a river runs through it." I, too, am "haunted by waters."

Although your names never appear in the text, they are written on the face of every word.

Heather E. Bruce
Missoula, Montana
September 2002

Introduction

Before Shakespeare's sister can come, we must have the habit of freedom and the courage to write and say exactly what we think.

—Carol Gilligan

A Decade of Gendered Learning

I first became interested in the ways in which girls' experiences in schools dramatically shift between their elementary and secondary school years between 1983 and 1987 when I was teaching a group of "gifted" male and female adolescents, who also were identified as having multiple emotional, cognitive, or behavioral "disabilities" in an alternative public school program designed "to meet their special needs." Over the course of their fifth- through ninth-grade years, I was their English teacher. I found these students to be the most engaging, challenging, delightful, and frustrating adolescents with whom I have ever worked.

Because of the uncommon professional advantage of teaching the same students over the entire course of their middle school years, I noticed a pattern of development among my female students, which both baffled and intrigued me. Girls who in the fifth and sixth grades were gregarious, outspoken, academic achievers turned over the course of the summer between their sixth- and seventh-grade years into sullen, silent, angry underachievers. If I had not known these students during their last years in elementary school, I might have reasonably concluded that the girls I was teaching in the seventh-, eighth-, and ninth-grade years were simply "poor" students.

The only insight I gained into these girls' behaviors came one day when a drama troupe visited from the nearby high school to give a performance to our students. The troupe of young men and women performed an interactive simulation to demonstrate the potentially negative effects of giving in to peer pressure. My girls acted unusually silly throughout the performance, but seeing them act out at all was a change of routine, which I welcomed. To my view, they were acting both "dumb" and "foolish," and I wanted to know why.

So I asked.

Julie rolled her eyes to the ceiling and looked at me as though I'd just flown in from Jupiter. She said, "Didn't you notice how cute those boys were? I can't believe you don't know that cute boys don't like smart girls. Everyone knows that!"

After lashing them with a stupidly impassioned lecture on the nonsense of such assumptions, I vowed that I would investigate this matter further; and if, as Julie speculated, I was the only one who did not know that "cute boys do not like smart girls," then I would at least gain scholarly and practical knowledge to remedy my cultural ignorance.

Indeed, I have...

Girls' Developmental Trajectory and Schools' Response

To wrestle with the concerns Julie raised, I read a great deal about the developmental and academic experiences of adolescent girls during their secondary school years. I discovered several explanations for the behavior I observed in Julie and her female classmates. What I found greatly disturbed me.

Most of the information I read in the early 1990s about girls' development during adolescence was news to me. As a classroom teacher, I had not been exposed to the ways in which girls' experiences during adolescence differed from boys' experiences. The vast amounts of information that are currently available to teachers regarding gender issues in the classroom (e.g., Brown and Gilligan; Caywood and Overing; Gabriel and Smithson; Gilligan, Lyons, and Hanmer; Orenstein; Sadker and Sadker) were unknown to me at the time. What I knew in the late 1980s was that adolescence is a time when the self stands at the crossroads between childhood and adulthood.

What I did not know was staggering.

For example, I did not know that until relatively recently much that has been written about adolescence in the fields of psychology, sociology, and educational studies has been derived from work with male subjects. In the late 1970s, educational psychologist Carol Gilligan conducted interviews with women who were pregnant and thinking about the difficult choices they faced (*In a Different Voice*). As a result of this work, Gilligan developed a stage theory of women's development and consequently began to inquire about the role of adolescence in that development. Although I had studied with Kohlberg and Gilligan in the mid-1970s, I was unaware of Gilligan's groundbreaking work on female moral and psychological development.

Gilligan suggests that girls develop in remarkably different ways from their male counterparts. Whereas the adolescent male experience is typified as a time of separation, adventure, and confidence-building, Gilligan typifies the female adolescent experience as one of attachment rather than separation. She writes in *Making Connections* that early adolescence is

> a critical time in girls' lives—a time when girls are in danger of losing their voices and thus losing connection with others, and also a time when girls, gaining voice and knowledge, are in danger of knowing the unseen and speaking the unspoken and thus losing connection with what is commonly taken to be "reality." (Making Connections 25)

Gilligan calls this period for girls a "crisis of connection" (*Making Connections* 24).

Others have discussed the female adolescent "crisis" as well. Simone de Beauvoir describes it in *The Second Sex* and reports that it is the result of girls' realization that men have the power and that their only power comes from consenting to become submissive adored objects. De Beauvoir suggests that girls suffer from "power envy" (278). Girls who were the subjects of their own lives during childhood become in adolescence the objects of others' lives (337). As a result, adolescent girls experience a conflict between their powerful autonomous childhood selves and their need as adolescents to be feminine and ultimately to become the pawns in someone else's power games. De Beauvoir writes that adolescent girls can only be, not act (358). During adolescence, girls struggle to find a place between their status as human beings and their vocation as females (336).

More recently, clinical psychologist Mary Pipher, whose best-elling book *Reviving Ophelia: Saving the Selves of Adolescent Girls* has helped significantly to spread the word about girls' experiences during adolescence. Pipher has studied the lives of adolescent girls in counseling situations and calls this period in girls' lives "the developmental Bermuda Triangle," the location where the selves of adolescent girls "disappear mysteriously in droves" (19). Pipher demonstrates that girls seem to lose themselves in adolescence and they know it (20). It is during this period that they experience rigorous training for the female role, a role that insists on selflessness, servitude, and silence. Pipher additionally articulates that self-esteem is based on the acceptance of all of one's thoughts and feelings. Girls lose confidence and their self-esteem suffers enormously because they disown themselves when they stop expressing certain thoughts and feelings (38).

As Julie and her peers had so aptly showed me, during the secondary school years, "the polarization between feminine attractiveness and independent intelligence comes to an absolute" (Rich, "Taking Women Students Seriously" 243). With puberty, girls face enormous cultural pressure to become feminine. The pressure comes from schools, print and visual media, advertisements, and peers. At this time, the culture expects girls to sacrifice parts of themselves. The rules are be attractive, be a lady, be unselfish by serving others, make relationships work, and be competent without complaint (Pipher 38–39). Therefore, girls are forced to choose between the androgeny of their childhood and the powerlessness of feminine adulthood. Just as I had noticed with Julie and her peers, Pipher describes how energetic and confident girls transform into shy and doubting young women. "Girls stop thinking, 'Who am I? What do I want?' and start thinking, 'What must I do to please others?'" (Pipher 22). In early adolescence, girls learn how important appearance is in defining social acceptability. Attractiveness is both a necessary and sufficient condition for girls' success (Brumberg xxiv).

Because many young women want desperately to fit into the feminine roles the culture has prescribed for them all the while that they disdain those roles, they frequently fall silent and slip into invisibility struggling with a diminished sense of self. Developmental theorists report that girls in white, mainstream, middle-class Western culture have relatively few affirming places or tools from which they can speak their experiences. The issues they struggle with during these years are barely discussed publicly. The language of adolescence available to describe this period in girls' lives does not fit their experiences. As a result, several of those who have studied the lives of girls during adolescent years have used the metaphor of "the underground" to characterize the place where the selfhood of adolescent girls resides (Gilligan, Lyons, and Hanmer).

Research on schooling and adolescent girls indicates that schooling provides little help to girls during puberty and adolescence. If an alternative reality is out there for girls, they probably will not find it in schools as we now know them. There are indications that widespread problems exist with the treatment of females in schools (American Association of University Women [AAUW] *Hostile Hallways*; Orenstein; Sadker and Sadker). In general, schooling disadvantages female students (Project on the Status and Education of Women). Schools are gender biased and discriminatory. Schooling was designed primarily for men and only secondarily, and as an afterthought, for young women (Tyack and Hansot). Beyond that, schools have contributed significantly to gender differentiation and sex-role socialization that privileges males (Nicholson). As well, comprehensive research indicates that young women experience a great deal of sexual harassment during their secondary school years. Addressing harassment is complicated by the fact that many young women are either unaware that they can insist that the school protect them from harassment, or they are afraid to report incidents of harassment (AAUW, *Hostile Hallways*; Stein, Marshall, and Tropp), or as I noticed with the students in my study, they view aggressive sexual behavior (such as grabbing the breasts, crotch, or buttocks) as benign flirtatiousness.

Additional problems occur for young women because secondary schools are conservative institutions. Gender differentiation that exacerbates male domination and female submissiveness is evident in the public American secondary school today. The standard American high school curriculum is generally devoid of the mention of women's work and women's accomplishments except as sidebars (Brown and Gilligan; Gilligan, *Making Connections*; Gilligan, Lyons, and Hanmer; McIntosh; Rich, *On Lies*; Spender, *Women of Ideas*; Whaley and Dodge). Girls read a history of Western civilization that is largely a record of men's lives and they see that men have most of the political and economic power. As girls study the history of Western civilization they become increasingly aware that history is the history of men. "Women's accomplishments are relegated to the lost and found" (Spender *Women of Ideas* 6). In high school, young women come face-to-face with the written traditions of mainstream American culture, which primarily value the lives and work of white men. (Gilligan et al.; Rich, *On Lies*; Spender *Women of Ideas*). As young women discover that women's knowledge, questions, lives, and voices have been largely omitted from curricular traditions valued in the schools, they often conclude that educational achievement brings with it what Mary Jacobus characterizes as a feeling of "alienation, repression, [and] division" (10).

Other research indicates that many secondary school teachers do not listen to female students. They largely dismiss the questions, comments, and written work of female students as frivolous and unrelated to disciplinary discussions and knowledge (Hall and Sandler, *A Chilly Climate*). Girls generally are called on less than boys, denied opportunities to succeed in areas in which boys are encouraged to excel, and taught to value neatness over innovation, appearance over intelligence (Brumberg; Sadker and Sadker). As a result, young women may decide to shy away both from the traditional dynamics of academic discourse and from the schools that enshrine it.

Teachers may now certainly be more aware than I was a decade ago of the gender distinctions among boys' and girls' experiences during adolescence and the ways that schooling disadvantages the young women we teach. Yet we still have too few instructional tools available to us to respond equitably in the classroom. Helping our students face gender stereotypes and overcome deeply held prejudices and personal insecurities can be a threat to adolescents' developing sense of femininity and/or masculinity—a threat to the very fabric of the social order, and a nearly impossible undertaking in public schools. Nonetheless, I set out to find more effective teaching strategies to address issues of gender concern in secondary classrooms.

Writing Up to Potential: Girls Revise
the Developmental Tale of Crisis

Several researchers investigating the lives and school experiences of adolescent girls urge them to struggle against the "loss of self" occasioned in traditional tales of female adolescent development by writing a different story. Writing, in Mary Pipher's view, becomes an opportunity and a place where young women can clarify, conceptualize, and evaluate their personal experiences. By writing their thoughts and feelings, Pipher proposes that young women can strengthen their sense of self (255). Writing becomes a location in which young women may act to revise the tale of pathology and crisis that currently illustrates the experiences of adolescent girls, a space in which young women may "encourage growth and train for resistance" (259). Likewise, Carol Gilligan suggests writing as a means of developing girls' intellect and voice and of establishing camaraderie with "grown women [who] might sustain girls' gaze and respond to girls' voices during turbulent adolescent times" ("Teaching Shakespeare's Sister" 25). Both of these researchers suggest that writing may act as a means to aid the personal, intellectual, and political action of young women.[1]

Because I identify primarily as a writing teacher and researcher, I am inclined to agree that writing might provide a useful means for framing varied ways to enact a female sense of self during the adolescent years and for providing the means for adolescent girls in schools to experience academic success. However, little has been done to study the effects of writing in the education of adolescent girls since Janet Emig's influential study of 12th-grade writers (*Composing Processes*). In the late 1960s, Janet Emig asked a cadre of eight 12th graders of above average and average ability—five girls and three boys—to give autobiographies of their writing experiences and to compose aloud three themes in the presence of a tape recorder and the investigator (*Composing Processes* 3). Emig formulated four hypotheses about the students' accounts of and Emig's observations of their writing behaviors that informed a virtual revolution in the way we have come to view the writing processes of students during the last three decades. Emig's findings were principally drawn from the writing behaviors of her primary informant, a young woman named Lynn.

Because of the historical significance of Emig's work, a feminist revision of her analysis, findings, and recommendations provides a useful trajectory from which to articulate the gendered effects of writing work in composition classrooms. As Patricia Sullivan points out, a fully realized feminist voice requires both reactive and proactive components—both feminist rereadings and critiques of androcentric discourse practices in the academy. Sullivan argues that empirically based studies of the relationships between gender and writing can transform social inequities and the relations of power they uncover (49). In light of Sullivan's argument, a proactive feminist reexamination of gendered composing practices in Emig's work—"the most influential piece of researcher inquiry in composition studies" (North 197)—is warranted.

In particular, the writing of two students in Emig's case studies—her primary informant, Lynn, and another student, Victoria—prompts consideration of the ways in which written discourse constructs these young women's views of "reality." Lynn's and Victoria's writing samples illustrate how the discursive organization of femininity and masculinity in culture does not just represent social relations—it constructs them. To examine the ways in which written discourse might jumpstart transformative educational projects for contemporary young women, it is helpful to understand theories of discourse that underlie constructivist views of learning.

Discourse is a complex concept, largely because there are so many conflicting definitions formulated from various theoretical standpoints. However, constructivist views of discourse suggest that

> Discourses are ways of behaving, interacting, valuing, thinking, believing, speaking, and often reading and writing that are accepted as instantiations of particular roles (or "types of people") by specific *groups of people*.... Discourses are ways of being "people like us." They are ways of being in the world; they are "forms of life." They are, thus, always and everywhere *social* and products of social histories. Language makes no sense outside of Discourses. (Gee, *Social Linguistics* viii)

Constructivist views of discourse emphasize the social relationships instructing rhetorical interactions between speaker and addressee or writer and reader. Constructivism in discourse theory articulates the ways in which power relations influence rhetorical choices between interlocutors in specific language exchanges. Moreover, this view emphasizes the processes of producing and interpreting speech and writing within the social contexts of actual language use. It examines how various discourses differently position people as speaking or writing subjects and mark their status in the "discourse community." This view suggests that conventions of language use in specific discourse communities construct mores of acceptable and unacceptable behavior in various social situations.

Each human being is a member of many "discourse communities" simultaneously, and each discourse in which a human being interacts represents one of multiple identities. Every discourse incorporates a taken-for-granted "theory" of what counts as a "normal" person and the "right" ways to think, feel, and behave for members of its "discourse community." All human actions are instantiations of usually tacit theories that empower or disempower people and groups of people as they interrelate across various discursive boundaries (Gee). The "who" we are and the "what" we are doing occur through a three-way simultaneous interaction among (a) our social or cultural group memberships; (b) a particular social language or mixture of them; and (c) a particular context; that is, a set of other people, objects, and locations (Gee 69). Therefore, a person's position as a discursive subject can be a powerful determinant of her lived experience, although discursive positioning is not necessarily coincident with the lives of "real" people (Fairclough; Fowler; Kress).

For example, females in the West, for thousands of years, have occupied a subject position subordinate to or, at the least, deviant from, the male, who is considered the "norm" or fully developed exemplar of the species (reported in Gee 185). The effects of this discursive positioning on the lived experiences of girls and women as a class have been widely studied.[2] One particularly representative example applies strategies of critical discourse analysis. Valerie Walkerdine and the Girls and Mathematics Unit investigated gendered discursive positions in a longitudinal study of children aged 4 to 15. They report that the discursive production of *femininity* as antithetical to *masculine rationality* is demonstrated to such an extent that femininity is equated with poor performance, even when the girl or woman in question is performing well in school.

Even though school girls' actual intellectual achievements indicate otherwise, the discursive interpretations that teachers assign to female performances in schools construe their achievements as "inferior" and "lacking brilliance" in relation to the interpretations teachers assign to the performances of males. Walkerdine argues that these discursive phenomena differentially organize the performances and achievements of boys and girls in school because *feminine behavior* occupies a subordinate subject position to *masculine intellect* in Western culture. In other words, regardless of how well girls and women actually perform, their abilities and achievements are rendered invisible by the "reality-constructing" effects of language, which position female as "other and less than" male (de Beauvoir).

Walkerdine and the Girls and Mathematics Unit invoke theoretical perspectives that are at the heart of critical discourse analysis. Theoretical perspectives also reveal how girls who revolt against pathologized norms are punished for acting out of "sugar and spice and everything nice" character. For example, if a girl protests expectations for life in "the underground" by dying her hair carrot orange and piercing her lips, eyebrows, nose, and tongue, she is designated "repulsive," "disgusting," "rebellious," and "ugly" (Brumberg 134–135). If a girl expresses her frustrations verbally, she is called a "bitch" (Joreen). If a girl experiments with her sexuality, she is called a "slut" (Holland & Eisenhart; Sharon Thompson; Wolf). If she withdraws from the cultural chaos of adolescence, she is diagnosed as "clinically depressed" (Pipher). If she wails in despair, she is labeled "hormonal" or told she must be "on the rag" (Daly). As a result of these discursive positionings, high school girls in public institutions are interpellated among the most powerless, insignificant, and self-effacing categories of people (Fiske). Given the ways in which discourse has served to disenfranchise young women in educational settings, is it possible to imagine that written discourse might enable young women to write a different "reality constructing" script? Can writing allow writers "to imagine alternate, possible, and resistant worlds," as Deborah Brandt suggests, and enable adolescent girls to reconfigure the powerlessness and insignificance that currently represents their educational experiences?

Contained in these questions are complications that can be profitably analyzed through the discursive lens of feminist performance theory (Butler, *Bodies that Matter, Gender Trouble*). Performance theory's usefulness to this project includes its primary assumption that gender is produced in language—that gender is a fictional text culturally inscribed on sexed bodies at birth. Although fictively produced, cultural notions of sexual identities appear stable through incessant repetition. Performance theory suggests that gender identities are fantasies of masculinity and femininity played out on male-identified and female-identified bodies whether the sex underneath is "true" or not. Gender is a theatrical impersonation of conventionalized notions of what it means to be male and female (and, by extension, "other than") in mainstream culture.

Butler examines the ways in which rhetorical practices work in culture to authorize or delegitimate sets of social and sexual relations. Butler argues that multiple discursive possibilities exist for the reconfiguration of gender performance in culture. She also discusses the ways in which identity categories might be strategically deployed for political purposes. Butler does not view the body as separate from the "text" it produces. In her view, it becomes impossible to separate out "gender" from the political and cultural intersections in which it is discursively produced and maintained (*Gender*

Trouble). Butler views discourse as the precedent to and the condition for formation of the sexed subject. The sexed body invokes cultural significations that carry meanings inscribed over time. Gender, therefore, is a performative function of the discourse community in which it is engaged. Transformative possibilities emerge through a performative view of gender because in every assumption about sex and gender is contained the possibility of its opposite and a multiplicity of other assumptions. Consequently, I use Judith Butler's articulation of feminist performance theory to reread Emig's *The Composing Processes of Twelfth Graders* as a feminist tale. I examine how compositionists and writing teachers might think differently about the value of writing for female students.

Applying Judith Butler's articulation of feminist performance theory, I set out here to document the ways in which writing might enable young women to traverse with power the landscape of adolescence and young adulthood. My assumptions about the critical and transformative potential of written discourse are premised on the notion that discourse, which historically has condemned *woman* because of her subordinate positioning in culture, might also serve as a tool that disrupts female subordination. Many feminists in the fields of linguistics, communications, and literary and educational studies have sought to replace prevalent inequitable cultural models of gender roles, expectations, and behaviors with more equitable ways of thinking, interacting, speaking, and writing so as to imagine more just words and worlds for girls and women, boys and men to inhabit (e.g., Alvine and Cullum; Barbieri; Broe and Ingram; Gilbert and Gubar; Kramarae; Lakoff; Lewis; Orenstein; Spender, *Man-Made Language*; Tannen, *You Just Don't Understand* and *Gender and Discourse*). However, techniques fundamental to this discursive work have not been widely transported to studies of female writers.

The possible power derived from discursive reconfigurations suggests that writing accomplished in an explicitly gendered environment might enhance girls' personal, intellectual, and political development. Deborah Brandt (*Literacy as Involvement*) discusses the ways in which written language removes social life to a symbolic realm to be contemplated privately. Brandt claims that writing rises clear of its rooting in an immediate time, place, and voice and thereby objectifies both thought and language. Writing enables the writer to revise her worldview because it heightens her consciousness in a way that not only permits the reorganization of thought and language but also permits the construction of a worldview that is no longer beholden to the ordinary world, to social relationships in that world, or to the "reality" of material experience. Writing allows departure from the writer's otherwise necessary syncopation with pragmatic action. Following Brandt, I argue that girls might write to compose opposite, emergent lives rich with possibility.

My interest in conducting this study was to examine the cultural uses for writing within a specific discourse community, a high school women's studies class. I was particularly interested in the ways that gender issues may intersect with written language and be a transformative force in the education of adolescent women. The overarching objective of the study was to examine the ways in which writing could help women's studies students in a high school to rethink gendered experience. The three primary purposes for the study were (a) to investigate specifically the effects of incorporating writing into a high school women's studies class; (b) to study the ways in which students enrolled in such a class might use writing to reflect upon, reinforce, and interrupt sets of gender relationships; and (c) to open lines of inquiry into the effects of writing on adolescent girls' integration of gender-related dicourses in their lives.

Aspen Grove High School, Emma Walker, and the Women's Studies Students

To explore my assumptions about young women and writing in a classroom setting, I spent three academic years (September 1992–June 1995) of ethnographic investigation (Agar, *The Professional Stranger, Speaking of Ethnography;* Heath; Lauer and Asher; LeCompte, Millroy, and Preissle; Lincoln and Guba; Saville-Troike) as a participant observer (Spradley, *Participant Observation*) in Emma Walker's women's studies class at Aspen Grove High School.[3] As a participant observer in Walker's class, I incorporated several writing assignments into the women's studies curriculum.

Aspen Grove High School is a large suburban high school in a major city in the Intermountain West region of the United States. Approximately 1,900 students attend the school. Seventy-five percent of the students are middle- to upper-middle-class white students whose families are members of the Church of Jesus Christ of Latter-day Saints, or, as they are commonly called, Mormons. The remaining 25% are predominantly white students from other religious backgrounds. Students of color comprise less than 5% of the school population. Twenty-five to 35 students enroll in women's studies each semester. Most of the students are female. During the three years of the study, between zero and four male students enrolled each semester. The course, which is offered for general elective credit, focuses on images of women in history and the traditional Western canon, the women's movement (first wave), women's psychological and moral development (based on theories posited by Gilligan and by Kohlberg), women's representation in advertising and the media, women in the workplace, eating disorders, violence against women, male and female communication styles, and contemporary feminism (the women's movement, the second and third waves).

Emma Walker, a highly respected veteran history/humanities teacher, teaches the semester-long class. Walker's purpose for teaching women's studies is to raise high school students' awareness of gender issues. She believes that her students are a generation in crisis. Caught living at a crossroads between two eras, Walker claims adolescent women and men today are taught gender stereotypes that are completely out of step with reality. Walker sees a tear ripping in the social fabric such as she has never before noticed in her 20 plus years of teaching. Her students are struggling with the ambiguities underlying their gender socialization. She says they feel trapped. Walker wants women's studies to provide these young women with ways for thinking their way "out of the trap." Walker teaches primarily through lecture and discussion. Students are evaluated on the basis of class participation in discussion, reading preparation, completion of class projects, and two essay tests. To accomplish her goals, Walker has adopted a postmodern stance and uses deconstruction as one of her primary pedagogical strategies.

Postmodern feminisms trouble the categories *male* and *female* and reject constructions of gender that depend on binary opposition. Gender is seen as inextricably linked to other constructions such as race, class, religion, and ethnicity and to social contexts that tend to destabilize identity, including gender identity. Emphasis is placed on difference within the category *woman;* generalizations that attempt to transcend the specificities of time and place are questioned. Postmodern feminisms reject stabilized and essentialized views of masculinity and femininity; however, postmodern feminisms' rejection of essentialized views of *woman* can be carried so far that the meaningfulness of the category *woman* is eliminated altogether (Ebert). Walker sees this as a limitation in the theories, especially as they relate to her work with adolescent girls because she believes it is important to maintain connection with the material conditions of her students' lives. Deconstruction can dismantle any sense of agency in subjectivity, and Walker sees this as dangerous ground to walk on with 17- and 18-year-olds. Because of similarly grounded concerns with this particular flaw in the theories when they are applied to understanding the lived experiences of flesh-and-blood subjects, some feminist theorists have tried to recollect the strategic usefulness of identity categories for political purposes.

Writing in Women's Studies at Aspen Grove

The writing experiences I incorporated into Walker's curriculum were designed to enable an examination of the discursive displacement of *female* both in written English discourse and in Western culture. The basic assignments included a deconstructive writing response log (known colloquially by the students as "the journal"), a writing autobiography, a masculinity/femininity history, and several spontaneous, in-class freewriting exercises. The format of the assignments was less at issue in accomplishing the goals of my project than the questions I asked the students to address in their writing. In women's studies, writing became a strategic mechanism that allowed young women to give voice to and to critically examine their gendered worlds in an effort to construct other possible visions of gender performance. I used writing to dialogue with students in order to defamiliarize the familiar, to make visible the invisible, to rupture the boundaries between gendered oppositions, and to expand the limits of gendered thinking. The writing provided students with opportunities to question the status quo and to consider nuances without exchanging one set of beliefs for an antithetical set of beliefs. For example, I did not want young women to come to terms with feminized behaviors that contributed to female subordination by determining that "all men are brutes" or some similarly useless pose.   My particular strategies for accomplishing my teaching goals included an exchange of written deconstructive dialogue with the students throughout the course of each assignment.

I collected all the writing completed by the students enrolled in women's studies and my corresponding feedback during the course of the investigation. I analyzed these according to principles of context-sensitive discourse analysis (Huckin, "Context-Sensitive Text Analysis"; "Critical Discourse Analysis"). Principles of context-sensitive discourse analysis assume that text analysis is problem-driven rather than theory-driven, although various theories may inform both the selection of a problem and the analysis of the data. The analysis is naturally eclectic and interdisciplinary and tries to account for as much of the context as possible. Additionally, context-sensitive discourse analysis takes into account the rhetorical situation and theoretical motivations of any text under analysis, and relies openly on plausible interpretations rather than on any kind of proof (Huckin "Context-Sensitive Text Analysis" 89). In the case of this study, for example, the problem generally is to discover what uses writing serves rhetorically in the discourse of a high school women's studies class. Analysis is framed in postmodern constructivist feminist views of composition and in feminist performance theory. As I will discuss in Chapters 2 and 4, I identified a range of transformative discursive performances in the women's studies students' writing. A transformative discursive performance may range along a spectrum of possibilities from the trivial to the traumatic. I identify three major categories of performative utterances that occur in the students' writing. I refer to these as *experiential editing, reflective revisions,* and *transformative performatives.*

In addition to the writing activities that I incorporated into Walker's curriculum, I took extensive field notes of classroom discussions, taught several class sessions, and completed nine case studies of students enrolled in the course—eight girls and one boy. I collected historical and other ethnographic data through archival studies, several interviews with Emma Walker, and a formal interview with Rod Harris, principal of the school. These data and theoretical perspectives provide the tools by which I analyze the discursive, interpretive, and performative effects of composing in the feminist education of high school students enrolled in a women's studies class.

Orientation to Literacies, Lies, and Silences: Girls Writing Lives in the Classroom

Literacies, Lies, and Silences: Girls Writing Lives in the Classroom examines the literacies and writing practices of adolescent girls in an unusual context in a mainstream public suburban high school. The context is unusual because women's studies at the high school level is anomalous; it does not exist with any degree of frequency to be considered part of typical culture in most public American secondary schools. Although the context is unusual, the lives and experiences of the young women who participated in this study are not.

During three years of participant observation in the women's studies class at Aspen Grove High School, I discovered a unique opportunity to examine the potential that writing might hold in the education of adolescent women. The principally 12th-grade girls involved in the study report that writing enhances their personal, intellectual, and political development. They report that writing contributes significantly to learning, allows them to express themselves personally and emotionally, and to assert opinions and argue positions in favor of self- and social transformation. Analysis of these findings indicates that writing is a critical part of a process in which students enrolled in a high school women's studies class are able to analyze traditional gender roles, to question conventional assumptions about gender-appropriate behavior and school-sponsored writing in the high school, and to consider a wider array of gender performance options.

The stories and writing experiences of women's studies students at Aspen Grove have much to offer educators interested in young women's education during the secondary school years. These young women's stories also offer much to think about for those compositionists who have wondered, as I have, why we have responded so inadequately to the literate and pedagogical needs of the young women we teach. This book is written in part as an effort to bridge that gap.

It is also written both to integrate insight and to explore the synergistic connections made by one precariously situated at an interdisciplinary crossroads where composition and rhetoric, teacher education, and women's studies intersect—to speak across disciplinary boundaries. I have had many opportunities to tell these students' stories to audiences in women's studies, to audiences in teacher education, and to audiences in composition and rhetoric.

I am always intrigued by the various angles of the stories that interest each audience. Those in women's studies are often most curious about and critical of my reconciliation of the essentialism of Gilligan's work with the constructivism of Butler's work. Audiences in teacher education are often most curious about Walker's women's studies curriculum and the process by which she gained administrative and parental approval for a women's studies course in a high school, especially in a conservative Mormon community. Audiences in composition and rhetoric generally find the rereading of Janet Emig's case studies and my consequent analysis of feminism in composition intriguing; however, composition scholars generally are uninterested in making the connections between young women's composing experiences in the high school and young women's composing experiences in the college composition course. I find this reticence most remarkable because I have gained multiple pedagogical insights about teaching writing to female students when I compare my experiences teaching writing in the high school women's studies class at Aspen Grove with my ongoing experiences as a first-year composition instructor at the university. I hope here to speak collectively in order that all readers—regardless of disciplinary or institutional location(s)—who are interested in young women's education and girls and their writing might hear these students' stories and experiences and find ways from them to combine efforts interdisciplinarily and intra-institutionally to transform young women's developmental and academic experiences during their adolescent years in both secondary school and college.

In this chapter, I have introduced the Aspen Grove site, the women's studies course, Emma Walker and the students involved in this project. I have also given a brief overview of the complex intersection of discursive, composing, and feminist theories that undergird this project. In Chapter 2, I revisit Janet Emig's pivotal work, *The Composing Processes of Twelfth Graders*, in an effort to recollect the first feminist visions in composition studies. I use Emig to frame current understandings of patterns of female adolescent development as writers and apply the assumptions of postmodern feminist theories. I specifically use feminist performance theory to identify possible feminist aims relative to schooling and adolescent female subjectivity relative to composition education. I argue that composition studies' overarching quest to be recognized as a legitimate field of inquiry obviates the substantive work, which might attend to the needs of gendered writers. Chapter 3 provides an in-depth examination of Emma Walker's women's studies course at Aspen Grove High School and the students who enroll in her course. I also articulate my research position and the pedagogical assumptions that underlie the teaching and writing interventions in this study.

In Chapter 4, I describe literacies of writing and of teaching writing in women's studies at Aspen Grove High School characterized by women's studies students and Emma Walker. I analyze the impact of writing on the students' and the teacher's personal, intellectual, and political development. According to principles of context-sensitive discourse analysis, I discuss the texts and contexts of a representative body of student writing to examine the performative effects of writing on the discursive assumptions of the women's studies students at Aspen Grove High School.

In Chapter 5, I discuss the cases of JoAnna and Alisa, whose atypical experiences in women's studies give me reason to pause and to view writing in relation to young women's education through a compound filtered lens.

Chapter 6 offers tentative conclusions about composition education and girls and their writing along with an array of questions to contemplate as we reconsider transforming education for young women during the 21st century.

Notes

1. One promising study that has recently emerged in the field of composition studies as the result of a doctoral dissertation by Sara Jonsberg involves writing with a group of formerly teen mothers to construct a new script for their lives.

2. For theories that analyze the effects in English discourse of the ways that privileging the male subject disadvantages the female subject, see, for example Lakoff; Penelope; Probyn; Smith, *The Everyday World; Texts, Facts, and Femininity*; and Spender, *Man-Made Language*.

3. Throughout *Literacies, Lies, and Silences*, I use pseudonyms for the school and the individuals who participated in my project in order to protect their privacy as well as to

safeguard Emma Walker's employment and the existence of women's studies at Aspen Grove High School in an increasingly conservative era. I agonize over this decision because I think that the teacher who masquerades in this text as Emma Walker deserves public recognition and praise for the exemplary teaching that she accomplishes year in and year out. However, she and I have both agreed that maintaining anonymity in today's political climate is our wisest course of action if women's studies is to be allowed to continue and to serve as a model of possibility for female-friendly curricula and pedagogy in the high school.

Written on the Body

Written on the body is a secret code only visible in certain lights; the accumulations of a lifetime gather there. In places the palimpsest is so heavily worked that the letters feel like Braille.

—Jeannette Winterson

Erase our bodies and we merely dance to music we cannot hear.

—Kristie S. Fleckenstein

Respected composition researcher and theorist Janice Lauer suggests that the fields of composition studies and rhetoric have been relatively silent on issues involving "the emergent woman writer: adolescent problems and pedagogy" (355).[1] Regardless of Lauer's recommendations to redress the mysterious inadequacy of investigations of the young female writer in composition research, recent scholarship has largely ignored female (and male) writing bodies in the classroom. Indeed, much theoretical and historical feminist work in composition studies appeared during the 1990s; however, little was done to investigate the ways in which writing influences the personal, intellectual, and political development of young women. I explain this neglect in two integral ways: Studies of writers have fallen prey to the inflamed debate surrounding theoretical discussion of the essentialism/constructivism binary.[2] Investigations of embodied writers are too comfortably critiqued as essentialist. Few other analyses in contemporary critical theory raise such persistent malignment, such little interrogation or such predictable fallibility as the claim of essentialism (Fuss). As a result, critical investigations of the composing practices of [female] writers have been viewed as theoretically suspect and unable to support composition's perpetual quest for legitimate disciplinary status in the academy. Despite Susan Miller's call to trump the quest for disciplinarity and tend to the work of composition by conducting "interpretive analyses of how students write, of what they write, or of how well they succeed in doing so depending on their specific instruction" (*Textual Carnivals* 200), the writerly body continues to be overlooked.

To respond to these concerns and to think about pedagogy appropriate for adolescent women writers, I tactically deploy Carol Gilligan's theory of female development and Judith Butler's feminist theory of performativity to reexamine Janet Emig's account of young women's experiences writing in her landmark work *The Composing Processes of Twelfth Graders*. Rereading the work of Janet Emig from a feminist standpoint provides a framework in which to articulate evidence regarding (a) the composing concerns of young women in schools, (b) the effects of writing on adolescent female subjectivity in a high school women's studies class, and (c) the potential for framing more empowering subjectivities for adolescent girls in school through performative views of composing. This exegesis is critical to reframing thinking in the field of composition studies for three principal reasons. First, this historical revision is crucial to understanding how those who teach writing might pragmatically attend to the gendered identities and writing performances of their students. Second, this account is tantamount to reclaiming the political usefulness of expressivist strategies to adolescent women writing. Finally, this move allows postmodern constructions of a female writing subject that recover the writerly body in the classroom. To fully appreciate the critical value of this approach, it is first useful to review the interrelated critiques of essentialism in feminist theory and the critiques of expressivism in composition.

Critiques of Essentialism and Expressivism: Two Sides of the Same Coin

Essentialists in feminism believe that female identity is the result of fixed, biologically determined essences—innate qualities that constitute femininity, which exist outside of and untainted by the patriarchal order. Feminist essentialism is linked most persistently to claims of a "true" or "original" female identity and in accounts of universal female subjugation. Additionally, essentialism underlies appeals to "the autonomy of a female voice and the potentiality of a feminine language" (Fuss 2). Essentialism is most commonly critiqued by anti-essentialist postmodern feminists who embrace constructivism and reject any attempt to naturalize an essence of womanness. Such feminists assume that female traits are historically, geographically, and socially embedded—highly mutable across time, place, and cultural identifications—and that there are no universal essences of femininity. Essentialist perspectives, they claim, elide the complexities of female identity—the multivarious historical, psychological, social, and cultural differences that constitute the female subject. The most volatile postmodern feminist critique of essentialism is that it safeguards patterns of subordination that hurt many flesh-and-blood women. Anti-essentialist constructivist projects not only reject a belief in essentialism but also demonstrate that taken-for-granted assumptions about particular kinds of "women" or "men," for example, are the effects of semiotic and linguistic representation. Socially constructed notions of femaleness (and maleness) are complexly organized and produced in discourse, such as we saw with the study by Walkerdine and the Girls' and Mathematics Unit recounted in Chapter 1.

Many feminists of color and lesbian feminists, among others, have taken issue with postmodern critiques of essentialism. For example, bell hooks argues that we cannot cavalierly dismiss a concern with identity politics, which derive from essentialist positions, given the pervasiveness of white supremacy that seeks to prevent the organization of a radical black subjectivity (*Yearning* 26). She suggests that "totalizing critiques of 'subjectivity, essence, identity' can be very threatening to marginalized groups, for whom it has been an active gesture of political resistance to name one's identity as part of a struggle to challenge domination" (*Teaching* 78). Indeed, Eve Sedgwick captures how postmodern constructivist critiques are similarly dangerous for gay and gay-friendly people in her book *Epistemology of the Closet*:

> It is so difficult to intervene in the seemingly natural trajectory that begins by identifying a place of cultural manipulation; and ends in the overarching, hygienic Western fantasy of a world without any more homosexuals in it…against them, essentialist understandings of sexual identity accrue a certain gravity. (42)

Gayatri Spivak argues for strategic uses of essentialism. By this, Spivak means essentialism put into practice by marginalized peoples themselves as a disruptive intervention "in a scrupulously visible political interest" (*In Other Worlds* 205). Spivak suggests that in the hands of the dispossessed themselves, essentialism can be a powerful strategic weapon operating as a displacing repetition that clears the way for those who have been disenfranchised to gain power by speaking or writing the particulars of their disenfranchisement ("Imperialism" 229).

The critiques of anti-essentialist constructivist positions offered by lesbian feminists and feminists of color have caused several other postmodern feminists to readdress the question of the body, its interrelation with identity, and the need for a politics of identity. This question pulses at the heart of my project. Adolescent women learning to write in a women's studies class are just beginning to form articulable positions on their developing sexualized gender identity. To deconstruct identity at this point in their development poses certain vexing problems. As Julia Kristeva ponders, "what can 'identity,' even 'sexual identity' mean in a new theoretical and scientific space where the very notion of identity is challenged?" (209). Mary Ann Doane expresses a similar concern: "In an era which is post-author, post-Cartesian subject, in which the ego is seen above all as illusory in its mastery, what is the status of a search for feminine *identity*?" (9). So many writing teachers build from the basis of embodied experience to help developing writers gain confidence and success with their writing. When identity is deconstructed and the author dead, there is nothing secure on which to base an identity politics from which developing writers might write with power. This dilemma sorely challenges process-oriented strategies of composing and composition instruction derived from composition studies' expressivist history, which I explore in the following section.

The most thoroughly critiqued essentialist position in composition studies is the writing process theory of expressivism. Expressivism is one of three prominent "process" theories of composing and models of composition teaching that have emerged over time and in juxtaposition with each other since the commonly recognized beginnings of the field in 1963. The poststructurally derived constructivist theory articulated in opposition to expressivism (and cognitive process theory[3]) is known either as social, social epistemic, or social rhetorical (Faigley "Competing Theories"). Lester Faigley articulates the commonly accepted ways in which the three approaches are most often positioned in his book, *Fragments of Rationality: Postmodernity and the Subject of Composition:*

...an "expressive view" that emphasizes qualities of integrity, spontaneity, and originality from Romantic expressivism, a "cognitive view" that emphasizes the rational working of the individual mind, and a "social view" that considers an individual writer as a constituent of culture. (17)

It is generally assumed that expressive views of composing and composition teaching emanate primarily from Romantic expressivism because expressivists (e.g., Elbow; Macrorie; Murray; Rohman and Wlecke; Stewart) variously cite writers traditionally associated with Romanticism to support the claims they make about writers and writing (Faigley "Competing Theories"; Berlin "Rhetoric and Ideology," *Rhetoric and Reality*). Rohman and Wlecke, two of the first of the so-called expressivists, define good writing as

> that discovered combination of words which allows a person the integrity to dominate his subject with a pattern both fresh and original. "Bad writing," then is an echo of someone else's combination which we have merely taken over for the occasion of our writing…. "Good writing" must be the discovery by a responsible person of his uniqueness within his subject. (cited in Faigley "Competing Theories" 529)

According to both James Berlin (*Rhetoric and Reality* 146–147) and Lester Faigley ("Competing Theories" 529), these are the same qualities M.H. Abrams uses to define "expressive" poetry in *The Mirror and the Lamp*. Rohman and Wlecke see writing as an act that "authenticates" and "affirms" the self (Berlin *Rhetoric and Reality* 147). With gestures that mimic its Romantic roots, proponents of expressivism generally teach students to write informal, personal narratives out of their lived experiences. The purpose of writing in expressive writing classes generally is to "empower" individual writers through the use of types of writing that enable personal autonomy, self-expression, and the reclaiming of "voice." [4]

"Authentic voice pedagogy" is woven through several expressive views. Authentic voice pedagogy argues that the aim of writing courses should uniformly be writing with integrity (Stewart cited in Faigley "Competing Theories" 529), which occurs through spontaneity. Ken Macrorie, concerned with the "way language works in us," was one of the first writers to develop explicit expressive pedagogies. He describes a method known as "freewriting," a process whereby the writer writes spontaneously and without pause whatever comes to mind in response to a prompt. Freewriting is supposed to help student writers develop authentic voices by getting past the writing "disease" that Macrorie coins "Engfish," the stilted prose of developing student writers. Freewriting enables developing writers to spontaneously tell the "truth of themselves" (Macrorie *Writing to Be Read*).

Expressivists maintain that asserting one's "voice" through writing is the creative power by which the individual writer discovers, thinks about, and gains control of knowledge and the self. Expressivists hold the view that all individuals have an innate need to represent their experience through writing, and that individual personal knowledge is the knowledge of most worth (e.g., Elbow; Macrorie; Murray).

Critics, who identify themselves as influenced by critical theory, neo-Marxist analyses, or social constructivist or all three theories, including some feminist theories, dismiss expressivism for its overarching dependency on modernist conceptions of the subject, which are frequently traced to Descartes and Enlightenment notions about the individual. These critics argue that expressivism embraces Cartesian notions of the self (e.g., Berlin "Rhetoric and Ideology," Faigley "Competing Theories"); underestimates the social, cultural, and historical conditions that shape selves, subjects, and the conditions out of which writers write (Sullivan and Qualley); and presumes "that language provides an unproblematic access to reality" (Faigley *Fragments* 8).

Drawing from essentialist positions that claim autonomy of a female voice and the potentiality of a feminine language, many cultural feminists adopted the expressivist view of composing as a way to counteract the textual and historical silencing of women. They suggested narrative as a mode for speaking the lives and voices of women where they previously have not been heard.[5] Although teaching narrative has some pedagogical value as a starting point for teachers of writing and of young women, feminist social rhetorical composition theorists argue that feminist uses of expressivism leave unquestioned the sociocultural, historical, political, and educational structures that have disenfranchised women. By not critiquing the differentiated power relations that trouble communicative efficacy across widely varied discursive communities, expressivism leaves itself open to appropriation by the patriarchal forces already institutionalized by the schools (Jarratt "Feminism and Composition"). By adopting a pedagogical approach that assumes that the expressive storying of students is empowering in and of itself, expressivism does nothing to recognize how students' different relations to discursive structures and cultural power might enable or inhibit social change.

Several writers influenced by postmodern feminist theories have similarly critiqued positions that essentialize women's ways of writing in "early" feminist work in composition studies and rhetoric (Brady; Flynn, Lamb, and Smith; Heather Graves; Ritchie). In particular, Elizabeth Flynn's 1987 landmark feminist essay "Composing as a Woman" has been scrutinized because Flynn mapped out the commonalities of "woman's experience" writing as opposed to "man's experience" writing. The insights gained from Flynn's groundbreaking work have been critiqued for offering essentialist analyses and for failure to account for differences in women's positions due to class, race, ethnic, sexual, geographic, and other multiple identifications. Indeed, Flynn herself has recognized the problems with essentialized views of women writing, distanced herself from her early liberal and cultural feminist perspectives and endorsed postmodern anti-essentialist feminisms in her ongoing work ("Feminism and Scientism"; "Review: Feminist Theories"; see also Clark "Argument and Composition").

The antagonism produced by the essentialist/constructivist debate limits progressive thinking about embodied writers. In spite of Joy Ritchie's remarkable efforts in "Confronting the 'Essential' Problem: Reconnecting Feminist Theory and Pedagogy" to help us think more broadly about gender while not abandoning our commitments to the material lives of women in classrooms, criticism of emerging feminist research in composition that deals with female-friendly pedagogies, women's texts, or female writers and describes female patterns of writing behavior continues to be characterized as "essentialized." For example, Elizabeth Flynn reviewed several feminist-identified book-length publications that have appeared since 1991 and advised that "feminist composition has entered a new phase of development" ("Review: Feminist Theories" 201). Included in Flynn's review is work that examines the practices of women faculty in colleges and universities (Kirsch); work that looks at the writing practices of college-age students from a gendered perspective (Rubin); a collection that focuses on defining gender-sensitive pedagogical practices in college English classrooms (McCracken and Appleby); a volume that foregrounds gender in a revisionist history of rhetoric and composition (Brody); and a study that examines the relationship between gender and journals and locates the journal as a site of writing that might help historically disenfranchised writers, especially women, move between "dominant and muted" discourses in an empowering way (Gannett xi). Each of these works attempts to counter the oppositional claims posed by anti-essentialist postmodern feminist critiques and to reconcile criticisms that might dismiss the work because it deals with embodied writers' subjectivities and material acts of writing.

In her review, Flynn acknowledges that these volumes are "the first extended explorations of composition from a feminist perspective"("Review: Feminist Theories" 201). However, she claims that this work arises out of diverse traditions and sometimes reports contradictory conclusions. Flynn theoretically situates these works in traditions of cultural, liberal, radical, and postmodern feminisms, draws some tentative findings, and warns that it is far too early in the development of the subfield of feminist compositions to identify consensual knowledge ("Review: Feminist Theories" 201). Flynn critiques the theoretical viability of feminist work that struggles to reconcile theoretical positions with the actual dilemmas of practice, implying that it is not possible to be both theoretically honest and pedagogically sensitive at the same time.

Although the second-wave feminist compositionists that Flynn discusses have attempted to grapple with anti-essentialist critiques and attend to the writer and her writing vis-à-vis application of postmodern critical analyses, they have struggled to come to terms with postmodern constructivist attempts to efface the gender binary. And struggle they must because, as Flynn rightly argues, the frameworks they have had at their disposal are inadequate to mediate irreconcilable differences among essentialist and postmodern constructivist feminist positions. The problem I wrestle with is the wholesale dismissal of the writer, which is served by Flynn's astute critique. Polemical oppositions inherent in the essentialism/constructivism binary not only mask important connections between feminist theory and practice, but they also obscure both feminisms' common purposes and the female student herself. Rather than suggest that feminist compositionists continue to puzzle with strategies for reconciling theoretical with pedagogical positions in composition, Flynn retreats by invoking the trope that composition needs to work along theoretically particular lines to establish disciplinarity for the field.

Perseverating on the controversy of disciplinarity inhibits work that examines the material lives of the students in our classrooms. In support of the ongoing quest for legitimacy, feminist compositionists (e.g., Flynn, "Feminism and Scientism"; "Review: Feminist Theories") proceeded, as Flynn advocated, with theoretically particular work before amply examining opportunities to find a way through the twisted labyrinths of the essentialist weaknesses in the "early" work in order to analyze critically the merits of gendering the writer in the contemporary composition classroom. Feminist work accomplished primarily to establish disciplinary status for composition serves as handmaiden and maintains patriarchal privilege in the academy. Feminist scholarship that critiques as "essentialist" work that locates female writing practices in female experiences is complicit in turning from view women's texts, women writing, and the contexts in which women write. In so doing, it effaces both women as writers and women-friendly writing strategies. It also helps lead composition back, as Modleski concludes, to a "pregendered" past where there was only the universal (male) subject. Because research that is concerned with identifying woman-friendly and female-oriented writing strategies has been dispensed with as "essentializing" and unworthy of further theoretical examination, the boundaries of discussion are set outside the category of woman altogether. In doing so, composition studies returns to its own "pregendered" past. Indeed, it is difficult to imagine how we might accomplish the inclusive aims of composition if we fail to re-envision the subjectivity of the female writer and provide her a central place in our now-established discipline. Feminist work in composition ought to proceed along pedagogical as well as theoretical lines if it is to respond to the writing problems and desires of female as well as male writing students.

Performance Theory Allows Us to Translate the Essentialism of Expressivism

Among the most recent projects examining issues of female subjectivity in composition studies are those found in the collection *Feminism and Composition Studies: In Other Words,* edited by Susan C. Jarratt and Lynn Worsham. In this volume, Laura Brady scrutinizes the uses of experience as evidence in early feminist work by examining Flynn's "Composing as a Woman," Mary Lay's "Feminist Theory and the Redefinition of Technical

Communication," and Catherine Lamb's "Beyond Argument in Feminist Composition." Brady considers the strategic deployment of Nancy Chodorow, Carol Gilligan, and Mary Belenky and her colleagues in that work. Drawing on Certeau, Brady explains that "tactical uses of essentialism can disrupt assumptions about gender roles, identity categories, and the intersections of language and material bodies" (26). However, when such tactical disruptions become repeatedly cited, they are transformed into strategies, which can be politically useful but institutionalized if resistant to change. (See also Diana Fuss *Essentially Speaking* 32.) Brady suggests that early feminist work drawing on women's ways of composing has outlived its tactical usefulness to transformative projects and that "it is time to move beyond existing uses of personal narratives and consider new citations and significations" (39). Brady turns to Judith Butler's theory of performativity in an attempt to find new "sites-cites for discussions and differences" (43) by examining the slippages between positions made available through "reexamining (perhaps repositioning)" (40) the personal experience narratives of Chodorow, Gilligan, and Belenky and colleagues, which have influenced our thinking about gender and identity in writing.

The usefulness of Butler derives from her examination of the ways in which linguistic practices work in culture to legitimate or delegitimate social and sexual relations. Feminist performance theory attempts to use ludic play as a means to rewrite issues of struggle hidden from view in essentializing systems to recover transformative politics sorely needed in a flesh-and-blood world. It attempts to intervene rhetorically in power relations by redescribing unified patterns of domination in order to contest them. The underlying premise of feminist performance theory is that "gender is a kind of persistent impersonation that passes as the real" (Butler *Gender Trouble* viii). On this view, gendered behavior derives from a culturally dictated script, which sexed bodies begin to perform the moment they are identified: "It's a girl!" "It's a boy!" "It's a hermaphrodite!!!"

Performance theory suggests that the limits of culturally available gender options can be loosed through stylized performative enactments that parody and disrupt the gender status quo. Such performatives create a discursive space for engaging a transformative gender politics beyond the culturally imaginable constraints of sexual identities. The critical task of performance theory is first to locate subversive strategies of gendered parody, mimesis, and irony to describe the ways in which sexed bodies "cross-dress" or stereotypically role-play other sexed bodies. The next task is to affirm the specific possibilities of intervention that occur during such performances. Finally, the analyst is able to contest notions of an essential gender through such performances. Disruption opens up options for variable gendered transactions to slip into view. Such slippages are especially valuable for liberating bodies that fail to comply with dominant cultural scripts—for example, gay, lesbian, and transgendered bodies; bodies of color; Jewish bodies; fat bodies; disabled bodies.

Performance theorists outline rhetorical and theatrical strategies that accomplish transformative goals when translated into pedagogy. These include laughter, parody, and "drag." Butler characterizes "drag" primarily as parody; however, she also defines "drag" as mime, hyperbole, exaggeration, impersonation, imitation, citation, appropriation, assuming the status of a particular sex, "cross-dressing," sex-role stereotyping, playing upon the distinction between the body of the performer and the gender that is being performed, imitation, and dramatization. Parodic drag identities provide clues to the ways in which essentialized gender interpretations might be reframed.

For example, Butler examines gender as drag in a chapter on performative subversions in her 1990 book, *Gender Trouble*. She quotes from *Mother Camp* by Esther Newton to illustrate how drag works to subvert essentialized gender meanings:

> Garbo "got in drag" whenever she took some heavy glamour part, whenever she melted in or out of a man's arms, whenever she simply let that heavenly-flexed neck bear the weight of her thrown-back head.... (as cited in Butler *Gender Trouble* 128)

In other words, a drag performance plays upon the audience's awareness that the performer's anatomy is distinct from the gender performed, whether the body underneath matches the performance or not. A good drag performance causes the audience to laugh as they recognize both self and other. A drag performance illustrates the ways in which gender is both written on the body and read by other bodies. Drag makes visible the invisible and "natural" ways in which sexed bodies perform their gender. Parodic performances of drag suggest a dissonance not only between sex and performance, but sex and gender and gender and performance, which write spaces on the body for multiple other gender performance possibilities to appear.

In her later work, *Bodies that Matter*, Butler describes additional discursive strategies assumed by drag. Drag exposes the presumed normality of gender presentations in which the gender performed is constructed by the performers' disavowal of various identifications. Disavowals construct a different domain of the "unperformable." Butler suggests that a drag performance constitutes the *sexually* unperformable, which is performed instead as *gender identification.*

> The straight man *becomes* (mimes, cites, appropriates, assumes the status of) the man he "never" loved and "never" grieved; the straight woman *becomes* the woman she "never" loved and "never" grieved. It is in this sense, then, that what is most apparently performed as gender is the sign and symptom of a pervasive disavowal. (236)

Butler explains that heterosexuals' rejection of homosexual attachments performs gender identification much as a drag performance does.

Within a drag interpretation of gender performance, the audience perceives how one's gender identification is constituted by a system of pervasive disavowal, which constructs a domain of the "unperformable," or that which must be "closeted" (invoking Eve Sedgwick's usage in *Epistemology of the Closet*). Consequently, the identity performed outright is read or interpreted as the "real" or "true" gender identification. In "drag," the body is able to become that gender which one has never loved and never grieved. One is able to make oneself into that gendered self, which one wants desperately to love but cannot because of social taboos. Like Garbo, one performs the gender identification they desire but cannot legitimately (sexually) have.

Another example of the ways rejection of homosexual attachments performs gender identification is illustrated in Margaret Finders's brilliant study of literacy and life in junior high (*Just Girls*). A group of "popular girls," whom Finders calls "the social queens," have very rigid views of acceptable femininity for members of their group. Guided by images of beauty and sexuality transported through print and other media, the "queens" carefully monitor their physical appearance, dress, social behavior, academic achievement, and reading and writing preferences to present a unified vision of "popular" femininity. In public, the social queens present a unified front; however, in private conversations, the queens disagree, compete, cast blame, and deny allegiance as a way to check and test their ways of being female, popular, and adolescent. These girls use critical competitive comments both to define feminine attractiveness and to create strong bonds of solidarity among members of their group.

The social queens perform for each other. Such performances most often focus on body images and attractiveness to boys. The social queens mime images of beauty and sexuality encoded in photographs of models in teen magazines. Miming the models presented in zines, the social queens appropriate "cool" images to be attractive to boys. In this way, the queens assume the status of acceptable heterosexual femininity. However, the performances are not really aimed at any particular boys; the queens selectively choreograph their parodied performances for each other. It is the female images of beauty and sexuality that they desire. Imitating cited images from teen zines, these girls perform "the signs and symptoms of a pervasive disavowal," which in turn is read as appropriate gender identification by their intended audience—each other. The social queens perform in the domain of the "unperformable" as do we all every time we produce ourselves to conform with socially desirable images of femininity, masculinity, or "other."

Expanding notions of gender impersonation through performance translations allows us to examine the gendered performances of writers writing in ways that trouble essentialist critiques. The writerly body examined does not contain an essence of femininity (or masculinity or other) underneath; the body is the writer's page ready to be written upon. Performance theory opens up possibilities for subversive "drag" alternatives to accompany pedagogy in the composition class. Used in the context of a composition class, writing may perform instances of gender impersonation, drag performances, and disavowals of the self one "never" loved and "never" grieved. Vis-à-vis the resultant laughter and recognition, writing makes visible the invisible and otherwise "natural" world of gendering, which students tacitly assume. Through writing, students find ways to create other sexed possibilities. In the next section, I examine the tools that perform this transformative revision.

Rereading Janet Emig's Case Studies: Reexamining Lynn's and Victoria's Texts As Subversive Drag Performances

The findings of Janet Emig's study reported in *The Composing Processes of Twelfth Graders* are largely responsible for writing process approaches to composition instruction. Emig's work has been linked both to expressivist and cognitive process theories, but not to social rhetorical theories. Even while recognizing the significance of Emig's research on our understanding of writers' processes in general, several compositionists have variously critiqued the conclusions of *Composing Processes* for essentialist conclusions. For example, Emig has been faulted for inherently modernist and new critical presumptions (Schreiner), for cognitivist premises derived from empiricism, which fail to question the values of the goals they enable (Berlin "Rhetoric and Ideology"; Faigley "Competing Theories"), and for a general insensitivity to sociocultural and political concerns (Berlin "Rhetoric and Ideology"). Others have condemned Emig for generalizations drawn from a limited sample (Voss) and from too few data (North), and for braiding literary idioms with scientific inquiry (Faigley "Competing Theories"). It strikes me as odd that feminist compositionists have neither responded to the multiple critiques of Emig's work nor returned to Emig to reinterpret her findings about writers in general to mark the gendered implications that arise from her investigations of a young female writer.

In *The Composing Processes of Twelfth Graders,* Janet Emig laid the groundwork that might have helped compositionists and writing teachers to begin to understand sooner the processes of writers as sociocultural concerns. For example, in the case of Victoria, a Chinese-American female student who attends a predominantly (95%) African-American high school in which most of the teachers are white, Emig remarks:

> Victoria astutely realizes the usefulness of satire to a girl who feels exceptionally hostile to adults, particularly teachers and administrators: ...V[ictoria]: Well, you can't really when you get angry with a situ-, when you get disgusted with something, you can't really come up to that person or that organization and say, "Boy, you really disgust me." You have to do it kind of subtly, and, ah, so I write these things: it's ah, it's kind of a release of feelings and tension, but yet you don't really hurt anybody. (80)

Emig also recognizes the importance of female peer connections to the adolescent female writers in her study.

> All five girls refer to a friend or friends with whom they talk regularly about and share their writing—some in an extra-curricular activity, such as the publishing of a yearbook or a literary magazine; others solely and simply as personal friendships....Significant others among peers tend to be of the same sex....(78)

Emig unmistakably poses possibilities for gender-based inquiry:

> What can be the explanations for these striking differences between the boys and girls in their accessibility to invitations in a range of fields of discourse, and in both major modes of student writing? (82)

She offers explanatory sociocultural analyses:

> One explanation—and one not wholly satisfactory—is that as a woman, the investigator reminds the boys too much of all the teachers of composition they have had in high school... and they are not rejecting the stimulus so much as the giver of the "assignments." The second is also cultural: perhaps the white boys genuinely believe writing poems and stories is an unmanly activity. Bradford [an African American], in contrast, seems perfectly comfortable writing his poetry. (82)

However, the cultural influences that she recognizes are erased in characterizations that designate her findings about writers, in universal, nonspecific terms. Because of perceived needs in a newly developing discipline at the time Emig completed her work, the greatest issue of concern to her was to understand more fully the nature of writing processes in general.[6] As a result, it is disappointing but not surprising that Emig's gender, racial, sexual, and class identifications and analyses are suppressed by language describing writers and their processes in not only hers, but in ensuing studies, which for all practical purposes have ignored the female (and male) writing subject altogether.

Gerald Nelms, and more recently, Peter Mortensen, have rearticulated the importance of Janet Emig's work on ensuing scholarship in rhetoric and composition studies. Beginning to forge Emig's link to constructivist theories in composition, Mortensen reminds us in his essay "Going Public" that what is most remarkable about Emig's work is her affirmation of "concern for the value of persons and their ties to place represented in her study" (198). Emig constructed a foundation that certainly could have been invoked earlier to support feminist research and social epistemic theoretical work in composition studies and rhetoric, most especially as it pertains to "the emergent woman writer" (Lauer).[7] Reconsideration of Emig's case studies, particularly the cases of Lynn,[8] a white, middle-class Jewish student; and Victoria, a Chinese-American student, highlights what are potentially the first socioculturally aware feminist tales in contemporary composition studies. This rereading provides a theoretically viable framework for addressing the questions about the writerly body and its interrelation with identity and the need for a politics of identity, which young women writing in a women's studies class specifically might find transformative.

Attempting to reread Emig's groundbreaking work through a feminist performance lens, I am struck initially how the case of Lynn in particular resonates with Carol Gilligan's stage theory of female psychology and girls' development. I am also struck by the ways Lynn's case resonates with findings from empirical investigations into the situations of adolescent girls in American schools that express female "norms" of development, behavior, and treatment by the schools (AAUW reports; Orenstein; Sadker and Sadker). In their book *Meeting at the Crossroads*, Lyn Mikel Brown and Carol Gilligan describe the ways in which girls move from a period of outspoken assertiveness (ages 7–9) through a period when they can name their feelings, but they don't speak them because they know that "nice girls" want to avoid conflict in relationships (ages 10–12). They begin to dissociate from their feelings. Finally, young women learn to pretend they do not see what they see or feel what they feel until they lose their awareness of the feelings they may have (ages 13–14). Young women "take themselves out of relationship for the sake of maintaining relationship." By this, Brown and Gilligan mean that young women disconnect from feeling things that might hurt them or their friends. They gloss over and dissociate from their feelings in order to maintain a facade of harmony. They think that absence of conflict will preserve the relationship. They voice over their inner feelings so completely that they lose touch with them. They become observers of their own lives, losing a sense of self.[9] Most women who come out of this stage (typically, if this occurs, it occurs during middle age) have a very difficult time "finding their voice." During this crisis of connection experienced by females in adolescence, girls tend to speak of themselves as living in connection with others, but cast in a relational crisis that is inherently paradoxical. To fill the female role of making relationships work, females in adolescence begin this abandonment of self and give up their voice for the sake of becoming a good woman and having good relationships. The worst thing that can happen to them is to be cast out of the relational web.

In her essay "Teaching Shakespeare's Sister," Gilligan explains the relevance of this aspect of female adolescent development to girls' education. Girls will only speak, she reports, when they feel that someone will listen and will not abandon them in the face of conflict or disagreement ("Teaching Shakespeare's Sister" 24). Girls often choose silence ("Teaching Shakespeare's Sister" 21) or divide themselves from their knowledge by regularly prefacing their observations or concluding their explanations with the comment, "I don't know," the sign of girls' repression (14–15). By using the retreat, "I don't know," girls avoid telling the truth and potentially opening up a space to be hurt. Gilligan reports that girls will say they don't like to talk to people about what they are really thinking because it might reveal their vulnerability. Girls decide that it is much safer to keep things to themselves ("Teaching Shakespeare's Sister" 21). Brown and Gilligan conclude that the silencing girls experience is directly related to the fate of their education. Until women can speak in a relational realm where they are convinced that a teacher will listen and will not leave them out, will take them seriously and will not put them down, they are unlikely to participate fully in their education. They will keep quiet, notice the absence and subordination of women, and say nothing (*Meeting at the Crossroads* 26).

There have been numerous constructivist critiques of Gilligan's work for generalizing findings from interviews with (primarily) white, middle-class girls to describe unilateral stages of female development. Gilligan has also been criticized for essentializing the female experience. These multiple critiques of Gilligan and her assessment of girls' and women's development point to the difficulties in accepting a strictly developmental rereading of Emig drawing on Gilligan. However, I am haunted by the ways in which Gilligan's work seems to "ring true" as I reread Lynn's writing performances in particular.

For example, Lynn is a good student; however, she has a fairly cynical view of teachers and of school-sponsored writing. Lynn writes about a topic that will take the least amount of time, effort, and personal investment, and which will least require the expression of emotions from her, "although the decision makes her feel guilty" (Emig *The Composing Processes of Twelfth*

Graders 50). When Emig inquires why Lynn abandons writing about issues of personal concern to her, Lynn attempts to expose her rationale to Emig but concludes, "I don't know why this is, I could, get some sort of explanation, rather I'm sure, but I don't know" (Emig *The Composing Processes of Twelfth Graders* 48). The only audience Lynn can conceive that might be interested in the social concerns of an adolescent girl is readers of *Seventeen* magazine (Emig *The Composing Processes of Twelfth Graders* 64), a magazine she thinks is "silly." Although her experience is engaging enough to sustain her interest in writing privately about it over the course of at least a four-month period, Lynn is certain that her story would be viewed as "trite," "not very original," or "not very interesting" by any other readers (Emig *The Composing Processes of Twelfth Graders* 136).

Because her teachers have told her not to use clichés when she writes, Lynn struggles to find ways to avoid clichés while still protecting the privacy of her thoughts and feelings. Lynn's solution is to write about topics that do not engage her personally or emotionally. It is not that Lynn does not have strong feelings. She is reluctant to voice them in the arena of school-sponsored writing "where most writing does not require the deep personal engagement of the writer" (Emig *The Composing Processes of Twelfth Graders* 50) and the audience is viewed with cynicism by the writer.[10]

The developmental stages outlined by Gilligan and her colleagues (*Making Connections;* Brown and Gilligan, *Meeting at the Crossroads*) offer one possible representation of (white, middle-class) girls' writing experiences during their adolescent years. As Gilligan and her colleagues suggest (white, middle-class) girls do at this stage of development, Lynn dissociates from her feelings even though doing so makes her feel guilty; she invokes the response indicative of girls' residence in the emotional underground, "I don't know"; she represses discussion of things that she finds personally interesting and dismisses them as trivial; she concludes that the audiences available to adolescent women are "silly." Gilligan's work gives voice to the lived experiences of young (white, middle-class) women and, when examined in the context of Emig's study, Gilligan's representation of adolescent female development and experience allows an examination of young (white) women and their writing through a more experientially representative lens. Consequently, it is useful to conclude initially (drawing on Gilligan) that much of what Lynn "feels" and "believes" remains hidden in her school-sponsored writing because it provides insights about (female) students that led Emig and countless others influenced by her findings to draw tactical pedagogical conclusions about teaching writing to both women and men.[11]

However, I wish to respond to essentialist critiques in advance by strategically repositioning my analysis of Lynn's experiences writing for Emig and in school à la Gilligan and attempt to recuperate an embodied "subject" of composition in postmodern constructivist terms. Drawing on Butler, we are also able to see the contradictions in Lynn's and Victoria's conversations about their school- and inquiry-sponsored writing experiences as performative utterances.[12] These performative utterances act to disavow the intensity of Lynn's and Victoria's passions, which are motivated by the social inequities of the day rather than by developmental prerogatives. By looking through a performative lens, we see not only the ways that Lynn and Victoria "feel" and "believe," but the ways that Lynn and Victoria perform a parodic theater of "the good student"—sign and symptom of a pervasive rejection of the self they wish desperately to love.

For instance, Emig explains that all the students in her case sample "should be considered to possess above-average intelligence." Each participant in Emig's sample was characterized as a "good writer" by the chair of the English department at their high schools (*The Composing Processes of Twelfth Graders* 29). Emig's analysis of Lynn's and Victoria's writing processes reveals that these girls' writing behaviors can be interpreted as efforts to conform to directives given by English teachers who have told them that "good" (student) writing "avoids cliches" (*The Composing Processes of Twelfth Graders* 49) and "should be clear, concise and memorable" (*The Composing Processes of Twelfth Graders* 60). In particular, Lynn's efforts to respond to her teachers' directives are procedurally operationalized in her dealings with syntax as well as her "lexical, rhetorical and imagaic" choices (*The Composing Processes of Twelfth Graders* 60). These students have clearly figured out how to perform in ways that please their teachers, gaining them academic standings in the top 5–10% of their class.

However, Lynn's and Victoria's work both cites that which is expected of the "good writing student" and becomes a site for resignification of expectations for the "good writing student." At the same time both Lynn and Victoria perform "the good student," they contest their "schoolgirl" performances. They mimic their teachers' expectations: "They seem to have this thing about spelling…and this business about length" (Lynn in Emig

The Composing Processes of Twelfth Graders 70, 71). They parody their teachers as "disgusting" (Victoria in Emig *The Composing Processes of Twelfth Graders* 80) and "trivializing" (Lynn in Emig *The Composing Processes of Twelfth Graders* 68). Lynn finds her teachers "uninspiring"; she accuses them of "oversimplification and casualness, if not cynicism, in evaluation (They demand correction of trivia, but they will not read and reevaluate a serious effort to recast essences)" (Emig *The Composing Processes of Twelfth Graders* 68). While performing in ways that their teachers applaud, these girls laugh at the absurdity of their teachers' scripted expectations. They give their teachers what they want—three-, five- and seven-paragraph themes in the expected length with accurate spelling and correct syntactic constructions—while they reserve their most engaged writing performances for self-selected audiences whom they value more highly than their teachers. Lynn and Victoria make themselves into the gendered writers they want desperately to love but cannot—both "citing-siting" (Brady 41) the norm and creating "an occasion to expose the norm itself as a privileged interpretation" (Butler *Bodies that Matter* 108).

Lynn and Victoria cover over their desires with a costume that will be read according to the expectations of their teacher-audience. However, Lynn always imagines a larger audience for her writing and even sees the possibility of making money by writing about a topic she would never address in school—dating two different boys at once (Emig *The Composing Processes of Twelfth Graders* 64). She regularly shares her writing with peers both privately and in extracurricular activity as coeditor of the yearbook (Emig *The Composing Processes of Twelfth Graders* 78). Victoria writes with peers who imagine themselves already as "embryo professional writers" with a "great seriousness of intent" and "already-initiated practice of their craft" (Emig *The Composing Processes of Twelfth Graders* 79).

Their rhetorical desires are concealed when given the opportunity to write on a topic of their choice in inquiry-sponsored writing. Lynn, on the one hand, draws from what she has learned during school-sponsored writing episodes and selects perfunctory topics that she sees as "easy" while she muses about length and spelling demands, which are important to her teachers (but of small account to Emig). Topics that might engage Lynn's passions—the aging of her grandmother, the war in Vietnam, the dilemmas involved in dating two boys at once, a failed relationship—are not selected. Presumably Lynn does not select engaging topics all　because of the personal demands required and the fact that writing about them would require more than 250 words—the length of the typical school writing assignment (Emig *The Composing Processes of Twelfth Graders* 53)—and more time than is usually given for writing in school (Emig *The Composing Processes of Twelfth Graders* 56).

Victoria, on the other hand, writes nearly exclusively in parody and satire as a way to mask her "exceptionally hostile" feelings toward teachers and administrators. She chooses parody and satire in order to say, "Boy, you really disgust me" (Emig *The Composing Processes of Twelfth Graders* 80) to teachers who only respond to superficial concerns (spelling and punctuation, for instance [Emig *The Composing Processes of Twelfth Graders* 87]). Victoria only revises writing that she accomplishes for herself and her peers (Emig *The Composing Processes of Twelfth Graders* 87); Lynn does not revise at all because she views it as teacher-initiated punishment (Emig *The Composing Processes of Twelfth Graders* 68). As Emig characterizes it, there is "the inescapable impression" that these students "are more sophisticated" than their teachers, both as to "the level of their stylistic concerns and to the accuracy and profundity of their analyses of themselves as writers" (*The Composing Processes of Twelfth Graders* 73, 83).

In these ways, Lynn and Victoria produce "cross-dressed" representations of texts that are outfitted to fit the rhetorical, institutional, and gender occasion while they simultaneously play upon the distinction known to their imaginary audiences that they disdain the polite conventions of the body underneath—evidence of their subversion of institutional power rather than their dissociation from it. Their performances "pass as the real" winning them the "goods" that the society they are in views as valuable. According to Emig's analysis of the ways in which teachers react to the students' texts, not only do their teachers *not* read their texts as subversive, but they only note superficial features that are out of place—the length of the hem and coverage of the midriff—rather than seeing the rich range of the textual possibilities of the performance.[13] Their teachers appropriate these girls' texts, an act that serves to maintain teachers' discursive privilege—giving them good grades for "the accidents rather than essences" of their writing (Emig *The Composing Processes of Twelfth Graders* 99), but Lynn and Victoria have the last word and the last laugh.

Lynn and Victoria burlesque the discursive expectations valued by the school. Their teachers are persuaded by their parodic performances according to socially acceptable norms both of femininity and high school discourse. They see these girls as "polite writers"—ones who worry about the elements and amenities of discourse (Emig *The Composing Processes of Twelfth Graders* 72) rather than as disenchanted students concerned with sociopolitical issues (Lynn "This is Enough to Make Me Start Smoking" in Emig *The Composing Processes of Twelfth Graders* 124; Victoria in Emig *The Composing Processes of Twelfth Graders* 83) and the contradictory mindlessness of school-sponsored writing. Their performances suggest a dissonance between the writer and her writing. This rereading exposes the presumed normalcy of feminine discursive presentations as "dutiful and disciplined enough to want to please" (Emig *The Composing Processes of Twelfth Graders* 56). Read through a performative lens, Lynn and Victoria reveal how gender expectations are constituted by identifications that are simultaneously disavowed by the performer. Like those of Finders's social queens, these girls' performances constitute a different domain of the "unperformable."

Lynn and Victoria assume the status of the writer they desire in their self-sponsored writing while exposing their contestatory connections with school- and inquiry-sponsored writing. Their performances acknowledge how their writing identities are constructed both through opposition to and exclusion of other possibilities (Butler *Bodies that Matter* 115). In these ways, Lynn and Victoria make visible the gendered nature of their performances and rupture the surface of common readings of their heretofore ungendered writing bodies. The drag performance they produce works to the subjects' advantage because the dissonance between the writing they perform and Emig's representation of these girls' writing processes cites a fractured reality, which both contests notions of a "real" or "ideal" gendered writer underneath and affirms other transformative possibilities. In the performative slippages in between, Lynn and Victoria write spaces on the body of composition scholarship for multiple other writerly performance possibilities to appear for female (and perhaps male) writers.

Butler converts the essentialism of expressiveness that undergirds Gilligan's and Emig's frameworks into a performative framework that recovers writing bodies lost to essentialist critiques. The distinction between expression and performativeness is crucial. If the various ways in which a body shows its gender are performative, then there is no essential identity "by which an act or attribute might be measured; there would be no true or false, real or distorted acts of gender, and the postulation of a true gender identity would be revealed as a regulatory fiction" (Butler *Gender Trouble* 141).

According to this line of reasoning, the rewriting of composition's process-derived expressive strategies is possible. In converting expressive notions of process to performative notions of process, compositionists might recuperate the "subjective" losses the field has sustained. In this rereading, the embodied "subject" of composition may be revitalized. The formerly derided "object" of composition takes a speaking "subject" position and becomes the "agent of social change rather than a victim" as Berlin suggests ("Rhetoric and Ideology" 478).

I have reread Lynn's and Victoria's cases assuming that their experiences with writing in school and for Emig were indelibly influenced by cultural scripts of female development and female experiences in school, but I do not view this rereading as an essentializing explanation. I have offered a performative translation of expressivist and cognitive process interpretations of these girls' experiences writing in order to recover an embodied discourse—to both redescribe the writing choices made by Lynn and Victoria and to interpret the writing choices made by female students in the women's studies class at Aspen Grove High School. These developmental and performative refigurings of Lynn's and Victoria's composing practices enable critical considerations of gender influences in the writing performances of the students in women's studies without backing us into an essentialized corner.

By rereading Emig's study from this perspective, the door opens to invite inquiry about other possible ways writing might serve to alter the gender representations of female (and male) writers and to transform gendered writing norms. Feminist performance theory and the writing of young women retold give compositionists reason to rethink the ways in which the body has been "written off" in our work and to (re)consider ways to write on and through the body so that we may walk through the door and meet the embodied "subject" of composition again.

Writing on/through the Body in the Classroom

The students in the women's studies class at Aspen Grove High School use writing to reconfigure their understanding of the discursive gender performances available to them. Writing gives these students the impetus to expand and to transform their social roles: to name, consider, and to act in ways that give voice to diversity; to explore the belief in a stable, unified self; and to offer means of exploring how identity is multiply constructed. In several instances, writers call into question the conventional narratives of gender performances available to adolescent girls in their culture.

To cite an instance, one student writes:

> Through my writings I've learned that I shouldn't always depend on a man and that I want to be who I want to be, not who someone else wants me to be. Before taking this class, I used to never be able to say how I feel about something or someone and now at least I've begun to be able to express myself to others. Writing in a journal gives me the opportunity to better understand myself, giving me endless opportunities.

This is an utterance that enacts a performance of a different sense of self than was previously understood. The writer proclaims a subjectivity performed differently from that of many adolescent girls in schools. The writerly performance sanctions a range of different gender options.

Through this study, I characterize three categories of performative utterances: (a) *reflective revisions*, propositions whereby a writer declares a revised sense of self; (b) *experiential edits*, propositions in which a writer constructs enabling conditions for change—for reconsidering personal responses and actions to specific stimuli and events; and (c) *transformative performatives*, propositions in which a writer scripts a sense of future self—writes a life she wishes to perform. The performance of these textual categories in the writing of the students involved in this study, which are analyzed in Chapter 4, indicates that writing may provide adolescent girls enrolled in a high school women's studies class with an occasion (a) to construct discursive spaces that interrupt the discursive position of subordinate reality for female subjects, (b) to think and (re)think gender options, and (c) to script more empowering discursive alternatives, which ultimately may differently organize their lives.

Even as composition studies has problematized expressivist and cognitive process approaches to understanding and teaching writing initially inspired by Emig and advanced a "social epistemic" stance (Berlin "Rhetoric and Ideology"), pedagogy appropriate to an embodied identity politics remains elusive. Julia K. Ferganchick points to composition's unwillingness to deal with the complicated messiness of the (gendered) teaching and writing bodies in writing classrooms:

> Without stating so explicitly, our field's "body" of scholarship about teaching and teacher training ignores the body. We collectively pretend, at least in pages of our journals and books, that our physical characteristics are irrelevant to discussions of pedagogical theory and practice. (8)

Every time the fear of essentialist critique causes compositionists to ignore the gendered, raced, classed, sexed writerly body, we fail our students. Postmodern constructivist feminisms seek to rupture the totalizing surfaces of gender and sexuality identifications; however, theories are only useful to a point. Pedagogy is needed that attempts to write on/through the body. Feminist performance theory provides alternative strategies that leave the body intact, while rewriting its meaning.

The purpose of writing on and through the body is transformation of compulsory cultural (i.e., gender) and institutional (i.e., public school) systems that privilege one sex and one gender (and one race and one class) over other(s). Writing on and through the body works to revise inescapable systems that punish those who cannot or will not comply. Systems can be reformed when parodic performances—such as Lynn's and Victoria's—put readers out of synch with their usual expectations for girls and girls' writing in high school and create critical reformulations of the gendered status quo.

If those who teach writing translate the reflexive/expressive writing that Emig called for into performative processes that enable socioculturally scripted writers to write on/through the body of their lived experiences, we might enact "postmodern qualities of antiform, play, chance, anarchy, and silence" (Faigley *Fragments of Rationality* 14). Once expressivist strategies of freewriting and personal experience narrative, for example, are performatively translated, they can no longer be dismissed as essentialized precursors to a more desirable finished product nor as artifacts that represent the authentic voice and essential identity of the writer underneath. Expressive strategies are performatively recuperated as process for its own sake, as composing possibilities for proliferating "subject" configurations outside the restricting frames of the status quo. Through Butler's performative translation of expressivism, we recuperate the value of expressivist strategies for their usefulness in giving voice to (female) diversity; in exploding the belief in a stable, unified self; and offering means for exploring how (gender) identity is multiply constructed and how agency resides in the power of connecting with others and in building alliances.

Performance analyses enable those who teach writing to see other readings for female students—disenfranchised subjects who remain silent or stifled during "school-sponsored writing" (Emig *The Composing Processes of Twelfth Graders*), yet who in effect write a more empowering subjectivity through the text of the body. Writing that provides opportunities to question the very notions of an essential sex and a true or abiding masculinity or femininity reveals the writing subject's performative character and the performative possibilities for proliferating other possible identity configurations. The critical strategy is not necessarily in changing the ways we write but in changing the ways we read the writer and allow the writer to write.

When female writers participate critically in the discourses that shape their lives, they fully participate in discourse communities that previously have erased their writing. Writing on the body helps young women enact the political ideals of inclusiveness that are the goals of feminist theory and composition studies. Young women writing through the body in a high school women's studies class helps them understand the power relations that operate everywhere to create inequality among women and men and among women and women. Writing on and through the body in a high school women's studies class that hopes to transform the oppressive mechanisms of compulsory systems may create conditions that discursively put both the writer and the reader out of synch with the written text she is culturally and institutionally expected to write. Writing on and through the body in a high school women's studies class provides location and opportunity for multiple other, potentially transformative discursive possibilities to emerge. Writing on and through the body helps us value the experiences of every woman and value feminist collectivity in the form of solidarity.

Historically, solidarity begins with consciousness raising and remains an ideal—whatever its present state among women and among feminists. Weaving knowledge gained from "feminized" experience as evidence into academic arguments in a high school women's studies class helps young women recognize overlapping sets of ideas around which continuing common and uncommon struggles for equality are organized: position and location, identity and voice, sexuality and gender, differentiation and commonality, community and solidarity. Writing on and through the embodied expertise of experience allows us to use the scripts of young women's particulars of the present for transformative purposes. There are no essentials indicated in these girls' scripts of the particulars of their lives. Meaning is always fluid, dispersed, and in some sense beyond completion. Feminist lives and texts are always a work in progress.

Notes

1. Lauer's description of the adolescent female writer as "emergent" and "problematic" locates adolescent female writers in an unconsciously infantilized (see Susan Miller *Textual Carnivals* 196) and pathological space (see G. Stanley Hall on female adolescence), which I vigorously contest. What is noteworthy for my purposes in Lauer's assessment is her recognition, as an influential composition scholar, that indeed young women are missing from the action of composition research.

2. Essentialism is most generally defined as a belief in the true essence of an entity, the invariable qualities or properties that define the essential nature of a thing. Constructivism is the belief that identity is socially constructed and not the result of innate biological qualities. In feminist theory, the essentialism/constructivism debate applies most particularly to assumptions about the qualities that constitute understandings of gendered entities such as "woman," "femaleness," and "femininity."

3. Cognitive process views of composing and composition teaching are influenced by developmental psychology and cognitive psychology and trace the cognitive processes of individual writers writing. The most prominent cognitive process views of writing have been forwarded by the research team of Linda Flower and John R. Hayes, who invoke American cognitive psychological models to make pedagogical recommendations that first identify the problem-solving processes that comprise composing, and consequently teach the composing processes of "expert" writers to "novices" (Flower; Flower and Hayes).

4. Expressivists generally define voice as the ability to express oneself forcefully,

authentically, with art. When a student writer is writing with an "authentic" voice, the writing is fresh, surprising, authoritative, and memorable. The writing sounds much like the writer speaks—natural and right, fitting the material and the audience (Kirby and Liner; Macrorie *Writing to Be Read*).

5. Heilbrun, Grumet, and Witherell and Noddings would be examples of feminists who might ascribe to this view of writing and women.

6. Before embarking upon this rereading, I spoke with Professor Emig to gather insights about her current reflections on the poststructural influences in composition (personal interview 1997). Emig explained that she did not focus centrally on gender and other sociocultural factors both because of the pioneering nature of her work and fieldwide skepticism in literary studies about composition investigation in general (see Nelms's account of Emig's dissertation "nightmare"). Clearly, Emig was not naïve in this regard because she comments elsewhere in her analysis about ways that gender and race might possibly have influenced the students' writing processes, which indicates her sensibilities regarding the potential effects of gender socialization and racial identifications on the composing processes of her case study participants.

7. Two prominent factors make possible a feminist revision of Emig's groundbreaking work (*Composing Processes*). First, Emig provided ample demographic information in *Composing Processes* to reconsider the relations of gender to the conclusions she draws about writers' processes; Emig's primary informant was a young woman named "Lynn." Second, Emig self-identifies as feminist; she writes about her lifelong commitments to feminist principles in the introduction to *Feminine Principles*.

> I had consciously lived my entire life as a literal feminist: I had been economically wholly self-sufficient since the age of 22, a lifelong lesbian, an early survivor in fiercely male academic settings. I regard my two university graduate programs in English education as conceptually and actually feminist, at a time when, to my knowledge, no others were. (Emig and Phelps xiii)

8. With the case of Lynn, Emig's primary informant, Emig consciously chose to study a girl rather than a boy according to an interview with Gerald Nelms (118).

9. Gilligan and her colleagues worked primarily with white, middle-class girls to derive these patterns of development. bell hooks presents a different view of African-American women. Deyhle and Margonis indicate that Gilligan's patterns do not hold true for Navajo women either. Since the girls in my study and in Emig's study are primarily white and middle-class, these patterns are more likely to hold in our cases than with differently situated writers in schools.

10. Harriet Malinowitz provides a similar accounting of the writing processes and written texts of gay and lesbian writers in her study of an attempt to create gay/lesbian-friendly discourse communities in a composition class. Gay and lesbian students in Malinowitz's study struggle in ways similar to Lynn in that they feel awkwardly positioned by a homophobic cultural context, as Lynn feels awkwardly positioned in a misogynistic cultural context, to write in ways that disavow their interiority and the complex of actions they might take in their selection and response to certain writing themes and topics in school-sponsored writing. Similarly, the "tough cookies" in Margaret Finders's study of literacies and life in junior high talk about making things up when asked to write about personal experience in their language arts classes.

11. By permitting Gilligan to *retrospeak* to Emig, however, I do not wish to suggest that patterns of adolescent female development identified by Gilligan and others are overly deterministic or indicative of an essentially female nature. I do wish to point to relevant developmental literature through a powerfully focused lens that sees these patterns in relation to Emig's work and ultimately within view of the day-to-day lives of many adolescent girls. I also wish to note its particular relevance to writing in the context of a primarily female college composition class in the final section of this chapter.

12. Performatives in speech acts are those words or utterances that perform or produce what they say. Butler recalls J. L. Austin's example of a judge performing the marriage ceremony with the words "I pronounce you man and wife" both citing the law and becoming a site "for the reconstitution and resignification of the law" (Butler *Bodies that Matter* 107). The ability to perform derives from repetition. Repetition implies that performatives refer to prior acts and become part of a signifying chain that constitutes norms of meaning.

13. Mary Louise Pratt also gives examples of this type of subversion in her landmark speech "Arts of the Contact Zone" in her accounts of Guaman Poma's discursive attempts to persuade the king of Spain and in her son Manuel's attempts to let his fourth grade teacher know that the work he was expected to complete in school was useless to him.

Writing in Women's Studies at Aspen Grove High School

Teach a woman letters? A terrible mistake:
Like feeding extra venom to a horrifying snake.
                                            —Menander (c. 342–291 B.C.)

Choosing Ethnography, Finding a Site

The research methods used in this study draw from the ethnographic tradition of participant observation and case study research (Agar *The Professional Stranger, Speaking of Ethnography*; Heath *Ways with Words*; Lauer and Asher; LeCompte, Millroy, and Preissle; Lincoln and Guba; Saville-Troike; Spradley). Ethnography is one means of reporting the findings of composition investigation, which fulfills composition studies' hopes for more democratic research methods (Faigley "Competing Theories"; Flynn "Review: Feminist Theories"; Heath *Ways with Words*). Ethnography accomplishes these goals because it richly represents the strategies of writers who are embedded within complex cultural situations. Describing and analyzing the social and contextual factors surrounding acts of writing are fundamental to understanding interpretations of writing (Moss 156). Ethnographic methods provide essential tools for exploring how writing may enable adolescent women in a women's studies class to consider their gendering and its effects on the decisions they make in their lives. Several sets of data were gathered and analyzed during the course of the study. These include field observation notes, a semester-end writing evaluation, case study interviews, teacher interviews, ethnohistoric data gathered through examination of school reports and interviews with school- and district-level administrators, and writing samples (Bruce).

I selected Aspen Grove High School as the site of the study because it provided the most viable match with my twofold selection criteria. First, I wanted to work in a public school site with a teacher who was willing to examine gender issues in the course of her curriculum and teaching. Second, I wanted to work with a teacher who would be amenable to using writing as a tool in this examination. I had the most difficult time satisfying the first criterion. It was difficult to locate a public school site where gender issues, specifically women's issues, were being discussed or could be discussed openly because most public schoolteachers that I approached said that discussion of gender issues was either unnecessary, too controversial to take up in the public school, or too divisive.[1] After several months of searching, I contacted Emma Walker at Aspen Grove High School. Walker taught the only women's studies class in the state at the high school level. Walker's class provided a perfect site for this study because gender issues were already the central focus of the curriculum. Walker and I discussed our experiences of teaching in public schools, teaching female students and the potential uses for writing in women's studies curriculum.

At first Walker was hesitant to work with me because she could not see the value of incorporating writing in a women's studies class. She is not a writing teacher and does not feel very confident about teaching assignments that rely on writing. Additionally, she had tried and "failed" (her own assessment) to use written journals successfully in women's studies the first year she taught the class. Students had generally used their journals as diaries to discuss Friday night activities at school or problems with boyfriends. Walker thought journals had been a waste of time and she felt badly about it because journal writing is an integral part of many women's studies classes at the college level. I talked about the many, different ways I thought writing might be incorporated into her existing curriculum and said that I had an idea for using a journal-like writing activity that might work differently. She eventually agreed to let me become a participant observer and incorporate writing into her women's studies class.[2]

The School, Student Body, and Staff

Aspen Grove High School is one of 10 high schools in the largest school district in the state. The school sits on a 55-acre campus and was built according to an "open space" design. The 350,000-square-foot building opened in 1970. The original pod spaces have been retrofitted with walls. Eighty percent of the student body entering Aspen Grove as 10th graders receives a diploma three years later. The 20% that do not finish generally move out of the area or go into alternative programs, home study, or night school. Approximately 35–40 students drop out during their sophomore year. At Aspen Grove 120 of the nearly 2,000 students participate in the free lunch program, and another 55 participate in the reduced lunch program. Elsewhere in the district the percentage of students participating in the free or reduced lunch program ranges from as low as less than 1% to as high as 100%.

The climate in the school is mostly relaxed, friendly, and free from severe behavior problems. Many students describe Aspen Grove as a place where you can come and be yourself. Preppies, cheerleaders, straight-edgers, hippies, cowboys, punk rockers, Mormons, and non-Mormons coexist harmoniously. The pressure to conform to certain community norms that exists in other schools is less so at Aspen Grove. Walking around the halls, one notices that most of the students wear blue jeans or baggy shorts and T-shirts or polo shirts to school. The only noteworthy exceptions to this "uniform" are worn by the cowboys, who dress in cowboy boots and ten-gallon hats, and by the punk-rockers, who generally dress in black, dye their hair in primary colors, and pierce and tattoo various parts of their bodies. Alternative groups of students such as these comprise a relatively small portion of the student body.

Three administrators oversee the school—the head principal, Rod Harris; the assistant principal in charge of discipline and facilities, Nanette Kantola; and a second assistant principal in charge of curricular and extracurricular scheduling, Tom Brigham. The principal and the male assistant are Mormon. All three are white. The approximately 100 (61 women and 50 men) teachers and aides are divided into 15 instructional departments, each led by a department head. Teachers are given a great deal of instructional latitude in their respective classrooms as long as students do well on standardized test measures and not too many parents complain. Course content is selected on the basis of a combination of factors. Some classes offer concurrent enrollment at the community college or at the university and the curricular content is determined by the relative institution. If the class is a core class, the state core standards and the district in compliance with those standards establish curricular benchmarks.

Individual teachers in collaboration with their departments determine other offerings.

A Portrait of the Teacher in the Women's Studies Class

Emma Walker is considered a highly effective teacher by the Aspen Grove administration. She teaches advanced placement American and European history classes, women's studies, and two sections of an interdisciplinary humanities class, which she designed and team teaches with Lyn Blessing, an English teacher. Walker is a white, middle-class, 49-year-old female, born and reared in the Aspen Grove community.[3] Walker's mother was Mormon and her father was Catholic; she received varied ecumenical training. She now is involved in a self-study of Eastern religions, particularly Zen Buddhism. Walker has never been married. She is closely involved with parenting her younger sister's two children, a boy of 16 and a girl of 8. Her nephew moved in with her during the 1996–1997 school year. Walker also assumes care responsibilities for her younger brother who requires kidney dialysis several times a week and generally needs the use of a wheelchair to get around. Walker has taught at Aspen Grove for more than 20 years. In her years of teaching, she has received many teaching awards, which include District Teacher of the Year, EXCEL Foundation Teacher of the Year, PTSA Teacher of the Year, and a BYU teaching award. She has been relieved of some of her teaching duties so that she might help the school obtain grant monies from district, state, and national sources to support the achievement of school goals. She has been highly successful in these efforts.

Walker believes that education is a lifelong process. She thinks that good teachers are those who inspire students to make the all-important decision to learn, to be open to other ideas, and to be analytical enough to see alternatives. She believes her students live in a troubled world. Her goal is to ease their way and to prepare them to succeed in the future. She has no desire to make her students' choices for them, but rather to give them the tools to make competent decisions. Walker designed the women's studies course for junior and senior students at Aspen Grove after a highly publicized bulimic-related tragedy took the life of a popular Aspen Grove girl. At the same time that everyone else at the school was wondering,

"How could this happen at a place like Aspen Grove?" Walker was busy developing a women's studies course proposal to present to the principal and the district offices for curricular approval. Walker had taken several courses in the women's studies department at the university and was concerned about the young women that she taught. She had a good idea why the young women at Aspen Grove were suffering from unprecedented instances of eating disorders and depression and why no one was talking about it until a young woman at the school died.

Walker collaborated with Aspen Grove's principal, Rod Harris, to develop the women's studies curriculum. Harris had a personal as well as a professional agenda for the class. He is the father of five daughters. Harris's eldest daughter, a "bright, talented, beautiful" young woman, suffered during adolescence from both bulimia and anorexia, as did a growing number of girls at Aspen Grove, and he could not understand why. When Walker presented her idea to Harris, he saw women's studies as a class that might help young women enhance their self-esteem and prevent other young women from suffering the way his daughter had. At first, Harris was reluctant to allow Walker to broaden the scope of women's studies beyond issues in self-esteem, thinking Walker's proposed curriculum might cause a political fiasco at the district offices and in the community. However, because he is extremely supportive of her work, he lobbied for the curriculum she had designed before the central administration.

Walker's course proposal did raise a number of eyebrows, but the district thinks very highly of Harris and accepted the women's studies course Walker designed to be offered once a semester for general elective credit at Aspen Grove High School (AGHS) on a three-year experimental basis. Women's studies at Aspen Grove has since been permanently approved, which means that Walker can teach it as long as students continue to enroll and that other schools in the district can adopt a similar curriculum. Two other schools have sporadically offered classes modeled after Walker's curriculum.

Designing Curriculum that Fosters Gender Equity

Although the course was accepted in response to a school tragedy that primarily led parents and administrators to be concerned about girls' self-esteem, Walker's purpose was much broader. She hoped to raise students' awareness about a wide array of gender-related issues. The semester-long course Emma teaches includes literature that focuses on women's history, women's images in literature and the media, women's psychology and moral development, women and violence, women in the workforce, eating disorders, male and female communication styles, and an array of feminist theories.

Working with Walker to help achieve the critical goals for the course and to understand the ways in which composing processes might support those goals, I spent three years of participant observation in the women's studies class at AGHS integrating a writing component into Emma Walker's eclectic curriculum. The work became the focus of my dissertation research (Bruce). I attended every class session—observing, taking field notes, participating in class discussions, and debriefing each class with Walker at the end of the day. I taught several writing lessons each semester, responded to all student writing, and analyzed it for emergent patterns and themes. I also completed case studies of nine students—eight girls and one boy—during my years of coparticipation in Walker's class.

Gender awareness is important to both Walker and me because we believe high school students crossing into the new millennium constitute a generation in crisis. Caught living at a crossroads between two eras, adolescent women and men today learn gender stereotypes that are completely out of synch with the way they will grow up to live. As if perseverating on images they have never seen of Ozzie and Harriet and the Cleaver family, students today still hold on to a 1950s-esque fantasy of the American dream. Outdated illusions of romanticized, heterosexual, middle-class adult lives proliferate regardless of the statistics, which indicate that a majority of these students will divorce, will raise children in widely extended and diverse family structures, will have to work longer and longer hours outside their homes, will experience long periods of unemployment in their lives, and will have to make decisions about sex and children of which Harriet Nelson and June Cleaver never even dreamed. Even though many of Walker's women's studies students have lived lives very different from those in these long-expired, white TV families, they expect to live in middle-class comfort where the father works and "brings home the bacon" and the mother stays at home, raises lovely children, and has warm cookies and milk waiting for them when they get home from school.[4]

Walker believes that although many of her students have not lived this fantasy life, they desire it, perhaps because they have never known it. It is not uncommon, for example, to hear a story similar to Alisa's:

> My parents have been divorced 4 times and I am only 16....I always tell them that one day I'm going to show them how it's done. I believe that I would do anything for my husband....I would love to be a housewife. I love kids. I LOVE to clean. But I would still have a career, go out and have fun with friends....I believe you can fall in love and live happily ever after, but it will take some work.[5] (freewrite)

As a result of this pastiche of fantasy layered through the real-life experiences of her students, Walker sees high school students struggling with the ambiguities underlying their socialization: "My students are caught in a trap that threatens to pull them apart. Women's studies is a location for questioning these fantastic assumptions and providing students with tools for thinking their way around the traps." Walker believes that high school students need critical opportunities to question the contradictions between their beliefs and the experiential realities they are bound to face in their lives.

Such opportunities, Walker insists, are not available to students in many of the English, history, and social studies courses or in alternative core electives offered in conventional high school fare—a fact that strikes me as odd given the multiple calls for schools to be more gender fair (e.g., AAUW *Hostile Hallways*, *Out of the Classroom*, *Campus Climate Revisited*; Orenstein; Sadker and Sadker). Granted, Whaley and Dodge report that textbook publishers have worked to include more female authors in their textbooks, but on closer examination the selections included in textbooks available to students tend to be shorter works or works that often fail to show strong, successful, satisfied female protagonists (44). In support of this claim, Walker's female students report that the relative absence in their courses of meaningful curricula that support investigations of and discussions about women's lives and issues by and large leaves them feeling that the world is made for men and that their place within it is as a subordinate, 1950s-esque, indeed.

Women have only been "added and stirred" into the curriculum fostering an illusion that equity has been reached. For example, during all the years she has taught the course, Walker has asked her students on the first day of class to explain their interests in enrolling in women's studies.

Answers generally echo that of Jen, "All my classes have taught about men. I want to know what women were doing while men were doing the stuff I've already learned about." During the course of my investigation in Walker's class, we have listened to the reports of hundreds of mostly female students who speak much like Jen about their high school education. If a gender-balanced curriculum has been reached because of efforts to push educators to achieve gender equity in schools, then our students have not experienced it. There is a great deal more that can be done to ensure sensitivity to gender issues among our students and colleagues.

Women's Studies' Students at Aspen Grove

Approximately 35 to 40 students per semester enroll in women's studies at AGHS. Most are juniors or seniors although there are no restrictions on enrollment. Male and female students are equally encouraged to enroll; however, between zero and four male students generally enroll each semester.[6] Except for the fact that most of the students in the class are female, the demographics in the class generally mirror those of the rest of the school. The academic ability level of the students varies from those who spend most of their day in "resource" classes to those who take predominantly honors and AP classes. Most women's studies students, male and female alike, report that women's studies is the most important class they take in high school. They think it should be required for all students. They characterize Emma Walker as one of the best teachers in the school.

A Portrait of the Typical Women's Studies Student

When Walker asks students on the first day of every semester why they have enrolled in women's studies, they generally report that they want to learn about women in history and about historical development of sex roles. Male students also report that they want to learn about "the other half of the population" or that their girlfriend or sister insisted they take this course to learn how "to get along better with women." However, in end-of-semester evaluations, both female and male students universally report that other topics, such as portrayal of women in the media, women and psychology, communication between men and women, and violence against women are the most meaningful portions of the course. History has never placed among the students' most valued topics in the class.

Neither Walker nor I have been able to acquire any systematic information about whether the women's studies students are any more or less typical of other students at AGHS.[7] It is our overall impression that there is no such thing as a "typical" women's studies student and that the students who enroll in women's studies have some experiential or intellectual reason to question the gender status quo. They have a sense of the societal inequalities between men and women in their culture and are skeptical about the ways things are for males and females. In comparison with students in Walker's other classes, a disproportionate number of women's studies students during the course have reported experiences of sexual, physical, and mental trauma or abuse of some kind.[8] Something has caused students who enroll in women's studies to sense that all is not well in the traditional Edenic view of male and female sex roles.[9] It is our view that they come to women's studies to ponder their confusions and to get some answers to their questions.

Walker and I also believe it is very possible that other AGHS students have faced similar questions-at-issue but either do not enroll in women's studies or talk about these things in their other classes or with their counselors or teachers. We neither wish to presume that the students in women's studies are typical of other students at Aspen Grove nor do we wish to presume that they are not. Given the extraordinary amount of trauma, rape, and abuse that women's studies students have self-reportedly faced, we would *prefer* to believe that these students' experiences are atypical for most adolescents. However, our inclination to pathologize more than likely results from a desire to relieve our own discomfort about these students' experiences. Consequently, we are left with a haunting premonition that identifying these students as "abnormal" is altogether naïve, uninformed, and blindly complicit with status quo assumptions about the innocence, interests, and experiences of many adolescents.

Women's Studies in the High School

Emma Walker has assembled a reader that serves as the textual center of the women's studies curriculum. In preparing to teach the first section of the class, she talked with a number of women's studies faculty members at the university in an attempt to collate materials that she might use. She assembled various readings in a student reader and uses these as the basis for her curriculum. One of the tenets of women's studies that Walker adopted in her first class was to ask the students at the beginning of the semester what they wanted to learn. She discovered that the students had interests that went beyond her original vision; she expanded the topics and the reader to address the students' concerns. The selections that appear in her current reader include images of women in history and the traditional Western canon, the women's movement (first wave), women's psychological and moral development (Gilligan; Kohlberg), women's representation in advertising and the media, women in the workplace, eating disorders, violence against women, male and female communication styles, and contemporary feminism (the women's movement—the second and third waves).

Materials in the reader represent a variety of feminist perspectives. The course surveys prominent feminist theories such as liberal feminism, Marxist feminism, radical feminism on reproduction and mothering, radical feminism on gender (sexuality cannot be addressed directly in Walker's course packet because of state mandate[10]), psychoanalytic feminism, social feminism, existentialist feminism, and postmodern feminisms, including challenges by feminists of color both to patriarchy and to white middle-class feminist discourses. A table of contents for the student reader appears in Figure 3.1.

Figure 3.1

Women's Studies Student Reader
Table of Contents
Section One: Ancient Views
"Demeter and Persephone," Charlene Spretnak, *Lost Goddesses of Early Greece*. Avalon Metaphysical, 1992: 105–118.
Harmony of Man and Nature, author unknown, unpublished teaching materials, E. Walker.
Traditional View of Chinese Women, unpublished teaching materials, E. Walker.

(Figure 3.1 cont.)

Traditional Views of Western Women, unpublished teaching materials, E. Walker.

"The World Without de Beauvoir," Robin Morgan, *Ms.,* July 1986, 85–86.

"Matter," Susan Griffin, *Woman and Nature: The Roaring Inside Her.* New York: Harper and Row, 1978, 5–46.

Section Two: History and the Women's Movement (First Wave)

"Declaration of Sentiments and Resolutions, Seneca Falls Convention of 1848," Elizabeth Cady Stanton.

"Marriage," Sarah M. Grimke, *Miscellaneous Essays, Weld-Grimke Papers.* Courtesy of the William L. Clements Library, University of Michigan, Ann Arbor. (1792–1873).

"The Story of Sadie Sachs," Margaret Sanger, *Margaret Sanger: An Autobiography.* New York: W.W. Norton, 1938, 86–92.

"Constitutional Argument," Susan B. Anthony. *Life and Work of Susan B. Anthony, vol. ii.* Indianapolis: Bowen-Merrill, 1898.

"Why Women Should Not Meddle With Politics," Lydia Drake. 1840. Manuscript copy, Western Reserve Historical Society, Cleveland, Ohio.

"The Constitution and Women's Legal Rights: Chronology of Women's Rights Under the Constitution," compiled by Kathryn L. MacKay from Leslie Friedman Goldstein. *The Constitutional Rights of Women: Cases in Law and Social Change.* Madison: University of Wisconsin Press, 1988.

"Ain't I a Woman," Sojourner Truth, 1791–1883. Originally in Elizabeth Cady Stanton, Susan B. Anthony, Matilda Gage, *The History of Woman Suffrage (1881–1886).* Vol. 1. Reprinted Ayer Press, 1979.

"Rediscovering American Women: A Chronology Highlighting Women's History in the United States and Update—The Process Continues." *The Spirit of Houston: The First National Women's Conference.* An official report to the president, the Congress, and the people of the United States, March, 1978. Washington, DC: National Commission on the Observance of International Women's Year, U.S. Department of State, 1978.

"No Rights but Human Rights," Sandra F. VanBurkleo. *Constitution.* Spring/Summer 1990, 4–19.

"The Yellow Wallpaper," Charlotte Perkins Gilman. (1899). Ed. Robert Shulman. Oxford, UK: Oxford U.P., 1996.

"The Story of an Hour," Kate Chopin, *The Awakening and Other Stories.* Ed. Judith Baxter. Cambridge, UK: Cambridge U.P., 1997.

"In Search of Our Mother's Gardens," Alice Walker, *In Search of Our Mother's Gardens: Womanist Prose.* NY: Harcourt, 1983.

Section Three: Psychology

"Carol Gilligan: Leader for a Different Kind of Future," Lindsey Van Gelder. *Ms.* January 1984. 37–40, 101.

"The Heinz Dilemma," Lawrence Kohlberg. *The Philosophy of Moral Development: Moral Stages and the Idea of Justice.* San Francisco, CA: Harper & Row, 1981.

"Kohlberg's Levels and Stages of Moral Development." Unpublished teaching

(Figure 3.1 cont.

materials, E. Walker.

"Comparison between Kohlberg and Gilligan." Unpublished teaching materials, E. Walker.

Section Four: Women and the Workforce

"Occupational Statistics." U.S. Department of Labor, Bureau of Labor Statistics. Unpublished teaching materials, E. Walker.

"The Femininization of Poverty." Arlene Burraston-Wood. *Ladies' Home Journal.* January, 1993. 127–132.

"Poverty Is a Woman's Problem." Kathleen Shortridge. *Women: A Feminist Perspective.* 3rd edition. Ed. Jo Freeman. Mt. View, CA: Mayfield Pub, 1984.

"The Approaching Obsolescence of Housework: A Working-Class Perspective." Angela Y Davis. *Angela Y. Davis Reader.* Ed. Joy James. Blackwell Pub., 1998: 193–209.

Section Five: Women and Violence

"Violence Against Women: A Ms. Report on Life in Our Times." *Ms.* September/October 1990. 33–56.

"The Mind of the Rapist," David Gelman, Karen Springen, Regina Elam, Nadine Joseph, Kate Robinson, Mary Hager. *Newsweek* July 23, 1990. 46–52.

"A New Way of Looking at Violence Against Women." Lisa Heinzerling. *Glamour* Vol. 88 Iss. 10, October 1990: 112.

"Many Bright Teens Believe 'No' on Date Means 'Yes.'" Cox News Service. *Salt Lake Tribune*, November 18, 1992. http://www.tribaccess.com/lpBin21/lpcxt.dll?f =templates&fn=slmain-j.html. 15 Apr 2002.

"Women Cry for Protection from World of Violence." Cox News Service. *Salt Lake Tribune*, February 7, 1992. 1.

"The Rape of Mr. Smith." Unknown. *Women Helping Women: Volunteer Resource Manual.* Rape Crisis Services. Urbana, IL.

Section Six: Women and Female Stereotypes at Work

"The Secret of My Success: How to Be a Contender at Work and in Love." Susan Squire. *Cosmopolitan.* 174–176.

"How To Make an Impact on a Man." Unknown. *Cosmopolitan.*

"Men Trouble." Nina Keilin. *Ladies' Home Journal.* August 1990. 84–89.

"A Slap at Sex Stereotypes." Andrea Sachs. *Time.* May 15, 1989. 66.

"The Bitch Manifesto." Joreen. (pen name for Jo Freeman). Reprinted from *Notes from the Second Year.* Ed. Shulamith Firestone and Anne Koedt. New York Radical Women, 1970. April 1997. *Documents from the Women's Liberation Movement: An On-line Archival Collection.* Special Collections Library, Duke University. http://scriptorium.lib.duke.edu/ wlm/bitch. 15 April 2002.

Section Seven: Communication Styles

"Can We Talk?" Peggy Taylor. *New Age Journal.* November/December 1990. 31–36.

(Figure 3.1 cont.)

"Women: Can We Get Along? and Men: Should We Even Try?" Kay Leigh Hagan. Excerpt from "Women Respond to the Men's Movement: A Feminist Collection." 1992. *Utne Reader.* January/February 1993. 52–55.

"The Fight Is Far from Over." Rebecca Walker. Reprinted with permission of Ballantine Books. *The Black Scholar,* 1992, *Utne Reader.* January/February 1993. 56–58.

"Do Gays and Lesbians Get Along?" Laura M. Markowitz. *Utne Reader.* January/February 1993. 61.[11]

"Figures about Child Abuse and Domestic Violence Have Been Inflated and Biased against Men." Unknown. Excerpt with permission from *Texas Monthly*/February 1992. *Utne Reader.* January/February 1993. 60–61.

"It's a Jungle Out There, So Get Used to It!" Camille Paglia. *Utne Reader.* January/February 1993. 61.

"Television as Gendered Technology." Karen E. Altman. *Journal of Popular Film-Television.* 17.2. Summer 1987. 46–56.

"The Body Game." Carol Alt, Kim Alexis, and Beverly Johnson. *People.* January 11, 1993. 80–86.

Section Eight: Images of Women in the Media

"Body Doubles." Greg Collins. *GQ.* April 1988. 260–266.

"The Body Beautiful." Rosalind Coward. *Female Desires.* 1985. New York: Grove Weidenfeld. 39–45.

"Pouts and Scowls." Rosalind Coward. *Female Desires.* 1985. New York: Grove Weidenfeld. 57–60.

"Some Day My Prince Will Come: Female Acculturation through the Fairy Tale." Marcia K. Lieberman. *Don't Bet On the Prince: Feminist Fairytales in North America and England.* Ed. Jack Zipes. Aldershot, Ger: Gower, 1986. 185–199.

"The Esquire Survey: What Makes the Perfect Woman?" Arnold Roth. *Esquire.* March 1990. 176.

Section Nine: Eating Disorders

"Eating Disorders: Bulimarexia." Nancy Vrechek. *Adolescent Counselor.* October 1992. 79.

"Are You Dying to Be Thin?" (questionnaire). Unpublished teaching materials. E. Walker.

"Symptoms for Early Detection of Anorexia Nervosa/Psychological Characteristics and Physical Complications Associated with Anorexia Nervosa." Unknown. Unpublished teaching materials. E. Walker.

"Signs and Symptoms of Bulimia Nervosa." Unknown. *Anorexia Nervosa and Bulimia Nervosa.* Unpublished teaching materials. E. Walker.

"You Call This Progress?" Lois Anzelowitz. *Working Woman.* October 1992. 95.

Section Ten: The Women's Movement (Second Wave)

"Listen. This Is the Noise of Myth." Eavan Boland. *An Origin Like Water: Collected Poems 1967–1987.* New York: W.W. Norton, 1996. 187.

"The Feminist Mystique: Why College Women Don't Like the Feminist Label." Maria Buhl. Based on National Health and Leisure Time Poll, National Opinion

(Figure 3.1 cont.)
>   Research Center. *Working Woman*. October 1992. 96.
>   "Why Can't a Man Be More Like a Woman...and Vice Versa." Kathryn Phillips. *Omni*.
>   October 1990. 42–43, 68.
>   "Sizing Up the Sexes." Christine Gorman. *Time*. January 20, 1992. 42–51.
>   "Feminist Activism: Issues and Events." Unknown. *Women Move*. 443–456.
>   "Blueprint for a Second Wave." Anita Shreve. *Women Together, Women Alone: The Legacy
>   of the Consciousness Raising Movement*. New York: Viking, 1989. 241–275
>   "Defining Feminism(s)." Linda Ellerbee. *Move on: Adventures in the Real World*. New
>   York: HarperPerennial, 1992.

Walker also uses several videos throughout the course of the class to teach concepts she is trying to convey. A list of these videos appears in Figure 3.2.

Figure 3.2

Films and Videos Used in Women's Studies

Traditional Myth of Demeter and Persephone, School District Resource materials.

The Yellow Wallpaper, Charlotte Perkins Gilman, Alistair Cooke's Masterpiece Theatre.

Rosie the Riveter, documentary.

Killing Us Softly: Women's Image in Advertising, Claire Kilbourn, University of California, Santa Cruz.

The Little Mermaid, cartoon from Walt Disney Pictures.

Pocahantas, cartoon from Walt Disney Pictures.

Tootsie (starring Dustin Hoffman, Jessica Lange).

All of Me (starring Lily Tomlin and Steve Martin).

The Human Animal, Sexuality, Nature vs. Nurture, Phil Donahue, talk show host, narrates.

Anorexia Nervosa, 20/20 segment on the work of Canadian psychologist Peggy Claude-Pierre.

Women's Studies Pedagogy

Emma Walker draws on formats used in women's consciousness raising groups in the early 1970s to organize procedural aspects of the class. She investigated the literature and discovered that consciousness raising procedures were products of the Redstockings, the New York Radical Feminists, and the National Organization for Women. She reports that later groups amended and edited these early blueprints to suit the needs of their members. Consciousness raising procedures include (a) select a topic, (b) go around in a circle, (c) do not interrupt, (d) never challenge anyone else's experience, (e) avoid the temptation to promote one woman to the position of leadership, and (f) sum up. Walker has adapted these principles to fit the classroom context.

Walker organizes women's studies around the students' interests. She varies the time and emphasis spent on each of the topics based on students' indications on the first day of class. She adjusts the curriculum throughout the semester. Students decide how the class will operate on a day-to-day basis. Class consensus determines the weight each assignment will carry toward report card grades. The assignments that the students decide among are two short-answer essay tests, two formal and several informal papers, an ongoing reading response log (journal), an oral book report, and daily preparation and participation. Walker explains the assignments before the students discuss and vote on the options:

> The test is short answer essay and I give you the questions ahead of time. The papers are reflection and analysis. The "journal" is a daily assignment where you respond to the readings and discuss what you're learning there. The book report is an assignment that was designed by women's studies students. You read a book from the list I give you and then you talk about something in the book that strikes you in some way and makes you think about it. I take preparation points every time I take roll. I ask you to say "yes" if you did all the reading, "half" if you did half, and "none" if you did none. Participation is measured by your participation in discussions. I grade participation not just on quantity, but on quality....The only way you can be hurt by participation is if you say nothing at all. (field observation notes)

Each class decides the weight of the assignments differently every quarter.

The class is organized around a discussion format, which Walker also explains to students on the first day of class:

> The next rule of the class is quite easy, I think. Your opinions and ideas in this class are of equal value. The idea here is to talk about things that are difficult, that are often invisible to you at this point. It's hard to talk about those things, I will give you the toolbox to be able to see things and say things that you didn't know before. It can be fun, but it can be discomforting at the same time.... This is a discussion-based class. (field observation notes)

Walker does not begin class until all the students are sitting on the front row of desks, which are organized in a horseshoe arrangement. She does this so the students can address each other in face-to-face discussion, which she believes is essential for the class to work successfully. She tends to begin each class session with open-ended questions that allow the students to direct the day's discussion around their interests. For example, during a discussion of Sarah Grimke's abolition-era essay on marriage, Walker begins the class with the question, "She is saying that marriage is legalized prostitution. What do you think about that?"

On another day when the discussion topic is women in the workplace and the students watch the documentary film *Rosie the Riveter*, Walker begins the class with the question, "Did you get those transitions—how they got women to go out and get those jobs and then go back into the home? What do you think of Rosie?" Students generally respond freely; the discussion evolves fluidly. Walker keeps talk going by asking additional open-ended questions throughout the period.[12]

Occasionally Walker lectures on topics that do not appear in the reader. Lectures are rare and are used to introduce concepts that would be difficult reading for the students in their original form. These include a summary of scientific perceptions of women throughout the ages (Griffin); an overview of Freudian psychology, Lacanian psychology, and the French feminist perspective of Luce Irigaray; and an analysis of challenges to white, middle-class feminisms by contemporary feminists of color, particularly bell hooks and Patricia Hill Collins. She uses these frameworks of analysis as a basis for the students' examination of a number of literary texts and films, which include Gilman's *The Yellow Wallpaper*, Sojourner Truth's "Ain't I a Woman?" speech, Kate Chopin's *The Awakening* and The Story of an Hour, Disney's *The Little Mermaid* and *Pocahontas*; and *Tootsie* starring Dustin Hoffman.

Additional strategies that Walker uses during the course include the following three small-group activities:

1. During a section on girls and education, students tour the school in pairs and investigate kinds of classes offered throughout the school and tally (a) number of male and female students in each class, (b) sex of the teacher, and (c) any gendered artifacts that are on display

in or around the class.

2.   During the education section, Walker conducts a simulation of the Broverman study. Students divide into three groups and receive lists of paired characteristics (e.g., aggressive/passive, competitive/not competitive, talkative/not talkative). Walker gives directions privately to each group. One group selects one of the pair that most characterizes stereotypically male behavior, another group selects one of the pair that most characterizes stereotypically female behavior, and the third group selects one of the pair that most characterizes characteristics of healthy adults. Students choose and discuss.

3.   Following several sections in which sex-role characteristics arise in discussion, Walker asks students to pair up and role-play a simulation in which they must negotiate a contract with a partner about role functions in a typical living unit. The purpose of this activity is to raise students' consciousness about the need to negotiate expectations prior to agreeing to living with someone.

Toward the end of each quarter students give oral reports on a book that they read on their own time.[13] Books are selected from a reading list that Walker hands out the first day of each quarter. She initially assigned students to read a book of their choice and write a report on it. However, students preferred oral instead of written reports and decided they should give a brief synopsis of the book, then talk about parts that struck them in some way. The purpose of the oral report is for readers to explain what impressed them, why it impressed them, and what conclusions they drew from the reading. Students sign up for the days they will discuss their reading and are graded on their critical analysis of the book. For example, Missy reports on *The Chalice and the Blade*:

The view of this book is that there was a time when matriarchy ruled but archaeologists don't tell that part. They figure that there was a time when goddesses were prominent and matriarchy ruled and so women had more power than men. I have to disagree with male dominance. Archaeologists have never told about female participation in historical periods. It's not right that women went unacknowledged. Throughout time women that should have been acknowledged were ignored. If we are going to have equality, then we need to know about the contributions of both women and men. That is where we ought to be, I think. (field observation notes)

Book reports provide students with opportunities to assert their opinions, express emotions, make personal connections to the content, think critically and analytically, and construct arguments. Missy's comments, although satisfying Walker's hopes for the assignment, are somewhat atypical. Very few students do more than make an emotional or value response, and this disappoints Walker. Solo's book response is more typical of that which the students produce:

> I read *Refuge* by Terry Tempest Williams. It's really depressing, it's good and hopeful and stuff. But the story is really depressing. Her mom dies of cancer, so does her grandma, six of her aunts have cancer. She parallels it with the flooding of the Great Salt Lake in Utah. I liked it but it was really sad. For me it made total sense to have connection with a place. (field observation notes)

Walker perseveres with the book reports because she wants students to be acquainted with a range of feminist materials. She hopes students will remember something of what they have been exposed to through the book reports. When the ideas seem more relevant to their daily lives, Walker wants her students to have something of substance to which they can return after they are long gone from women's studies. Even though not many students make critical connections between their lives and the women's studies content through the book report, Walker continues with it because it promises to accomplish her curricular goals.

Figure 3.3: Women's Studies Booklists

First Quarter
Lost Goddesses of Early Greece: A Collection of Pre-Hellenic Myths, Charlene Spretnak.
Women's Diaries of the Westward Journey, collected by Lillian Schlissel.
In Search of Our Mother's Gardens: Womanist Prose, Alice Walker.
Women's Reality: An Emerging Female System in the White Male Society, Anne Wilson Schaef.
Meeting at the Crossroads, Lyn Mikel Brown and Carol Gilligan.
In a Different Voice, Carol Gilligan.
Smart Girls, Gifted Women, Barb Kerr.
Joy Luck Club, Amy Tan.
Refuge, Terry Tempest Williams.
The Awakening, Kate Chopin.
A Doll's House, Henrik Ibsen.

(Figure 3.3 cont)

The Dollmaker, Harriette Arnow.

Creation of Patriarchy, Gerda Lerner.

Simone de Beauvoir, Deirdre Bair.

The Grimke Sisters from South Carolina: Pioneers for Women's Rights and Abolition, Gerda Lerner.

The Grimke Sisters from South Carolina: Rebels Against Slavery, Gerda Lerner.

'Til They Have Faces, C.S. Lewis.

Mistress Anne, Carolly Erickson.

Black Looks: Race and Representation, bell hooks.

Reviving Ophelia, Mary Pipher.

Nappy: Growing up Black and Female in America, Aliona L. Gibson.

Second Quarter

Backlash, Susan Faludi.

The Beauty Myth, Naomi Wolf.

Female Desires, Rosalind Coward.

The Cinderella Complex: Women's Hidden Fear of Independence, Colette Dowling.

Women of Ideas, Dale Spender.

Women's Ways of Knowing, Mary Belenky et al.

The Feminine Mystique, Betty Friedan.

Incidents in the Life of a Slave Girl: Written by Herself, Harriet A. Jacobs.

Sula, Toni Morrison.

Possessing the Secret of Joy, Alice Walker.

The Second Sex, Simone de Beauvoir.

My Life, Golda Meir.

Portrait of An Artist: A Biography of Georgia O'Keefe, Laurie Lisle.

The Body Project, Joan Jacobs Brumberg.

This Bridge Called My Back: Writings by Radical Women of Color, Cherríe Moraga and Gloria Anzaldúa.

The Bluest Eye, Toni Morrison.

The Women of Brewster Place, Gloria Naylor.

Reviving Ophelia, Mary Pipher.

Every semester Walker organizes a "Women in Careers" panel presentation. She surveys the students and prioritizes a list of their career interests. Because time is limited, she tries to invite representatives from professions that are most commonly requested, and asks four or five women working in these professions to talk about what they do, about what kind of education and training they have received, and about their work experiences. Professions represented during the course of the study include writer, college professor, counselor, teacher, television news broadcaster, artist, businesswoman, battered women's shelter help line counselor, nurse, lawyer, doctor, and professional model. On occasions, Walker has scheduled a prostitute and a truck driver to speak. The panel presentation introduces students to professional women and gives them ideas about the varied issues different women face in the workplace.

The Role of Postmodern Feminisms in Walker's Pedagogy

Emma Walker's pedagogy is influenced by a study of postmodern feminisms, a stance that we share in common. Walker asserts a view of culture that is decidedly constructivist in its perceptions:

> Society is desperately looking for a new sociocultural metaphor. The binary logic of Western thought is no longer sufficient to explain modern culture. The industrial capitalist model of organization that undergirds our institutions from the family to the corporation is not working. To clear the way for multiple new possibilities, we must learn to take apart the logic of that which is faulty in our current metaphors. (personal interview, February 1993)

Instrumental for Walker is the postmodern constructivist problematizing of categories such as male and female, African and Euro American, heterosexual and homosexual, which results in the rejection of constructions of gender, race, and sex that depend on binary opposition. She puts constructivism to task in the women's studies classroom by relying on deconstruction among other strategies as one of her primary pedagogical tools. Deconstruction is the effort to critique all language as unstable and indeterminate in its meanings. Deconstruction, as Walker teaches the strategy to her students, aims to reverse power hierarchies and displace systems that keep asymmetrical relations in place. Deconstruction is a tool that can be used to unsettle the logic of polemical thinking, to consider the multiplicity of possibilities that range between binary oppositions, and to learn to accept differences.

Walker believes that deconstruction is the best tool currently available for finding transformative possibilities for social and cultural change:

> You can't name the gendering [or racializing or sexing] that is going on until you reverse the situation. What comes out of that is the power structure that holds [inequities] in place. You set up the binaries so you see what is in operation and

how it's working and you consider all the possibilities between that are never considered in that polemical figure of construction. I think it's going to be a lot of years before I understand the intricacies of how maleness and femaleness are constructed in masculinity and femininity. It's like the deconstruction tool will give them a way to begin to understand it. Once you have those basic tools, you're thinking changes and you can begin to unravel it on your own, with your own life experience, and that's really what I want them to have. (personal interview, June 26, 1995)

In Walker's teaching, deconstruction reveals a variety of ways that females and males might escape and resist binary categorization. Deconstruction opens up an endless range of gendering possibilities and rhetorically dismantles the domination of one sex, one race, one religion, and one sexual orientation over (an)other.[14] Through deconstruction, women's studies students at AGHS are able to envision cultural possibilities that they never imagined were available.

Walker uses deconstruction strategically. For example, she uses deconstruction as a tool to tactically demonstrate images of women that are portrayed in the media. First, students identify types of roles that are assigned to white women and men and black women and men in several media: print and visual advertising, television, and film. Once various roles have been identified and distinguished, Walker asks the students to imagine an inversion of the roles. In this process, the students generally can define the power structure that holds in place the hierarchy. They see how the status quo benefits white men and disadvantages white women and people of color. They begin to identify other possibilities that might be associated with both men's and women's gendered, racialized, and sexed identities and roles. In this moment, deconstruction opens up an array of possible escapes from simplistic either/or categorization such as "White men are strong and muscular" and "White women are coquettish and demure"; "Men and women of color are 'disadvantaged' to white men and women."

Another example of Walker's uses of deconstruction in the classroom is an audiotape of "The Meeting," a "phase two" deconstruction of a Christian church meeting. In the sacrament meeting scenario represented on the tape, typical sex roles and responsibilities ascribed to churchgoing Christian men and women are reversed. For instance, women are in charge of the meeting, and men are assigned childcare responsibilities. Women go on proselytic missions and men stay home to pray for and support the female missionaries. "The Meeting" explicitly demonstrates by role reversal how power is differently assigned to males and females in traditional American Christian culture. Because these students live in a predominantly patriarchal Christian community and are quite familiar with the roles and responsibilities assigned to churchgoing men and women, the deconstruction is particularly revealing. It makes visible sex stereotypes that these students tacitly accept as the "normal" and "appropriate" ways of being male or female in their community. This example helps them to understand both the process of deconstruction and to imagine what it would take to escape from lives held in simplistic binary opposition.

"The Meeting" deconstruction is a session that is often cited in the student evaluations as one of the most memorable because it helps students to understand the tacit assumptions they hold about gender roles and expectations. Other texts that Walker has used deconstructive tools to analyze include film clips from *White Man's Burden* starring Harry Belafonte and John Travolta, a "phase two" deconstruction of race relations in the United States; the films *Tootsie* starring Dustin Hoffman, *All of Me* starring Lily Tomlin and Steve Martin, and *The Little Mermaid* and *Pocahontas* by Disney, each of which illustrate the social construction of polemical gender, race, and sexuality roles in Western culture.

Walker sees an important limitation within postmodern theory, especially as it relates to work with adolescents. As I discussed in Chapter 2, the deconstruction of identity can be carried so far that the meaningfulness of gender, race, or sexuality categories is eliminated altogether (Bordo; Gilyard "Literacy, Identity, Imagination, Flight"; Royster and Williams; Sedgwick; Villanueva). Walker teaches the students about viewing gender, race, and sexual identities from a constructivist rather than an essentialist perspective, and she helps the students to understand that the gendering, racing, and sexing of identity and creation of relational roles in a masculine and feminine likeness is a matter of societal convenience that benefits white men more than white women and people of color. However, Walker hesitates to deconstruct the roles entirely.

> The reason that I kind of hesitate on deconstruction is I think deconstruction can result in a kind of nihilistic attitude, especially if you are 17 or 18 years old. And it's an important tool, but... I don't want to have them [the students] think a way into nothing basically because what is important is going to be the responsibility for them of making things work. In relationship [with the "other"], it's what you

have to do—to make [human relationships] work… (personal interview June 26, 1995)

Because it is highly unlikely that many of the women's studies students will reject entirely the societal roles that have been laid out for them, Walker feels obliged to be cautious in using deconstruction as an analytic tool at this precarious point in their development. She wants them to be able to analyze the power hierarchies that hold unequal relationships in place, but she also wants them to have something to believe in at the end of the day.

Other tools upon which Walker relies include Simone de Beauvoir's articulation of the structural position of woman as "other." De Beauvoir analyzes woman's positioning in culture as constructed on the basis of a positionality of "other than male"; this results in women functioning in culture from a deficit or less powerful location. Walker believes that the "othering" analysis allows the less powerful in culture to find a place of validation for how they feel; it gives them "the tools to look at things from a different perspective and name what bothers them":

> I think, for instance, with Rachel, who comes from a Jewish family or with LeTisha, who is Hispanic, who feel very "other" in [this state]. It gives some way of relating to "otherness"—some similar understanding of others, which we already know. It made [them] be able to name it and find a space besides the typical place. You see, you have to hope that they will see the different perspective of what being "the other" gender really does in relation to class, religion, [sexuality,] and race. (personal interview, June 26, 1995)

The "othering tool," which is derived from an existentialist feminist perspective, helps students understand the structural complexities that hold in place unequal cultural positions and provides them with ways to get past their rage at the resulting injustices. It also helps students see that the troubling issues of gender concern that they face are structurally and institutionally embedded and not the fault of any one individual. This can make the subordination of women seem like an insurmountable problem; however, it can also help students to find allies in empathic others.

Walker also incorporates a revisionist examination of the students' historical understandings of woman/women. She bases this examination in a postmodern conception of multiple other possibilities and reviews the historical marginalization of women's lives. Following a "pop quiz" during which she asks students to name the accomplishments of such notable women as Margaret Sanger, Susan B. Anthony, Ida B. Wells, Elizabeth Cady Stanton, Sojourner Truth, Lucretia Mott, and Emma Goldman, she comments:

> Walker: Did I pick women you should have heard about? They were famous in their day. Why don't you know about them?
>
> Solo: We've learned about mostly [white] men and what they've accomplished. [White] men are placed higher, as if they were better, like if a [white] man and woman were qualified for the same job, the man would get it. They've been placed higher, so we learn about them as more important.
>
> Lois: [White] men publish most of the books. They write about what they've done, what they have said. (field observation notes)

Walker demonstrates through historical analysis how white women and people of color have been written out of history and how this has resulted in the silencing of their accomplishments in historical perspectives. This tool also provides students with a perspective on the present and validation for writing themselves and the missing "others" back in.

Walker believes that the most important pedagogical outcome and ultimately the most important reward of women's studies is what she terms "consciousness raising," which she achieves through the application of the historical, existentialist, and postmodern tools just described.

> I think that our society has absolutely gone about designing roles that make relationships between men and women and between whites and people of color fail.... And in school, I think to take it as far as you can to help them create or fashion different kinds of roles, which we promote in the course—that's my goal, because otherwise it looks like a recipe for disaster. I guarantee that no one will be happy. And so consciousness raising for me is most important because I can hopefully affect their individual lives. That's my goal. (personal interview, June 26, 1995)

It is important to recognize Walker's postmodern goals for raising consciousness in terms of outcome: the creation of multiple other ways to become masculine or feminine or both in relationship with other masculine and feminine subjects, or both. Her use of "consciousness raising" as a pedagogical tool derives from a liberal feminist perspective. Anti-essentialist postmodern feminists generally oppose liberal perspectives. However, Walker is not trying to help young women become more powerful feminized subjects, as might be mistakenly concluded from her use of "consciousness raising" as a teaching strategy. She gives students a varied array of feminist tools to expand their thinking about gender socialization in culture. She teaches them to see that there is an endless range of ways to be male and female and other when these strategies are applied.

The Roles of the Researcher

I attended every class session during a pilot phase of the project (academic year 1992–1993) and during the study proper (academic year 1994–1995). In the second year of the study (academic year 1993–1994), I attended the class periodically to introduce writing assignments and confer with Walker about my developing theoretical framework for the study. During the pilot study, Walker and I developed a strong rapport. We were quite at ease working together as a collaborative teaching team and established a protocol of interaction that remained steady throughout the course of the study.

During both the pilot phase and the study proper, I sat at a student desk flanked by other students in the class and assumed the role of student and discussion participant. During the pilot phase, I took rough field observation notes by hand. During the study proper, I took rough field observation notes on a laptop computer that occasionally beeped and hummed. Students seemed to get used to my notetaking after the first couple of weeks of class.

Although most of my attention was absorbed in observing and taking field notes, I regularly participated in class discussions. Most of the time, my participation in discussion came in the form of responses to direct questions asked by Walker or at the specific insistence of a student. Typical questions of this sort took the form of, "Heather, what do you think about that?" or "Heather, what did you do when...?"

Walker clearly assumed the primary teaching role. When she first introduced me to the students, she said that I was a doctoral student from the university:

> Heather will help us with writing and be a member of our class. She will help me answer questions when I get stuck, which I frequently do. Heather takes notes in this class. She is working on her Ph.D. at the university. She keeps track of all the dialogue in the class; she analyzes what goes on. You may be aware of the typing

at first, but you will get used to the clicking. After a while you will not notice it. (field observation notes)

Occasionally she contributed other pieces of information about me that influenced my role in the class.

I think Heather gives a different orientation than I do. She married far too young. She has children. She's been divorced, and I think her being here gives a fuller perspective of life. Between the two of us we have covered all the life options. She will teach part of the class and participate in the discussions. Be very nice to her... (field observation notes)

At other times Walker told the students that I was a single parent of two adolescent boys, that I was an experienced writing teacher, and that I was conducting an ethnography of writing in women's studies for my dissertation.

I assumed the role of "teacher" when I taught the writing assignments that were incorporated into the class. The assignments and my pedagogical stance(s) will be discussed in a following section. I read all the writing assignments, gave written and verbal feedback, and graded all the written work that was assigned. I also substitute taught for Walker on several occasions when she was ill, attending professional meetings or making professional presentations. Once or twice, she asked me to teach the class even though she was there because she felt I had more experiential knowledge about some of the topics. These included the sections · on women and violence and any time questions regarding women and sexuality concerns were raised.

Walker and I debriefed each class at the end of every session, unless she had to attend faculty or department meetings. I used informal interview techniques during these sessions and asked Walker questions like how she thought the class session had gone, what learning goals had been achieved, where there might be need for reteaching or incorporation of a different approach. We discussed students individually and ruminated over their personal and intellectual progress. Our habit was to discuss the plans for the next class session during these debriefings. We exchanged ideas for teaching the daily curriculum, for raising pertinent issues, and for incorporating writing. We regularly discussed curricular goals, collected and exchanged materials, and planned strategies for teaching the course.

Walker identified my role variously as that of "equal," "team teacher," "writing specialist," "researcher," "self-identified feminist," "teaching partner," "comrade," and "ally":

> I always felt like, for example, we talked about things. We spent time discussing ideas and so forth. So in moments where I got stuck, you bailed me out. There were moments when you would say, "You did that really well." You know. "How did you do that?" There was always an exchange. It seemed like there was never a hierarchy, it was always an exchange back and forth.... [We worked] as equals and I think that comes from the tradition I assumed because of your background that you knew writing as a specialty—that you were a self-identified feminist. I knew the classes that you'd had. We had that same basis of knowledge. And that was what was going on in the classroom. So we could discuss ideas as comrades in the classroom. And as teaching partners in the classroom. I always felt from day one that it felt more like a team teaching situation than it did like the observer from on high from the ivory tower university, you know, who observes you and pokes at you and asks questions to make you better. I mean it never felt like that, ever, a day... I always viewed you as an ally. (personal interview, June 26, 1995)

The students perceived my role from numerous perspectives. I initially thought that because I would be conducting some lessons and responding to student writing as part of the data gathering that these roles would lead the students to perceive me as a "teacher." Many students mentioned my teaching role when asked to describe my participation in the class, but they never called me "their teacher." For example, Trisha said, "It really helped when you taught us that compare/contrast thing. I have used that a lot in some of my other classes and that has helped me to do much better on some of my assignments. It would be good if you did more of that (personal interview, May 11, 1995).

The students never used the word "friend" to describe my participation. They used terms like "concerned adult" and "an older, experienced female they had bonded with" to describe my role. Trisha explained:

> You took us seriously. So when you wrote back and said, "Yeah, I understand what you're saying" and "You know, you're right about this," and then "You should think about other things." You know? Cause it showed you actually cared about my development or whatever. You know? Not that I just relied on your responses, you know. It's more that you cared, you wanted to read it. (personal interview, May 18, 1995)

I attempted to acknowledge the validity of their perceptions about things we were discussing in class, but always looked for ways to open up their thinking and consider other possibilities. In this way, I was viewed as someone who could be trusted, who tried to understand, and who connected with them in a role other than "teacher as evaluator" or "teacher as friend." For example, the students described their perceptions of my role(s) in various ways:

> We trusted you (Solo writing evaluation).

> When you write back and stuff, you tell us the truth, your own personal experiences. It helps to have a connection—to know that someone else is reading what you're writing and listening to you. It breaks down barriers, you know? I think I can actually talk to this person, you know? You talk about it and it helps to know that even with the age difference, I mean even somebody older has the same feelings. And they think what I am saying, you know, is not just some screwed up teenager thing, you know? Like some high school kid. (personal interview, Trisha, May 18, 1995)

> It was really helpful to have something that was like, "I understand how you feel." (personal interview, Thomas, May 25, 1995)

> We were all on the same level. You and Emma never talked down to us. I can't stand to be talked down to. You sat here on your computer, and you had your own opinions and you had your own things to add in.... It was like female bonding or something. (personal interview, LeTisha, May 23, 1995)

I think a reasonable composite characterization of their perceptions of me is as a coparticipant who was personally interested in them, who would not give up on them.

Walker believed I also played another role for the students—that of role model.

> I think having another woman in the class, one who is older than the students, whose life has gone down a totally different course than mine—who has been married, who has children their age, who had the courage to get herself out of a marriage that didn't work, has a perspective that is valued because that road is the road most of our students are going to head down. Most of the students relate to you. (personal interview, June 26, 1995)

At times I perceived my role as that of counselor or advisor, although the role of "teacher as parent or counselor" was one I initially wanted to avoid. However, the students frequently asked my advice on what they should do about some situation with their parents, friends, and lovers. To fulfill their expectations of me as a coparticipant that they trusted, I felt obliged to respond to them thoughtfully. I became involved in providing students with information, comfort, and support on several occasions. Their issues included concerns about sexual activity, birth control, pregnancy, and abortion. They also sought advice on how to deal with violent partners or parents or both, how to deal with their awakening sexuality, and how to cope with the after-trauma of rape.

I tried to avoid the role of "teacher as evaluator" and I think I was fairly successful in that endeavor. Sharon explains:

> [I realized] it's OK. This is not going to be like little English comments that are like "Good job, you get a gold star." You know? You're not going to question me at all or anything. And like I really progressed and talked about more personal issues and more things I had experience in or I wanted to learn about. I wrote about how I felt about things and like the feminization of poverty. Stuff like that. (personal interview, May 23, 1995)

The students perceived my role as that of a listener and responder—one who was interested in what they had to say for its own sake. I do not think that they saw me in the evaluator role—as one who corrected their grammar, spelling, and punctuation and gave them grades.

I was often conflicted about how well I was drawing the line between researcher and participant. I believed it was important to work with the writing and with the students in the ways that I had defined at the start of the study and to remain an unobtrusive participant in the class, but there were many times when I was anxious about whether or not I was maintaining objectivity. Walker reflected upon the researcher aspect of my role in our final formal interview:

> When push came to shove, you were a teacher first. I know I had control over the curriculum and reader, but I think of us as team teaching the class, almost.... But what is interesting is even though you were participating and doing all that, I was impressed because you were always aware of the dynamics and what to say and what not to say. You did make those kinds of decisions. There were moments where I clearly saw you not say anything because you knew it would change the classroom dynamic. (personal interview, June 26, 1995)

I believe that my frustration at such moments was apparent to Walker. However, given my participation in this study as both teacher and researcher, it was not my purpose to describe this setting as an intact community without accounting for the effects of my presence on the situation. I believe I was able to manage to keep enough ethnographic distance to fulfill my intended roles.

The Role of the Researcher's Pedagogical Assumptions

Articulating compatible frameworks that draw both on postmodern theoretical and feminist pedagogical assumptions is not easily accomplished, as was reported in Chapter 2. The essentialism/constructivism rift mirrors a division that exists between feminist theorists and feminist teachers. Joy Ritchie explains:

> Despite the fundamental feminist assertion that knowledge cannot be separated from the knower, many feminist academicians continue to operate within a binary perspective, placing intellect against emotion, separating reason from experience, and, ultimately, setting theory against practice. As a result, important connections between feminist theory and practice are masked, and we lose sight of our common purposes. Furthermore, we lose sight of our students. (249)

Nevertheless, I have attempted to reconcile feminist theory with feminist pedagogy to support my teaching goals for women's studies students at Aspen Grove. To accomplish this admittedly lofty goal, I draw upon the work of feminist teachers who assert constructivist definitions of gender and sex. By relying on the pedagogical articulations of constructivist positions on teaching, I attended to the students' gender and writing concerns in ways that hoped to reconfigure the binary logic of oppositional views of theory and practice.

Mary Louise Pratt's description of the *Cultures, Ideas, Values* classroom at Stanford University figures prominently in my thinking. Pratt's view of the classroom as a "contact zone," a social space, "where cultures meet, clash, and grapple with each other, often in contexts of highly asymmetrical relations of power" (34) has been widely discussed for its theoretical and practical suitability for attaining the egalitarian aims of a course in composition.

> The "'contact zone"'…offers one curricular model of a more pluralistic and interactive approach to literatures and cultures represented in emerging student populations…. There is still much to be done in constructing the pedagogical arts

of the "contact zone," and…one of the most important steps is to reconfigure power relations in the classroom….This can be achieved only if I identify myself, like everyone else, as an individual speaking from a specific subject position and as someone who does not have all the answers…. We all need to become decentered subjects, to recognize that the illusion of a "core" self is at the heart of essentialist positions which privilege one culture over another. (Van Slyck 152–153)

If, as Pratt suggests, the classroom can be conceived of as "a space that is aware of itself as a location where conditions of coercion, radical inequality, and intractable conflict are usually involved and where participants can attempt to grapple openly with these issues" (37), then the contact classroom might provide a potential basis for envisioning a pedagogy informed by feminist identity politics. In the contact zone of the classroom, theory explicitly informs practice.

For example, in a contact classroom, peoples "geographically and historically" separated come into "contact" with one another and establish ongoing relations through which they are constituted (Pratt 32). The wide range of gender issues that are debated in women's studies at Aspen Grove provides the content with which these students "grapple." The students in women's studies examine gendered cultures, ideas, and values. The writing assignments that I incorporate to forward discussion offer effective grounds for producing multiple responses to the issues. As Mary Louise Pratt speculates, these writing experiences help the classroom to function

…not like a homogeneous community or a horizontal alliance but like a "contact zone." Every single text we read (add *and write*) [stands] in specific historical relationships to the students in the class, but the range and variety of historical relationships in play [are] enormous. Everybody [has] a stake in nearly everything we read (*and write*), but the range and kind of stakes [vary] widely…. Virtually every student [has] the experience of seeing the world described with him or her in it. Along with rage, incomprehension, and pain, there [are] exhilarating moments of wonder and revelation, mutual understanding, and new wisdom—the joys of the contact zone. The sufferings and revelations [are] at different moments to be sure, experienced by every student. No one [is] excluded, and no one [is] safe. (38)

In the women's studies classroom, students come to see that the readings, our discussions, and the writing assignments provide a site where an important kind of cultural dialogue can take place. Women's studies is a space where complex attitudes on different sides of a question are dramatized. Often, contradictory positions create a contact zone. The fact that some or all of these ideological stances are scrutinized suggests that positions taken by students may also be questioned. Students come to recognize that any discussion of gendering is clarified by an awareness that there are many different sides to an issue, that we can question the values our positions represent, and that the premises behind particular attitudes are often more universal and complex than they may appear at first glance. The questions we raise about culture, gender, and sexuality help expose the fact that all values are socially constructed, thus undermining essentialist and monocultural notions of "truth."

For example, Maria wrote a response to Carol Gilligan's analysis of female silencing (Gilligan, Lyons, and Hanmer), which we read during a class readaround. Maria claimed that she would enter relationships assuming that they were temporary and eventually destined to end. This presupposition, she maintained, would free her to speak whatever was on her mind throughout the course of the relationship because if she began any relationship assuming that it eventually would end, she would not need to risk voicing over her feelings to preserve a connection that would inevitably dissolve. She said that she never wanted to fall into the traps in which she had seen both her mother and her sister entangled, of voicing over their true concerns about a relationship for the sake of maintaining the relationship only to be abandoned in the end. Maria concluded that both true love and genuine friendship were a convenient lie we tell ourselves to accommodate our desire for connection.

Many students disagreed vociferously with Maria, who adamantly defended her position. They ardently defended true romance and the possibility for a genuine relationship based on "open communication and honesty." Their primary critique of Maria's position concerned what they saw to be Maria's ill-fated preconceptions about love. They were certain that her stance would necessarily undermine any potential for establishing a successful relationship. JoAnna argued that Maria was "setting herself up for failure from the outset," and JoAnna was convinced you could establish a genuine relationship by being open and honest with a friend or a potential mate.

Walker directed a series of questions to students in which she asked them to examine the constructedness of their positions and to see that adamant assertions do not constitute reasonable entertainment of other alternatives. We affirmed Maria's attempt to stand apart from group consensus and to question its practices and values. We actively reflected her position back to her for clarification. In so doing, Walker helped adamant opponents to make sense of Maria's reframed position within the context of current statistics on divorce. The students referred again and again to this writing exercise and discussion as an example of an instance in which they were asked to examine the viability of previously unconsidered positions for solving a particular pragmatic problem. Although many of them did not indicate that they had changed their original stance, they had seen an instance in which a student with a contrary view gained the strength and security to express that view. They also acknowledged that several students began to question some of their assumptions. The processes we engage in the contact zone of the women's studies classroom create possibility for dialogue through which Walker, the students, and I begin to model challenges to the "culturally coded" gender positions that constitute our viewpoints (Van Slyck 153).

However, although Pratt is content with confronting conflicting responses to cultural issues in her college classroom, the revelation that no one is safe in the "contact zone" of the classroom poses a point of tension for women's studies in a high school where public school teachers are expected to serve *in loco parentis*. In women's studies, students examine difficult questions about their own emerging subjectivities. As they come to realize that their presupposed ideals of coherence, unity, and stability, which lie behind belief in one's gender, culture, as well as in one's own individual identity, is a constructed fantasy, their worlds begin to unravel.

Students report alienation from friends, lovers, families. Many of them find that they cannot "go home again." Some sigh in relief. Some say they are glad to see gendering for the illusion that it is, but they admit that it was easier to live inside the safety of a coherent and stable fiction of sex roles and expectations. Others fiercely maintain that no disjunction between their own and their parents' or community's values has taken place (or ever will take place). Many are ambivalent, and they write about this ambivalence as a source of both strength and conflict. Writing and talking in the women's studies classroom opens a door to a more complex understanding of subjectivity for students to explore. Sometimes the space behind the opening does not always feel safe and comfortable.

With each step we take in trying to redefine gender roles and expectations, we also need to examine and redefine our pedagogy. Much of

Walker's curriculum "actively interferes" (Jay) with students' gender experiences and values. This active interference can have emotional and psychological consequences. On the one hand, Walker hopes to teach the students the tools with which they might radically reconfigure gender roles and expectations; on the other hand, she does not want them to suffer psychic or emotional damage in the process. Part of our task is precisely to lead students to the recognition that we must all learn how to exist both within and outside our individual gender cultures. However, existing outside of dominant norms is a troubling task for most adolescents. Walker's curriculum has the power to expand the horizon of the students' gender literacy to encompass views she (or he) has scarcely acknowledged as real. This can be a difficult maneuver when students come face-to-face with challenges to conventional gender roles that they hold dear. Sometimes, such as in the response to Maria, the classroom exchanges become heated and emotionally charged.

Under these circumstances, the goal of the feminist teacher in the high school is to create a "safe house." For Pratt, the term is used

> ...to refer to social and intellectual spaces where groups can constitute themselves as horizontal, homogeneous, sovereign communities with high degrees of trust, shared understandings, temporary protection from legacies of oppression....Where there are legacies of subordination, groups need places for healing and mutual recognition, safe houses in which to construct shared understandings, knowledges, claims on the world that they can then bring into the contact zone. (39)

Walker and I appreciate the importance of building a "safe house" in the women's studies classroom where students' views may be put into dialogue with one another while maintaining a sense of continuing community (Graff 62). Writing in women's studies helps construct a "safe house" for students who are already open about an issue that may go against the grain of typical gender norms (such as against heterosexuality, monogamy, or the romance script). Writing helps reluctant students to gain strength and a secure sense that it is acceptable to express alternative views. Writing helps students who are not as open to question some of their assumptions.

To create an atmosphere in which students are safe, a feminist teacher attempts to understand the teacher-student relationship not in terms of separateness, but in terms of copresence, of interaction, and of interlocked (not consensual) understandings and practices. The stance a feminist teacher takes in relation to "authority with or authority over" her students (Gore) is an omnipresent concern in the "contact zone" of a feminist classroom. Troubling boundaries between student and teacher expertise and privileging exchanges of authority among students and students and teacher(s) is a possible goal. In such an atmosphere, important questions about values and subject positions may emerge as students respond to texts that illuminate gender questions-at-issue and questions that examine the cultural location from which writers write. "To recognize that one's subject position is derived from social and cultural constructs which are always already in place" (Van Slyck 154) is always a goal of writing pedagogy in women's studies. In an effort to create safe houses within the contact zone of women's studies, I always write with and to the students by identifying myself as an individual speaking from a specific subject position (white, middle-aged, female, non-Mormon, heterosexual, divorced, mother of two adolescent boys, Ph.D. student, former English teacher, not their teacher, researcher, ethnographer, etc.) and as "someone who does not have all the answers." By marking myself with the identity politics by which I am encoded, I want the students to realize that each of us speaks and writes from an infinite array of culturally coded positions rather than from "universal," "innate," "natural," or "right" essential positions.

Another "contact" perspective that informed the pedagogical goals underlying my participation in women's studies at Aspen Grove is articulated by Elizabeth Ellsworth in her description of Coalition 607, a class taught at the University of Wisconsin, Madison. In Ellsworth's classroom, there is a realization that there are partial narratives that some social groups or cultures have and others can never know but are necessary to human survival. This awareness is a condition to embrace in order to build social and educational interdependency, which recognizes differences as strengths and as forces for change. As adolescents, women's studies students tend to cluster in and privilege members of specific groups. One's identity politics and the privilege of membership in groups of variable status (e.g., cheerleaders and jocks versus punks and cowboys) can create mistrust in those who feel excluded. Asking students to discuss solutions to gender stereotyping moves the dialogue to a new space in which they begin to take responsibility for themselves. Our challenge as feminist teachers is to create coalitions where students may find connection; however, we also explore the very difficult territory of gender identities and differences. Our intent is to help our students understand otherness better so they may begin to define what they as individuals *and* as members of communities need to do to connect across borders.

To instantiate this pedagogy during my day-to-day participation in Walker's classroom, Walker and I openly articulated the different roles and responsibilities among teacher, teacher-researcher, and students. We wanted to specifically identify our theoretical and pedagogical differences because we wanted to split open multiple possibilities within gendered teaching identifications. Multiple voices emerged through writing, teaching, and discussion. I tried to act as an active deconstructive lever in the classroom by which new gender possibilities could emerge. This meant that I had to know when to speak and when to remain silent.

Kathleen Weiler's (*Women Teaching*) uses of "voice" as a pedagogical category to examine the interaction of teachers and learners, the knowledge they both bring to the classroom, and the knowledge they produce together was especially helpful to me in making these decisions. In contradistinction to the "authentic voice pedagogy" of expressivist compositionists, which was discussed in Chapter 2, "voice" for Weiler is related to the processes through which "teachers and students attempt to make themselves present in history and to define themselves as active authors of their own worlds." Voice in Weiler's sense represents those varied subjectivities, discourses, and biographies that constitute teachers and students alike within relations of power, history, and experience, and allow for multiplicities of identifications to be honored.

> As a referent for empowerment, the category of voice interrogates the processes through which identities are ignored, constructed, or experienced; meanings are affirmed, marginalized, or questioned; and experiences are formed within the interlocking and related processes of subjugation, affirmation, and enlightenment. (Giroux and Freire, as cited in Weiler *Women Teaching* xiii)

Weiler's concept of voice and dialogue undergirds the pedagogical and analytic choices I made during the course of this study, which will be discussed more fully in the sections that follow.

The Role of Writing Teacher in
Women's Studies at Aspen Grove

I had great success using assignments drawn from expressivist traditions when I taught English in the middle and high school. My adolescent students seemed more energetic engaging writing tasks that called for personal experience narratives. However, during the decade I was in graduate school and working in women's studies at AGHS, social views of composing and composing instruction theoretically eclipsed expressive views as the favored framework guiding writing in the classroom. The relatively abrupt shift from a private, individualistic view of the writer to a view that frames the writer as a constituent of culture brought a shift in purposes for writing instruction. Writing teachers who once invited students "to master or transcend the strictures of written discourse" now were calling upon students "to participate critically in the discourses that shape their lives" (Sullivan and Qualley ix). Constructivist views of writers and writing altered the nature of the writer's expertise, which previously had been viewed within the province of individual achievement. Constructivist views aimed at social transformation by attempting to foster students' critical literacy and to view rhetoric and composition as consequential in a participatory democracy (Sullivan and Qualley).

Constructivist views of composing forwarded by social rhetorical and feminist theorists in composition studies were certainly compatible with my aims for writing in the women's studies class at AGHS. However, as I discussed in Chapter 2, the constructivist theorists who framed social rhetorical and feminist views of composing and composition instruction traced the developments of process approaches by pitting social views against the ideological naiveté of expressivism. These theorists critiqued expressivism for failing to enact the egalitarian aims of composition. Although opposed to expressivism, social rhetorical and feminist positions failed to adequately identify pedagogical strategies that enabled the democratic goals they forwarded (c.f., Faigley *Fragments*; Emig and Phelps; Sullivan and Qualley). Anti-essentialist constructivist claims have been theoretically potent, but pedagogically barren.

As a result, many writing teachers, especially those working in K-12 environments who have been influenced by the broad-reaching influences of the New Hampshire school, have acritically stuck with expressivist approaches to teaching writing (e.g., Atwell; Barbieri; Calkins; Donald Graves; Murray; Newkirk; Reif; Romano). Because I had so little to draw on when designing assignments that would foster the goals of the study and because I had experienced so much success with expressivist strategies in the past, I returned to Emig's work with 12th-grade writers to frame my approach to the writing assignments in women's studies at AGHS. I relied on Emig rather than writers in the New Hampshire school, who had been my previous guides, because I identified constructivist underpinnings in Emig's work, which do not emerge in writers from the New Hampshire school.

Additionally, composition scholarship regularly refers to the influential nature of Emig's work on *both* composition theory *and* practice. Composition scholars rarely if ever invoke writers in the New Hampshire school in discussing the influences of their theory to inform pedagogical practice (with the exception of Donald Graves and Murray). Although New Hampshire school-influenced pedagogy is popular and effective, especially in K-12 settings, it has not explicitly addressed anti-essentialist, anti-expressivist critiques. As a feminist researcher and writing teacher, I could not afford to ignore these critiques. I wanted to build a feminist bridge over tensions caused by constructivist/essentialist rifts in composition. I discovered my building blocks by rereading Emig through a feminist performance lens. A performance view of Emig's work repositions and recuperates the efficacy of expressivist strategies in light of the political goals of social rhetorical and feminist approaches to composing and composition teaching, and provides a constructivist framework for designing writing assignments for women's studies.

Each assignment I incorporated into the AGHS women's studies class asks students to rely in some fashion on personal experience narration or memoir as evidence in support of some point about gender questions-at-issue. The specific assignments include a deconstructive writing response log (known colloquially as "the journal"), in which students critically and informally respond to ideas raised by the reading; an academic writing autobiography in which students write their literacy history; a masculinity/femininity history in which students retell and analyze their most memorable gendering events and experiences; and several spontaneous, in-class freewriting exercises in which students respond to readings or class discussions. I designed these writing assignments (a) to help students open new perspectives on gender, race, religion, and class issues, (b) to lead students to question rigid perspectives on gender and cultural roles and expectations and to enlarge their awareness about gender and cultural issues of concern, and (c) to think through the difficult problem of how to position myself as a teacher in the margins of student writing as a mediator, guide, and provocateur of critical dialogue. See Figures 3.4—3.7.

Figure 3.4: Student Handout *Writing Response Logs*

WRITING RESPONSE LOGS

You are expected to keep a writing response log in this class. You will need an 8" X 11" spiral bound notebook for this purpose. You need to write a response in your writing response log for every assigned reading. Feel free as well to comment on ideas from class discussions and lectures in your log. Each response entry should take you about 20–30 minutes to write.

There are several forms your response entries may take. We will teach you different forms in class. You may be asked to complete double entry responses, dialogue responses, free responses, or rhetorical analysis. Whatever the form you use in your writing response log, you should consider the following:

- Read your assignments with an eye toward responding to the authors or discussing the reading material or ideas from class with other students. You may choose to quote or point out a part of the reading or discussion ideas that you find especially interesting or enlightening. Tell why you think the ideas are intriguing.

- Ask questions. Tell what confuses you. Tell what you don't understand. Explain why you think a writer, a teacher, or a classmate had a particular idea. Tell what you think the writer, teacher, or classmate needs to consider.

- Share experiences/memories/anecdotes that relate to the readings or class lectures and discussions. Tell what you are reminded of in the writing or discussions. Tell what comes to mind as you are reading, discussing, or listening. Write about these experiences or memories. Tell what made you make the connection—tell why you thought of them.

- React. Write about your reactions to the readings or discussions, giving examples and reasons for your reactions. You might think about telling whether you think the writer or discussants were hoping you'd have this response. Or another response.

- Connect. Tell how the reading or discussion relates to other things you've already read or experienced. Tell how you predict you might use this information in the future.

The purpose for this writing response log assignment is to get you thinking about discussing the readings with others as you are in the process of reading the course

(Figure 3.4 cont.)

assignments.

Evaluation of Writing Response Logs:

Credit is given for completing entries for each reading assignment. Informal, unpolished writing is acceptable. Grades are given on the basis of quality of thought.

To receive a "C," you need to respond to each reading assignment. Responses will indicate that you read the assignment because you discuss some of the main points of the reading.

To receive a "B," you should be able to answer these questions affirmatively:
- Have I read and responded to all of the assigned readings?
- Do I move beyond summary of texts, to connections with my own experiences and belief systems?
- Do I respond to the questions I receive from peers or from the teachers?

To receive an "A," you should also be able to answer these questions affirmatively:
- Do I try to respond to readings and discussions in ways that indicate my insights, my questions, my agreement or disagreement with the ideas in the readings or discussions?
- Do I extend my entries to use the writing to puzzle through ideas that I react to strongly?
- Do I attempt to discover new thoughts, ask questions about things that confuse me?
- Do I connect ideas together from different topics?
- Do I make connections between the ideas we read about and discuss in class and my experiences and beliefs?

Figure 3.5: Student Handout *My History as a Writer*

MY HISTORY AS A WRITER

Introduction: Women's writing has been much overlooked throughout history. We are interested in incorporating a variety of writing assignments into the women's studies course to help you be able to write texts that won't be overlooked. The central question in this first writing assignment is: "How did you learn to write?" We ask you to consider this question because writers who understand their own development as writers have greater insight into their writing processes—their successes and failures, problems, and promises. These insights ought to help you identify where you are in your writing development and help you to grow and develop as a student writer.

Using this rationale, we ask you to prepare a history of yourself as a writer. We want you to think back to your memories of learning to write—the "lessons" you learned both in and out of school about how to communicate on paper. Some lessons may be positive, others painful. Whatever their effect, they all contributed to your development

(Figure 3.5 cont.)

as a writer. Knowing more about yourself as a writer is a foundation experience this semester in women's studies.

Planning: You may wish to begin with planning by taking some notes. The idea is simply to list your thoughts as they come, letting the memories come as they will. If you can't remember at first, don't worry. Your "unconscious" mind will go to work on the problem. You will find yourself beginning to recall unexpected bits of the past at odd moments as you relax or dream. Jot down these fragments—situations, scenes, images. In other words, simply begin to collect "stuff about writing" from your memory. Here are some questions to prompt your planning or pre-writing in the form of notetaking.

1. Who or what was the earliest influence, either positive or negative, on you as a writer? How did those influences affect your attitudes toward writing? Toward yourself as a writer? Toward your writing habits?

2. How have you felt over the years about the task of writing? How do you feel now? How would you like to feel? Where do you see yourself as a writer right now? What do you think you need to work on at this stage of development?

3. What have been your behaviors as a writer? That is, how do you get the job done? When and where did you (and do you) seem to write best? How much could you (and can you) write at one sitting? Do you need to pace, eat, read aloud, talk aloud, rewrite as you go? Do you have special "tools"—a particular kind of pen, for example? What are your working habits? Where did you learn them?

4. To what extent have you written (and do you write) just for yourself? For other people? Does having an audience help or hinder you? What about writing for a "teacher audience"? What kinds of writing have you enjoyed most/least?

5. Go back to your files or scrapbooks and collect samples of your writing, if you are able. What are some distinctive features of your writing? How can you account for the changes over time? What, if anything, can you say about your voice as a writer? Your sense of purpose, tone, subject, and audience? Your commitment to writing?

The point about notetaking is NOT to answer EVERY question but to gather a rich database of impressionistic material to write from. Let your mind take you from early memories to more recent ones. Think about the teachers from your past, the assignments you turned in, the love letters and notes you wrote, the contests you won (or should have won), and the grades or other feedback you received.

The Assignment: Use your notes as an organizational aid to write an essay in which you describe the experiences that have had the most significant influence on you as a writer. Analyze the experiences to illustrate the influence they have had on your perceptions about yourself as a writer and the writing you have done. In the conclusion of the paper, draw some generalizations about what these experiences tell you about what you believe may be the best way to learn or be taught to write. The essays should be 3–5 pages in length (double-spaced and typed is best; handwritten is OK, if legible). These papers will not be graded, although you will receive preparation credit toward

(Figure 3.5 cont.)

> your semester grade. We are mostly interested in using these essays for planning the most useful and successful ways to teach the course and help you develop as a writer.

Figure 3.6: Student Handout *Masculinity/Femininity History*

MY FEMININITY/MASCULINITY HISTORY

Introduction: Characteristics of masculinity and femininity are socially constructed within one's culture. Our expression of masculinity or femininity about how males and females act in a particular culture influences our attitudes, behaviors, interests, and beliefs. What may be considered appropriate masculine or feminine behavior in one culture may be considered inappropriate in another. The central question in this writing assignment is "How did you learn to `act like' a girl or a boy in your culture?" We ask you to consider this question because masculinity and femininity are socialized traits. These insights into where your beliefs about how males and females in your culture are "supposed" to act ought to help you identify where you are in your development and help you to grow and develop in other masculine/feminine ways.

Using this rationale, we ask you to prepare a history of yourself as a masculine and/or feminine individual. We want you to think back to your memories of learning "to act like a girl/boy"—the lessons you learned both in and out of your family, school, church, and social and athletic groups about how to act as a feminized and/or masculinized subject. Some lessons may be positive, others painful. Whatever their effect, they all contributed to your development. Knowing more about how masculinity and femininity are constructed in a culture is a foundational experience this semester in women's studies.

Planning: You may wish to begin with planning by taking some notes. The idea is simply to list your thoughts as they come, letting the memories come as they will. If you can't remember at first, don't worry. Your "unconscious" mind will go to work on the problem. You will find yourself beginning to recall unexpected bits of the past at odd moments. Jot down these situations, scenes, images, fragments. In other words, simply begin to collect "stuff about gendering" from your memory. Here are some questions to prompt your planning or pre-writing in the form of notetaking.

1. Who or what was the earliest influence, either positive or negative, on you as a feminine and/or masculine subject? How did those influences affect your attitudes, interests, behaviors, beliefs about what boys and girls do, how they act, what their interests are?

(Figure 3.6 cont.)

2. What are some of the experiences you recall that have helped to shape your masculinity and/or femininity? List some of these experiences. Tell how you felt at the time. Describe how you think about them now.

3. In what ways, if any, have you resisted or escaped the categories of masculinity or femininity? How do you feel about your resistance or escape? How would you like to feel?

4. What are some of the pressures you have experienced trying to conform to the categories of masculinity or femininity defined by your culture? How have you dealt with these pressures? What are your reactions to the pressures? In what ways, if any, do you welcome or resist the pressures of needing to act or think in particularly feminine or masculine ways? How does your culture respond to resistant behavior?

5. List some of the "rules" you have learned about how "good boys" or "good girls" are supposed to act and think in your culture. How did you learn these "rules" about attitudes, interests, beliefs, and behaviors? What do you most enjoy/least enjoy about having to act and think in these particular ways in order to conform to the standards of masculinity or femininity prescribed by your culture?

6. In what ways, if any, have stories and other texts, and the media (print, visual, performance media) influenced your perceptions about masculinity and femininity? How do you respond to these influences?

Remember, the point about notetaking is NOT to answer EVERY question but to gather a rich database of impressionistic material to write from. Let your mind take you from early memories to more recent ones. Think about the people and experiences that have shaped your thinking and behaviors from your past up to the present day.

The Assignment: Use your notes as an organizational aid to write a narrative essay in which you describe the experiences which have had the most significant influence on you in developing your masculine and/or feminine subjectivity. Analyze these experiences to illustrate the influences they have had on your attitudes, behaviors, interests, and beliefs about masculinity and/or femininity. In the conclusion of the paper, draw some generalizations about what these experiences tell about what you believe about masculinity and/or femininity, and how you react to those beliefs. What would you like to change, if anything, about your own subjectivity; your own interests, attitudes, behaviors, and beliefs; the ways in which your culture socializes gender—the ways in which you might choose to socialize a child of your own, if you choose to parent one someday.

The essay should be 3–5 pages in length (double-spaced, typed is best, handwritten is OK, if legible). These papers will not be given a letter grade. You will receive preparation points toward your semester grade. We are mostly interested in

(Figure 3.6 cont.)

> using these essays for planning and to help you to make personal connections to some of the basic premises of the content taught in the women's studies class.

Figure 3.7: In-class Freewrite Experiences

IN-CLASS INFORMAL FREEWRITES

During the course of class discussions, we might stop and write about a topic or idea for 7–10 minutes. I would collect the papers and respond to them in several ways. We might collate the responses and read them anonymously as a class text during the next session to generate discussion. I might respond to the writer in writing. Emma and I might use the written responses as a basis for discussion and respond to the students at that time. Following is a description of the freewrite topics, which are constructed from the text of my field observation notes.

1. Gilligan (one)

I want you to think about this process that Gilligan describes is the crisis point for girls' identity. Go back through your life. Look at the "nice girl" thing, the "disassociation" thing, the "hitting the wall" thing. How are you in your own life? How are you going to solve the dilemma of wanting genuine relationships when you voice over your feelings in relationships? How do you expect to have a genuine relationship when you have learned how to do that? Go back through this process and explain how it happened to you. Then explain how you think you can solve it.

2. Gilligan (two)

We read an article in class titled "For Sexes, Communication is Key," a report of miscommunication that resulted in an accusation of date rape: I want you to write a postscript to your dilemma of genuine relationships responses. Think about what this article is addressing, and respond. How do you get at honest communication? If one person is speaking—say in Spanish, and the other is speaking—say in French, more than honesty may be required. What do you think?

3. Gilligan (three):

After discussion of the first two written responses: We have come this far, we may be sounding pretty cynical. I don't believe equal relationships are impossible, I just think they are nearly impossible. Why don't you write for three minutes. What haven't we let you say? Do you want to tell us we are just a bunch of old cynics?

4. Fairy tales:

We have been talking about the myth of happily ever after, silencing, and rescuing by the prince. I want you to think about it. How has this myth affected your perceptions? I would like you to write about how you have viewed the princess who gets rescued, the happily ever after ideal, how women lose their voice in the fairy tale. Examine a particular fairy tale and perhaps bring in your own experiences. What do you have to

(Figure 3.7 cont.)
say?

5. The effects of advertising

Please take a few moments and write about how advertising has affected your self-concept. You might want to consider what we've been talking about in discussing the feminine masquerade or how you have been affected by the media in general. What have you thought in the past? What do you think about this now?

6. Violence

We read several articles about women and violence and rape. What surprised you? What questions does this information raise for you? How do you react to this information? What have you been thinking about these various things? What do you think about doing to protect yourself? If you are or have been the victim of violence or know someone who is, do you know where you can go for help? If you need information, ask us in this response.

The students were occasionally asked to write any questions they might have about topics we had been discussing down and hand them in. We used these as a basis for several class discussions.

A sampling of questions includes the following:
1.   Is there ever a time when you know if you're really ready to have sex with a person?
2.   Why do the people who are rapists rarely get in any serious trouble?
3.   I want to know good comebacks to sexist remarks.
4.   What can I do to give women more power? How can women change the male dominance in society?
5.   Why does the government get involved in women's choices about abortion?

Although students were asked to draw from personal experience in their writing, the assignments pushed them to consider other possible viewpoints on gender, difference, and the complexity of gendered subjectivities. Once the students finished the assignments, I responded to them in the margins of their papers. My response strategies were guided by my pedagogical assumptions. I asked writers questions to point to the existence of binary oppositions, to suggest inversion of power hierarchies, and to ponder the alternate, possible, and resistant possibilities that may emerge. I worked from the perspective of attempting to trouble constructions of gender that depend on binary opposition. I questioned generalizations that transcended the specificities of time and place. I often questioned students' expressions of essentialized views of woman and man that asserted a universal female and male essence in an attempt to deconstruct the socialized positions they hold. Our exchanges constituted much of my and the students' reflexive engagement with the course curricula. These assignments and the response exchanges constitute much of the students' reflexive engagement with the course curricula. Although I invoked expressivist approaches, I refused both to underestimate the social, cultural, and historical conditions that shape selves, subjects and the conditions out of which writers write (Sullivan and Qualley) and to presume "that language provides an unproblematic access to reality" (Faigley, *Fragments* 8).

Let's examine an excerpt from Trisha's writing log response to Susan Griffin's "Matter," for example:

> If men say that women lead to corruption, then why would it be acceptable for men to gain pleasure from women? Shouldn't men be at fault just as much as women for wanting, or lusting after the pleasures that women are said to provide?

I respond to her:

> The logic you present shows insight. You raise a good question. Why do you suppose men might not see the logic the way you do? What responses might you pose to them?

Later Trisha writes back:

> It seems that these rewards are for men's self-worth. Women should not do things in order for a man to feel good about himself. (Trisha, Writing response log, "Feminine Dependency")

I attempt to create several complex interactions in this exchange. Trisha has questions for which she wants answers. She asserts a position that points out the contradictions implied in an essentialized orientation to masculinity and femininity. I acknowledge that perspective and push her to consider other possibilities. Trisha ponders this and suggests an alternate position. I try not to assume a position of authority over Trisha but to suggest a space in which she can voice a position that emerges from her own authoritative stance.

Another example from an exchange between me and Louise illustrates the dynamics of response. Louise writes:

I HATE FASHION MAGAZINES. I HATE MODELING. I HATE

SOCIETY. (Writing response log, "Pouts and Scowls")

I respond:

> We fall in these traps because there are great rewards for obeying the cultural codes and great punishments for disobeying. What do you think?

In another entry, Louise reports:

> I want to be able to accept me more and love me more than I already do. It's nice to be able to feel myself inside supporting me and holding myself up, amusing me when I'm sad or angry and entertaining me when I'm bored. I want to try to work my way out of the feminine rut so many women get into. I'm probably the only one who'll right now totally accept me. A lot of it [the problem with acceptance] is my recent discovery of my bisexuality and my sexual openness about it....(Louise, Writing response log, "Femininization of Poverty")

I suggest an alternate position to Louise because she is frustrated. I turn it back to her, however, so that she may determine her own position. Louise suggests that she is struggling with the "standard ideal" of femininity that is displayed in fashion magazines and the media and explains why it causes her alarm. Louise articulates her own alternative moves even though they rub up against the positions of others around her. Louise notes in her last class entry that she learned through these exchanges that "I am O.K. just the way I am" to which my reply was, "You certainly are."

The purpose behind my responses is to engage students in opportunities to write about their culturally gendered selves and experiences and to dialogue with someone who cares about them and who is attempting to unbalance the gender status quo. I want the students to reorganize their views of gender socialization and see other ways than the ones that historically have disenfranchised women and people of color. The writing assignments and response sequences were shaped to open other possible viewpoints on gender, difference, and the complexity of subjectivities through ongoing inquiry that asks student writers such questions as, "What other ways might this occur?" and "Whose interests are served by this position?" "What different ways could you view this?"

Another response method that I use occasionally is the readaround. Readarounds set up writing as both a "reflexive and extensive" act (Emig *Composing Processes*) and as a performance. A readaround is accomplished by selecting excerpts from the students' writing and collating them anonymously into one continuous text, which we "read around" in class round-robin style. The readaround accomplishes multiple purposes. One purpose is to include student writing as a text for discussion and additional writing in the class. The rationale for elevating student work to the level of textual focus is to recognize student ideas as central to work in women's studies class and deconstruct the hierarchy that generally exists among students, teacher, and researcher relations in educational settings.

Another purpose is to construct a conversation among students. When the researcher/teacher is the only audience for the students' writing, the students get no explicit views out from their own thoughts, positions, and experiences into the views of their peers. Readarounds are used to construct a conversational context for enlarging the borders of the written discussions and creating an open discussion among peers.

Yet another purpose for the readarounds is to provide students with opportunities to confront the alienating isolation that occurs when one questions cultural norms. Frequently, when students are able to read what their peers are thinking and writing about gender issues of common concern, they are surprised and relieved to discover that many of their peers have similar views and experiences. They find connection with others where before they experienced isolation from others.

However, connectedness is not always the outcome of the readaround and neither should it be. At times, the students take positions of radical disagreement on gender questions at issue. Walker and I encourage the students not only to express their views but to construct questions that allow them to negotiate issues and begin to explore difference without assigning "boundaries" or "hierarchies" and without demanding accommodation to any single or unified social vision. Recall the example of Maria (pp. 82–84 of this text).

Case Study Participants and Interviews

I selected seven students to serve as informants during the study proper and two students during the pilot study (Agar *The Professional Stranger*). I became especially interested in working with students who articulated during class discussions or in the writing response logs that they were experiencing a great deal of cognitive, procedural, or emotional movement in either their writing and/or their gender self-awareness. Code terms that seemed to signal movement include "I have changed," "I have noticed myself behaving in a [certain] way," "I want to change." Other criteria for selection include the following:

1. Students whose writing response log entries or comments in class demonstrate a high degree of struggle over writing and/or gender issues.

2. Students whose writing response log entries or comments in class demonstrate (a) a high degree of competence in and awareness of uses for writing (e.g., the student who writes profusely, expressively, and analytically) and/or (b) a complication of gender issues and performances.

3. Students whose in-class participation varies greatly from their writing participation (e.g., students who write a lot, but say nothing in class; or students who say a lot in class, but write little).

4. Students who may bring "other" awareness to the data (e.g., non-Mormon students, students of color, homosexual or bisexual students, foreign-born students).

As I indicated in the section "A Portrait of the Typical Women's Studies Student," there is no such thing as a "typical" women's studies student. The seven students that were selected during the study proper include six female students and one male student: Margaret, Solo, JoAnna, Trisha, LeTisha, Sharon, and Thomas. In the case study group, four of the students come from Mormon families, six of the students are white, one is Hispanic, four of the students have been sexually active for quite some time, and the other students did not divulge that information. Three of the case study students have been victims of sexual violence. Two have been physically and mentally abused by parents and parent figures. One has engaged in both same-sex and opposite-sex relations. One has suffered severe depression; two others have suffered milder cases of depression; another has lived with a severe eating disorder. Four of the case study students live with both parents, one lives with grandparents, one alternates between parents, one lives with her mother. Six of the students live in middle-income families. One, the Hispanic student, lives in a lower-middle-income family. Four of the seven have taken women's studies more than one semester.

Additionally, I examined in depth the writing of two other students, Louise and Alisa, who were unable to meet with me for outside interviews. Louise is non-Mormon and has lived in a residential treatment center to deal with severe depression, alcohol abuse, and stress-related traumas. Her father sold both her and her sister to his friends for sexual favors when she was young, and she was raped by a janitor when she was in elementary school. She is bisexual. Alisa is Mormon. Her parents have been married and divorced to each other on two different occasions, and they each have married and divorced another person, as well. She admits to self-mutilation as a way of dealing with anger and disapproval, especially from boyfriends. Alisa says she will be the one to show her parents that marriage can work if one works hard enough at it. I studied the writing of these students because Louise wrote more than anyone else, and Alisa seemed to write particularly resistant responses to concepts presented in women's studies.

Although you may think that Alisa's and Louise's cases provide extremely atypical examples of the range and kind of gender and sexual experiences that adolescents at Aspen Grove confront, I cannot legitimately characterize them as either "typical" or "extremely atypical." Such a conclusion is unwarranted, given the factors that limit any systematic study of the "typical" characteristics of Aspen Grove students.

Additionally, and more importantly, it is peculiarly dismissive to assume that these two students' experiences are atypical, simply because so many of the students in women's studies have confronted many of the same issues as Alisa and Louise, only to a lesser degree. However, even to mark one student's experience as "more" or "less" in kind or degree diminishes the effect the experience has had on his or her subjectivity. Walker maintains that an adolescent's experience of crisis is individually cataclysmic to them, regardless of the "degree" or "kind" of crisis measure that a more experienced individual might assign the experience. Adolescent crises, Walker insists, warrant no comparison with anyone else's experience of crisis. For this reason, I cannot suggest that any of the students in women's studies are typical of any other adolescents, or that they are not.

I remained in contact with two students from the pilot study throughout the course of the study proper. Rachel, who is Jewish, attended a premed program at the state research university on a full academic scholarship and is now in medical school. Kate is Persian-American and attended the state research university on a state teaching scholarship. She plans to become an art teacher. These students have provided longitudinal perspective on the effects of writing in women's studies.

I generally met with the case study informants during lunch and free periods, after school, and during the summer break. Three formal interviews of approximately one to one and a half hours were conducted with JoAnna, Trisha, and Thomas. Margaret, Solo, Sharon, and LeTisha were interviewed twice. Rachel and Kate were interviewed formally three times during the pilot study and twice during the study proper. Formal interviews took place in Emma's classroom. Informal interviews took place in the hallways or the parking lot at school or at restaurants and coffee shops near the school.

Writing Samples

I collected all student responses to the class writing assignments. I also collected all of my and Walker's feedback to the writers. Principles of context-sensitive discourse analysis were applied to the coding and analysis of the writing samples. The procedural steps that are followed when engaging context-sensitive discourse analysis are (a) select an initial corpus, (b) identify salient patterns, (c) determine interestingness, (d) select a study corpus, (e) verify the pattern, and (f) complete a functional rhetorical analysis in light of the theoretical framework underlying the study (Huckin, "Context-sensitive"). I selected an initial corpus by accounting for the number of whole texts collected from each student, including the number of pages and words that were represented in those texts. I compiled the information into a data chart so that I might compare the students' individual written texts for each writing experience across the entire corpus of assignments. From this initial corpus, I selected a representative sample, the work of nine students, which included the work of the seven case study participants. The examined sample accounted for 25% of the entire corpus. The writing sample data are cultural artifacts that are both critically contextualized and concretely distanced from the "bias" of authorial interpretation and analysis. This serves to offer a slightly more objective epistemological slant to the findings of the study.

In working with the representative sample, I coded each proposition that indicated topical change. Sometimes this occurred at the sentence level; other times it occurred at the paragraph level. The number of propositions coded in the representative sample is 2,528. I coded the writing samples for frequency of occurrence of propositions that emerged in the other data sets because the categorical patterns co-occurred in the writing. The pattern was verified through this procedure. A few new subcategories appeared, but no new overarching categories. A functional rhetorical analysis of the representative sample was completed.

First, the entire corpus of student writing and corresponding researcher responses is examined. The number of whole texts, the number of pages in those texts, and the number of words on those pages are calculated and compiled. The entire corpus represents the completed work of 39 students. Five hundred twenty-five reading response log entries, 23 writing autobiographies, 27 masculinity/femininity histories, and 136 freewrites are included in the corpus. The salient patterns, which emerge in a thorough reading of the initial corpus, are identification of propositions at the sentence and the paragraph level that function rhetorically within expressive and social rhetorical categories analyzed in previously examined data sets. The reading of the entire corpus produces no additional categories of analysis. In other words, the interestingness of the writing samples appears in the result that the students' written texts support the claims they made about the effects of writing in other data.

A representative sample, 25% of the entire corpus, which contains the work of nine students and includes the writing of the seven case study students, was examined in more detail. The purpose of this analysis was to verify the patterns that emerged in the entire corpus and to complete a functional rhetorical analysis in light of the theoretical framework underlying the study. Two thousand five hundred twenty-eight topical propositions were analyzed in the representative sample.

Analysis of the writing samples produced 15 categories of propositions that indicated students identifying writing as a tool for learning; three categories of propositions that identify students' interactions with classroom protocol; four genre and voice categories; two categories of evaluative responses; and two categories of propositions that act to build relational connections: first, construct a conversation and second, create a script (write/revise a life) (Bruce). The relation-building category divided into three categories of performative propositions, which I term *experiential editing, reflective revisions,* and *transformative performatives.* A discursive performative, in this case, is a linguistically coded utterance that signals or marks the writing or speaking subject's transformation or desire for transformation. The content of the performative utterance ranges along a spectrum of possibilities from the trivial to the traumatic. I explain these in depth in Chapter 4.

Notes

1.   Maureen Barbieri reports similar responses from the faculty at Laurel School, where Carol Gilligan and Lyn Mikel Brown completed their research on women's psychology and girls' development. Although the faculty were invited to read and respond to Brown and Gilligan's work in progress, Barbieri reports that teachers scoffed at the ideas. "Wasn't this a normal part of maturing, becoming socialized? Who among us can say exactly what we think all the time? Shouldn't girls become more sensitive to the feelings of others as they grow up? We were, some teachers insisted, oversaturated with talk of 'gender issues'" (Barbieri *Sounds from the Heart* 6).

2.   After Emma and I began working together, she told me that some of her hesitancy in agreeing to allow me into the classroom had to do with a school- and districtwide suspicion of university researchers. Emma said that the reason that she, the principal, and the assistant superintendent ultimately agreed to let me participate as an observer/researcher in the school was because I am certified to teach grades K-12 and have 13 years of successful public school teaching experience. Their decision ultimately had nothing to do with my research interests or research design. She since has turned down several other university researchers and maintains that she would not let anyone in the classroom that did not have extensive public school teaching experience.

3.   An important focus of the women's studies class is determining the contextual forces that motivate women to make the choices they make. All grown women who are invited to attend and participate in the class wittingly or unwittingly become a text of study in the class. Understanding Walker as a person is key to understanding the curricular choices she has made, which will be discussed in more detail in later sections

in this chapter.

4. TV and film images of single women in the 1990s-2000s portrayed in characters like Ally McBeal and Bridget Jones are presented as archetypes although they are little more than composites of frivolous neuroses who are obsessed with the ticking of their biological time clocks hoping that they'll eventually end up in worlds like Harriet Olson's and June Cleaver's. In the June 29, 1998, issue of *Time*, Ginia Bellafante reports that although the women's movement has changed our individual lives and expectations, 50% of young women age 18–34 surveyed claim to share feminist values, by which they mean that they "want a world in which they can choose to be anything—the President or a mother, or both" (58). Motherhood is not far from most women's primary anticipations.

5. All quotations from students and Walker appear in full text form in my dissertation *Writing in the Margins*, the University of Utah, 1997.

6. More male students might enroll in women's studies if it were called "gender studies"; however, there is a general stigma among AGHS males against taking a course that they erroneously perceive to be "for women only" and about "male-bashing." Emma has thought long and hard about this and decided that female students in particular need a safe place to address women's generally subordinate status in Western culture and therefore retains "women's studies" as the title for the elective course.

7. It is against privacy laws to inquire about students' personal experiences. The demographic and experiential information acquired during the study was obtained through student self-disclosure.

8. Neither of us is trained as a counselor. When students self-disclose such experiences—and they do blurt these things out during discussions of class readings or discuss them in their reader response logs—we often find ourselves in "counseling" roles. We do what we can but are ever ready to get them to the appropriate supporting professionals and/or to follow through with the required legal reports.

9. Among the various "somethings" that students have mentioned are reports of rape, sibling suicide, cancer diagnosis, homosexuality, sexual abuse by a trusted adult, an eating disorder, a clandestine sexual affair with an older (married) adult, sexual harassment (both same-sex and opposite-sex), drug and alcohol dependency, and parental divorce, to name just a few.

10. Resistance to homosexuality is a highly contentious, religiously based issue in the Aspen Grove community. A few years ago, a group of gay and lesbian students at a

neighboring high school petitioned for permission to meet as an after-school club under the name of the Gay-Lesbian-Straight Student Alliance. The school district, in response, withdrew the charters of *all* extracurricular clubs at the high school level in order to prevent the Gay-Lesbian-Straight Student Alliance from forming and to avoid any show of discrimination that would jeopardize federal funds to the district. The state legislature also got involved and passed a bill that prohibits the discussion of homosexuality in the schools. Nevertheless, many students at all the high schools—including Aspen Grove—have formed Gay-Lesbian-Straight Student Alliances in rebellion. Although the clubs at all the other schools in the city have to meet off campus after hours, the principal at AGHS asked Emma to advise a GLS alliance at Aspen Grove, which she most willingly agreed to do. In order to protect women's studies and the alliance, Emma has chosen not to deal with the issue of homosexuality in women's studies because it would be in direct defiance of a state law and could jeopardize the future of women's studies at AGHS. However, she is free to answer any questions students raise regarding sexuality and she tells them so. This opens a subversive space for students to ask whatever questions they wish about sexualities.

11. This article appeared as a sidebar in an article on communication styles. A parent complained to principal Rod Harris that students in women's studies were reading about homosexuality. Because discussion of homosexuality in schools is prohibited by state legislative mandate, Harris went straight to Walker and asked her about the article in question. Walker hadn't realized the sidebar had been reprinted in the reader and she immediately collected all the readers and had them reprinted without the article on communication between gays and lesbians. Although Walker disagrees with the legislative mandate, she did not want to jeopardize women's studies in any way.

12. Classes at AGHS are block scheduled. Women's studies meets for 90 minutes every other day.

13. Book reports generally take two to three class sessions.

14. I am indebted to Stephanie Pace and Claudia Wright for their help in deconstructing deconstruction as a pedagogical strategy.

Literacies of Writing and Teaching in Women's Studies

The point of writing is to bear witness.

—Alice Walker

Writing is making sense of life.

—Nadine Gordimer

Literacies

Every form of literacy always includes many social practices and has its own versions of context. In the context of any given discourse community, literacy is practiced in socially conventional ways. Characteristic ways of seeing, acting, thinking, talking, reading, and writing are taken for granted by literate members of the group. Members of various discourse communities demonstrate literacy practices by observing, receiving, and using language in situated "literacy events" (Heath "Critical Factors"). To understand literacy practices in particular discourse communities, one must observe, participate in, and make visible the ways in which language is used among its members.

In this chapter, I detail the ways in which adolescent females at Aspen Grove High School describe literacies of writing and of teaching writing in their women's studies class. The (principally) 12th-grade girls report that writing in the self-consciously politicized context of their high school women's studies class enhances their personal, intellectual, and political development. Writing, they report, contributes significantly to learning. Writing allows them to express themselves personally and emotionally, and, in some cases, to find therapeutic solace. Through writing, they learn what they think about gender issues of relevant concern and what they might possibly think otherwise—and this consequently enables them to assert opinions and argue positions in favor of self- and social transformation. Indeed, many of the students specifically identify writing's potential for constructing a discursive space that transforms their lives. Where once were spaces of silence, now are spaces of critical cognitive and experiential performance.

Literacies of Learning

Students distinguish writing primarily as a process by which they learn about women's studies content. Writing allows them both to express themselves and discover what they think, feel, and believe and, concurrently, to make personal connections with the major issues, ideas, and themes presented in class. Writing is "invaluable" because it helps students negotiate the terrain between classroom experience and daily life. Students see writing as a way to give voice to the many, varied ways they have come to know what they know:

> I think in women's studies that you are allowed to say what you really feel and actually talk about things that happened to you and not beat around the bush or talk about something that you are assigned to talk about—that you don't know what you are talking about. (Sharon, interview)

Before learning occurs, these students put a personal twist on the content, exploring feelings raised by the issues:

> Writing and understanding what I have written helps me learn. The writing has taught me how to be honest with myself. It has helped me express myself a little more easily. Writing has challenged me to listen to and see what I have written—to notice how it applies to me. (Maria, writing evaluation)

Students describe writing in women's studies as "different from" writing they do in other classes. Students unanimously indicate that the writing and work in women's studies matters to *them*. In other classes, writing is used to demonstrate knowledge *teachers* think is important. Women's studies students generally think other class work is generally meaningless, indicating that not much has shifted since Janet Emig (*Composing Processes*) accused American high school English teachers of teaching composition in a "neurotic" fashion:

> I would never write the way I write [in women's studies] for my English teacher. I would never write that way for Ms. Parsons because she would look past what I was trying to say and would write some whole other message dealing with grammar that I had no intention of trying. She would only deal with that. (Sharon, personal interview, May 23, 1995)

Sharon's assessment of her English teacher's responses to her writing sounds very much like the criticisms Lynn and Victoria (Emig *Composing Processes*) made of their English teachers over three decades ago.

Students use writing to construct the cognitive-expressive relationships that Emig ("Writing as a Mode of Learning") and others represent as the heart of learning. Students in women's studies are introduced to concepts of inequality between men and women, for example, and use writing to connect their comprehension of the concept to their own experiences, and to their experiences of others in the class. They understand it at both a personal and a social level. By making personal and social connections to the content, writing helps students grow as writers and as mindful and politically astute persons. Learning is group-mediated, an effect of writing about content they are studying together:

> In women's studies writing, you make your own connections. There are no right or wrong answers. This class has a lot more writing that counts, not busy work. My writing has become personal and I speak more about solutions or ask questions. I think that I have grown a lot in my writing and thoughts. I see problems and try to think about solutions or beginnings of the problem. (Trisha, writing evaluation)

> My writing has gotten more open. I've felt more able to express anger, sarcasm, pride, and happiness. I've learned it's OK to be me, to be different, to question people's ideas, how I act feminine, that male or female isn't really important. (Louise, writing evaluation)

Learning through writing occurs through problem solving and making connections—connections these writers claim as their own, but which are mediated by the understandings of the group. New understandings are a result of writing to problems and situations experienced by the writers and by others both like and unlike them everyday.

Students explain that writing pushes them to think critically and analytically about issues raised in women's studies. Writing helps them to take things apart and to apply concepts to other information and experiences. Writing provides students opportunities for "seeing how things work," which in turn helps them integrate new ways of seeing into their lives:

> My [writing response log] entries have grown and are more deeply analyzed. I have found ways that the articles [we read] are applicable to my life. My growth during women's studies has been a difficult one. In the long run, it's better for me, but being ignorant was so much easier. (Misha, writing evaluation)

Students use writing as a tool for critically analyzing information in various ways. Walker's promotion of "raising consciousness" exposes students to literate experiences, which offer more than simple recall and comprehension. As students distance themselves from their beliefs and ideas through writing, they explore the impact the culture has on their growth and development. They become aware of issues that previously were invisible to them. Writing in the context of women's studies about gender issues enables students to take stock of the distinctions between how they are valued in culture and how they differently value their own "participant structures and communicative competences" (Phillips):

> I have learned that men care so much about themselves and they look at women for their bodies. I have looked at men in a different perspective because now I really know how they act and what they are thinking. If I want to tell a man what I think of him, I'm not scared to say anything now. I will come out and say it. (unsigned, writing evaluation)

Students generally do not like the way they are defined in culture. They find they can take action to alter their situation. They learn that there are conscious choices they can make and that they have ultimate responsibility for their choices even if they cannot predicate the outcomes.

Students often approach writing in women's studies through the communicative competences the school values. They initially try to "psych out" the teacher—figure out what the teacher wants and approximate a version of it to get a good grade. Once they understand that the issues of importance to them are those wrapped in making connections with their own experiences and feelings and the experiences and feelings of others, and that it is acceptable with the women's studies teachers for them to do so, they pursue those connections actively. Writing enables them to assess critically an individual or a group of individuals based on their gender classification. This writing catalyzes the learning students most value.

Making connections to content produces active learning performed in lives:

> I think in women's studies class that you get certain points of view a lot, but then once you take it out of the class some people say, "Oh, they're full of crap" and stuff. But I think you have to work through it yourself, you know? And find something of your own, you know? You may not believe all of the statistics you hear and whatever...but it's like you just have to do it yourself, and connect it to how you feel and to how what's happened to you and what you see, you know? I am taking [ideas presented in women's studies] and applying them to myself, you know?...I think [writing] helps a lot because now I can remember what happened and put it in the right perspective. And then writing more—it just confirms what I think, you know? (Trisha, personal interview, May 18, 1995)

Writing enables students to interweave the mental work of figuring out with the experiential work of integrating learned ideas into their day-to-day experiences. Students typically refer to this process as "self-discovery."

Whereas in some cases students identify writing as a process of making personal connections to content, in other cases they describe writing as a learning process of coming to know what they think, feel, and believe about topics addressed in women's studies:

> [Writing] just makes me think more about myself. Having to write the assignments just made me learn about myself. It helped me to understand myself and understand why I react differently to ideas and I don't always know why I am reacting the way I do, but [writing] gives me kind of a place where I can see who I am or figure out why I am the way I am. (Solo, personal interview, May 24, 1995)

Writing provides opportunities for self-awareness and discovery of the high-stakes communicative competences of the culture, in which students generally believe they have no place:

> Just with the journals and the openness in class, if you had something you wanted to write or say you could just write or say it without having to listen to everyone else talk about how they feel and their opinions and everything. The writing helped me develop my own opinions. Cause I had to come in here and make a lot of decisions. I made a lot of opinions, I mean, I discovered my own opinions. About certain issues. (Margaret, personal interview, May 11, 1995)

Learning is group mediated. Students read about the experiences and ideas of others and come to know how what they believe fares in relation with or against views professed by their classmates, teacher, and researcher.

Writing in women's studies consequently enables academic growth. Students acknowledge that their writing and grades improve—a claim that Walker supports. The expressive and chaotic responses to content in women's studies help students address discourse practices and habits of mind of other disciplines:

> When you taught that compare/contrast thing…. I have used that a lot in some of my other classes and that has helped me to do much better on some of my assignments….it educated me and gave me confidence so I know what I am talking about now. I actually hold up my idea and that helps. I know how to back up things I have to say….My grades have been totally good this year compared to years before…(Trisha, personal interview, May 11, 1995)

Writing in women's studies transfers to work in other classes. Students discover ways to argue effectively.

Overcoming the silenced, marginalized position girls typically assume in school is one of the personal, academic, and political benefits of writing as the students see themselves writing more and writing better:

> I see myself writing a lot more on my own to think through things. I am doing that more now. I am writing a lot more on my own. Sometimes I can't go to sleep unless I write. I want to understand some things and it helps me do that. I am sure I will do that forever. I want to be able to look back on things that I have written and see exactly what was going through my thinking. (Trisha, personal interview, May 18, 1995)

Students also demonstrate several intellectual and writing processes at work in their texts. For example, Sharon responds to an article on women and poverty:

> "I believed I'd be cherished by a good man, taken care of, and respected as the mother of his children." (Burraston-Wood, "The Feminization of Poverty" 127).

> First, we find out that it's the parents who are playing this big awful joke on their young, impressionable daughters (*indication of comprehension; consciousness raising: parental models*). Then it's society's media who is backing it up (*consciousness raising: media*). It's a double whammy on the brainwashed things. They are never taught to grow up, just that they are baby machines, to sit around, grow fat, and have cute brats. How many girls do you think, if they weren't taught to think this way would really want to stay home with children? (*think critically/analytically*). (my emphasis, Sharon, writing response log)

Sharon comprehends the excerpt from the article "The Feminization of Poverty" by paraphrasing it in her own language, using a register that invokes a sarcastic tone. She demonstrates a rhetorical sense of an audience who will read this with insight and acceptance. She presumably does not fear punitive action from the teacher-researcher-peer audience. She also demonstrates analysis of the role that parents play in constructing models of behavior for their offspring. Her sarcastic tone implies that she is critical of ways in which parents unassumingly pass expectations, roles, and behaviors to their children. Her criticism indicates that she is aware of parental roles and expectations and the effects those play on children.

Sharon similarly demonstrates, again as she invokes a sarcastic tone, her critical awareness of media's reinforcement of gender stereotypes that effectually serve to disenfranchise women. "It's a double whammy on the brainwashed things," signals Sharon's use of high degrees of sarcasm and her suspicion of anyone who could be so naïvely led down a stereotypical path. Sharon indicates her disdain of the whole matter, using pejorated terms, "baby machines" and "cute brats" to characterize female domestic roles that confine women to a life of housewifery and, in her view, drudgery. Sharon's culminating criticism is that she cannot imagine that girls who critically analyze the roles and expectations would freely choose to live that lifestyle.

Sharon's text illustrates some of the several ways in which writing enables the sophisticated thinking that characterizes learning. Although considerable lip service is given to teaching students how to think critically about issues raised in school, simple recall and comprehension seem the knowledge of most worth (Ackerman). Sharon's written response also indicates that a level of trust and respect for differences exists in this classroom for a student to write such a text and not worry about negative consequences. Indeed, this is an aspect of women's studies that is acknowledged by several students:

> The best thing about this class is that it's safe to express yourself in here. In English classes and such you can't be sure you can trust the teacher with what you're writing about yourself. (Solo, writing evaluation)

Multilayered thinking processes are at work in the students' texts. Students not only demonstrate awareness of what the school values as learning, but also indicate thinking that might subvert dominant paradigms of thought represented in traditional discourses of schooling. Sharon's text acts out resistance to mainstream culture. She opposes the dominant discourse of the heterosexual romance myth and constructs an alternate subjectivity by suggesting that other possibilities exist than the dominant modes of women's participation in the traditional cultural narrative. Sharon derides the normative model in a text that performs a chaotic, sarcastic analysis of culture: "How many girls do you think, if they weren't taught to think this way would really want to stay home with children?" Sharon builds a sense of sorry connection with others who have been duped by the standard narrative. She adds historical depth to the narrative, acknowledging that many forces collude in keeping women in their place. She implies that she will not play out the punch line to this awful joke.

Sharon's excerpt provides one example that depicts how writing enables women's studies students to distance themselves from their embodied experiences and critically analyze traditional gender roles depicted in traditional forms of schooling and in predominant societal models. Students begin to realize how codes of femininity might not serve their best interests. Sharon's text also represents the anti-form and chaotic tendencies writing in women's studies may assume. Students scribble quick, derisive, fragmented articulations, which overtake the normative narrative with new visions of potential response. Writing serves to interrupt "appropriate" expectations for gendered behavior and enable women's studies' students to script possible alternative positions for their lives.

Trisha offers another example:

> These stories by Kate Chopin (Re: "The Story of an Hour," *The Awakening*) make me very worried to get married (*make personal connections to content*). I am scared that if I do get married I will not be able to live my own life (*express fear*). It feels hopeless that there are no men out there who let women do as they please (*express despair*). I know that the story was written a long time ago, but it still worries me. I see my own grandmother who had similar experiences (*discover a history*). Now she is living with us while my grandfather lives in Florida. She has a lot of problems mentally (she also has cancer) because she was not allowed to do what she wanted (*anecdote*). I am determined not to turn out like that!! (*transformative performative*). (my emphasis, Trisha, writing response log)

As a young Mormon woman who has been well socialized into the traditional, patriarchal trope of femininity prescribed by her culture, Trisha attempts to assuage her fears about assuming her place in that culture by noting that the stories were written long ago. However, in being provided with a bit of historical depth normally absent from postmodern culture, Trisha connects her own experiences with women populating a novel "written long ago." Based on the anecdote she provides, which represents her understanding of her grandmother's present experience, she remains skeptical at best. Woven throughout the excerpt is a sense of growing conviction that Trisha punctuates with a proposition for her own course of action in reaction: "I am determined not to turn out like that!!"

Trisha's excerpt provides another representative example of ways students weave women's studies content through their reconstructed understandings of personal experiences. Writing about the content helps them make sense of their personal experiences by building connections that are at the heart of critical learning. Trisha finds agency residing in the power of weaving connections among a character in a "Victorian" novel, the lived experiences of her grandmother and her own desire to change the circumstances of the standard trope of heterosexual love and marriage. In contradistinction to the authority of the "marriage for eternity" promise that her own culture prescribes for her, Trisha acts out a defiant, alternative narrative that opposes the Mormon promise.

On the surface, the connections between learning and writing that are articulated by women's studies students at Aspen Grove offer hardly new assumptions. Taken at first glance, these students' perceptions offer little insight into what compositionists have taken for granted—that writing "inevitably leads to learning" (Ackerman; Applebee; Emig "Writing as a Mode of Learning"). However, what is significantly compelling about the students' articulations about writing as a mode of learning is a systematic analysis of the effects of writing as a tool for learning in a self-consciously gendered context. Other studies have accounted for writing as a model of student learning by measuring the number of relevant concepts that appear in short answer and essay tests (Ackerman). Recall and comprehension of facts is the kind of writing most frequently assigned in school (Applebee) and the means by which learning is most typically measured. For women's studies students, writing to recall and comprehend facts is insignificant. They identify value in terms of learning about female subordination in Western culture and using writing to "figure out" femininity and "do it" differently. Furthermore, although the students' global assessments about learning mirror time-honored assumptions about writing-to-learn phenomena, their descriptions of the effects that writing enables provide a previously unpainted picture of the ways adolescent girls in American schools may value learning through writing.

Finally, investigations intended to verify connections between writing and learning have strictly examined the written product as evidence for learning. Women's studies students discuss the links between processes of writing and integration and application of content information into their lives. In turn, this leads to development of writing abilities, such as asserting a voice, arguing a position, and providing supporting evidence, which are valued in school. These students learn to use writing processes strategically—for academic, personal, and political gain.

Literacies of Voice

Students describe "asserting a voice" as an effect of writing in women's studies. They characterize voice as (a) asserting thoughts, beliefs, and opinions in writing that they keep to themselves in other arenas; (b) clarifying thoughts, beliefs, and opinions in writing, which in turn enables them to speak out in other arenas; and (c) formulating positions and arguments in writing as a result of not getting interrupted by others when they write. Voice in the writing samples becomes more than mere expression of opinion: "I think this sucks!", for example, is a frequently occurring response. More often than not, students "assert a voice" by presenting a thesis claim, arguing a position, or both, which is supported through experiential or textual evidence.

Concern for developing student "voice" has long been a focus of expressivism in composition studies. Expressivists have promoted "authentic voice pedagogy," defining voice as the ability to express oneself forcefully, authentically, with art (Macrorie *Telling Writing*). Additionally, cultural feminists have asserted that the "voices" of women writing might narrate women's lives to counteract the textual and historical silences of women (e.g., Grumet; Heilbrun; Witherell and Noddings). Most constructivist/postmodern feminist critiques assume that these views assert claims that leave unquestioned sociocultural, historical, political, and educational structures that have silenced women. Both expressive and cultural feminist views of voice have been critiqued for leaving female students to confront and negotiate on their own the uneven power relations resulting from gender, race, and class differences among students (Jarratt "Feminism and Composition"). Adolescent girls enrolled in women's studies at Aspen Grove High School find that writing allows them to "assert a voice"—to claim a sense of power in an educational system that otherwise disenfranchises them. Consequently, in response to Jarratt's critique, strategic reappropriations of "voice," which acknowledge the sociocultural and political location of the writer, can be beneficial to adolescent women writing within a classroom context.

Most women's studies students agree with research on the differentiated experiences of girls in school, which suggests that adolescent girls tend to go underground during their middle and high school years. In not so different a fashion than assessments made by Emig's subjects Lynn and Victoria, women's studies students at Aspen Grove acknowledge that they refrain from speaking up in class, asking questions, and pursuing topics that may be of particular interest to them because their teachers "confuse accidents with essences" (Emig *Composing Processes*) and trivialize the importance of meaning and of making connections to lived experience. Students feel alienated by the type of writing they are expected to do in their other classes. They experience feelings of disconnectedness from mainstream endeavors and conclude that their institutional and social position as silent, second-class citizens is warranted (Belenky et al.; Gilligan *In a Different Voice*; Gilligan, Lyons, and Hanmer).

Writing in women's studies gives students a location and opportunity to assert thoughts, beliefs, and opinions that they keep to themselves in other arenas. The writing is applicable and meaningful to their lives. Writing offers a means of exploring how gender is socially constructed and gives voice to diverse translations of appropriate and necessary gender norms:

> Writing helps to express what I learn because it's not always easy for me to share out loud. Writing has challenged me to find out what I'm really thinking and express the real emotions so others could see. (Sharon, writing evaluation)

> I've gotten better at expressing my opinions and myself. I think that writing has done a lot to help me.... I think the writing has challenged me to be honest with myself. Part of the process in women's studies is to really express yourself, and if you can't do it by speaking, it should happen through writing. (JoAnna, writing evaluation)

For many, the process is one of having the opportunity to assert what they think, feel, or believe in a way that helps them to clarify their positions and to speak out in other arenas. The benefit of asserting a stance in writing spills over into daily experiences:

> I would go home everyday and say, "Guess what I learned today?..." for the first time. And I would be at my boyfriend Max's house eating dinner and I'd be all, "Guess what Mrs. King?..." I would have all these ideas to share. (LeTisha, personal interview, May 17, 1995)

Writing provides a reason for speaking up and speaking out. In writing, students take on various roles and demonstrate both agreement and opposition to the dominant discourse on femininity even when they are unable to negotiate the demands of face-to-face interactions.

Writing helps students formulate and express positions because they do not get interrupted by others when they write. They discuss the ways in which other people's voices have silenced them:

> There's not really anything wrong with the people in our class but there are just a lot of people with strong opinions and they just want to talk about what they want to talk about.... And so I would rather, this is my family again, because I will try to express myself in my family and they'll just say, "It's wrong." And so I am just at the point where I keep my opinions to myself and that way nobody can run over them. So I write them out. That way nobody can see them and I can express myself. When I write it down, I don't have it all hyped up and hostile, you know? I really just can see what the situation is and I don't worry what everybody will think of it.... It helps me learn about (my)self. It helps (me) explain it, you know? (Sharon, personal interview, May 12, 1995)

Students are not as likely to risk the public airing of their positions in front of their peers. Students who find it difficult to negotiate the face-to-face demands of speaking in class discover that writing gives them a chance to assert what they believe, which in turn gives them the strength to speak up more in class.

It is not uncommon for a student who has had little to say during the course of the semester to begin speaking suddenly in the final weeks of class. Some students attribute this phenomenon to becoming more confident by asserting opinions in their writing and finally coming to feel like they might also speak out in class:

> [Writing] helps a lot with the learning process.... I think it helps your self-esteem, because then you know that you actually have some thoughts and ideas and stuff.... I was more reluctant to talk about it and now I talk more about where I am going to do stuff. (Trisha, personal interview, May 18, 1995)

Writing becomes a place for political action to begin—a location where students find "the freedom and the courage to write and say exactly what they think" (Gilligan, Lyons, and Hanmer).

The students frequently mention that the opportunities to "speak" (*read* "write") freely, without interruption in women's studies are unique to their high school experience. "Asserting a voice" is a process of self-discovery. Girls feel like they are forwarding opinions for the first time in their adolescent lives:

> Every time I wrote something, I learned something new about myself, about whoever I was writing about; so it's—it's every time I write something, I just learn something about myself or acknowledge something that maybe I didn't want to acknowledge earlier on. (LeTisha, personal interview, May 23, 1995)

For some students, the process of self-discovery is not so much a process of coming to know, but more a process of coming to terms with and accepting ideas and beliefs that they hold.

"Voice" effects of writing in women's studies derive from what the students term "writing authentically" and "writing honestly." Students say writing in women's studies represents their "true" or "real" feelings and is distinct from the "usual stuff" they say and write in school just to oblige teachers and not to disturb peer interactions:

Jeanne: It's the writing in school thing. Teachers ask you to write things all the time and you don't know what they are going to be used for. I think it makes a big difference knowing what we can expect from you. When you tell us the truth, we can tell you the truth.

Tabouli: I am constantly making things up for teachers. Why would I tell them the truth? I make stuff up for teachers all the time. I am not going to tell them what's really on my mind. It's different when I can trust them, know that they are going to be honest with me.

LeTisha: You tell us what is going on for you. I know I really appreciate your honesty. I am always willing to say what I think, because that is me and I am not ashamed to say what I think, but I really appreciate you sharing with us as if we are worth the risk.

> Tabouli: Yeah, writing seems more authentic.... (Transcription of class
> discussion, field observation notes)

Mary Pipher's clinical characterization of "authenticity" seems helpful
in understanding the students' usage:

> Authenticity is an "owning" of all experience, including emotions and thoughts
> that are not socially acceptable. Because self-esteem is based on the acceptance of
> all thoughts and feelings as one's own, girls lose confidence as they "disown"
> themselves. They suffer enormous losses when they stop expressing certain
> thoughts and feelings....With adolescence, [girls] begin to operate from a false self.
> (Pipher 38)

Students often distinguish the "claimed" self they present in women's
studies as their "true" self. In other classes, they say that they tend to
present a "false" self either to please the teacher or to hide the truth from
other teachers and students whom they suspect might injure them if they
are truthful:

> I think you can dig a little deeper into yourself than you could in an English class
> where there's not such a feeling of trust and openness. That's how I feel. I feel like
> there's nothing to hide in this class and everybody respects one another.
> Therefore, it opens an air to honesty and it makes you want to express yourself on
> paper, if not out loud.... I find that I'm able to open up and express myself with no
> hesitations. (Margaret, writing evaluation)

Students' abilities to shift and alter with the discourse situation give them
opportunity to take on multiple identities and alter traditional dispositions
of classroom power for girls in school (see also Barbieri; Finders).

Writing in the context of women's studies is self-revealing. It strips off
the cultural veil that shadows assertive thinking and believing especially for
adolescent girls. It allows girls to speak their mind without interruption and
to change their minds and words at will without punitive consequences.
When students feel free to speak without interruption to an audience that is
willing to take them and their ideas seriously, students counteract cultural
silencing, which results with dissociation from their interior selves.

I find that students' responses to the writing assignments interweave
both personal and argumentative moves and defy efforts to simply

characterize genres these students use in their writing. Students shift invariably among the forms typically valued in school using a pastiche of narrative/expressive (reflexive) and argument (extensive). In the reflexive mode their audience is the self and familiar others. In extensive writing, writers rhetorically intend a wider audience. Given the students' claims about writing as a tool for self-discovery, their writing is surprisingly devoid of anecdotal, personal narratives. Their writing assumes a chaotic shape in terms of standard modes of school-sponsored writing. Their writing also indicates a shift from common perspectives about "asserting a voice." Voice is less a matter of inserting female narratives into public conversation and more an appropriation of the discursive conventions valued in academic forms to argue alternative roles for women in their culture.

Expressivists and cultural feminists typically have valorized personal, informal, anecdotal, autobiographical writing as providing a forum for women to assert "voice." Students who employ personal, informal, anecdotal, and autobiographical moves in their women's studies writing typically invoke them strategically in support of a position or point they are shaping. For example, Margaret begins a response to an article on women's body image with a personal anecdote. Rather than simply tell a story, Margaret strategically invokes the anecdote to support a point she makes about women and the effects that ideal body image have on women's experience in general:

> I've always dieted and tried to fit the ideal and I often get frustrated about myself.... Women have to do that in order to feel in control of our lives. When you really think about it, we think we'll have more power and presence when we have a smaller, weaker body. It doesn't make sense. So many women are in this trap and it becomes a competition between women. (Margaret, writing response log)

Although Margaret uses informal diction to introduce some of her points (e.g., "When you really think about it..." "It doesn't make sense..."), she asserts a well-argued position that is supported by her own personal experience. This is not simply informal expressive writing. Margaret manipulates form to her advantage and speaks against the standard trope of female subordination. She participates as a critical onlooker in a discourse that has shaped her life and speaks back to it by showing its inadequacies.

In another example from a classroom freewrite, Solo invokes both informal and argumentative moves to support her position on establishing a genuine relationship:

> How I plan to have a genuine relationship? Hmmm….First of all, I'm taking that
> in the marriage/life time commitment sense. He would have to be a feminist.
> There is no way I could marry him otherwise. Communication would have to be
> there. He'd have to have the ability to listen, to question, and to tolerate me….
> Communication is the most important thing. Even if no major events happen in a
> day, you should discuss how you felt about things, a newspaper article, or a sunset
> because you need to talk about something other than your job assignment or
> whatever else is unrelated to how you feel inside. (Solo, freewrite)

Solo's thesis appears in the form of a question, a fairly sophisticated problem-solution organizational strategy. She uses the onomatopoeia "Hmmm..." to represent vocalized puzzling, which strategically indicates that Solo thinks planning to construct a genuine relationship poses a problematic task. In expressivist characterizations, this move might represent invocation of an "authentic, honest" authorial voice. However, attributing this as a "true" representation of Solo hides the strategic performance she enacts. Solo plays with form here. She manipulates the text in ways that allow her to situate personal experience narratives in a broader cultural context.

Solo uses the argumentative strategy of numbering her points: "First of all." She offers a definitional proposition to characterize the parameters of her debate—"I'm taking that in the marriage/life time commitment sense"— another strategically sophisticated rhetorical move. Solo positions herself as interested in a heterosexual relationship with a man who is a feminist, and she provides definitional evidence to support her intentions. Midway through the text, Solo shifts from a first-person stance (characteristically expressive) to a second-person stance (self-consciously expositional in that it moves into an arena requiring an outside audience). By invoking the second-person construction, Solo adopts the diction of procedural genres. She is no longer speaking from the voice of personal experience, but from an instructional voice, which performs an authoritative, rhetorically aware stance.

Whereas personal experience writing might be valued in expressivist terms for its moments of individual revelation, personal experience narration used to shore up a position, which might persuade a reader of the writer's intent, is a self-consciously rhetorical move. Women's studies writers seem to be much more rhetorically aware of the context in which they are writing and the audience to whom they are writing. Rarely does a writer in women's studies seem to be writing simply to see herself think or declare herself an identity. She writes as a member of a "community" that respects what she knows.

Women's studies writers assert positions, argue points persuasively and convincingly, and back up their positions with relevant and credible evidence. Personal experiences and anecdotes are strategically employed in support. Voice is established in and by the group as personal experience narratives are situated in a larger sociocultural context. The phenomena of "asserting a voice" shift from a matter of voicing one's opinions, likes, and dislikes in "authentic" and "honest" tones to a matter of arguing a position and providing evidence that is credible to the writers' intended audience. These rhetorical moves provide evidence for students' growing rhetorical facility. When invoked in connection with a women's studies content, it becomes the basis for building alliances and mediating political action.

For example, Louise asserts her opinion about the effects of advertising on her self-esteem. She argues against the prevalent use of ideal images to sell products, which create a desire for bodies most women do not have:

> Everywhere there are ads. In the newspaper, TV, magazines, billboards, stores, etc. To sell a product, they often display what is considered society's ideal body and face using the product. This stresses the importance of looking a certain way. I watch ads on TV and see them in magazines and sometimes I catch myself thinking, "I wish I was that skinny, that tall, that tan, that big-breasted." Because in ads there is only one ideal body type and facial structure, it's impossible for even a small portion of people to be considered as beautiful. I think ads also draw more attention to individual body parts and cause some of the "obsessions" (if you will), of "my nose isn't right," "my butt is too big," etc.; the picking apart of the body and only seeing parts instead of seeing the whole body and its symmetry. Ads objectify and reinforce society's stereotypes of how women and men are supposed to look and act. And I don't look like that or act like that. It makes me feel alienated, objectified, unattractive, and that my only importance is to look pretty, giggle, and bounce around and look "sexy." (Louise, freewrite)

Louise uses personal experience narration to support the argument she constructs: There is an ideal body image that is used to sell products, and when one's image does not conform to the idealistic standards represented by the images, one feels alienated and objectified. Louise's personal position, which asserts a presumably "authentic" and "honest" account of her response to advertising campaigns, does not represent the whole matter she constructs in this text. Louise argues a position, using her experience as evidence, in which she asserts convincingly that her experience can credibly generalize to other women, as well. She sees herself in relation with others who do not fit the standard.

At first blush, the claim that asserting a textual voice gives female students an opportunity to write themselves in from the silence of the margins offers hardly new assumptions. These students' perceptions offer little insight into what feminists have taken for granted—that giving female students opportunities to "write their lives" creates a semiotic space, which interrupts the unequal discursive positioning of "woman" in Western culture. In the same vein, students' claims about writing seem to support expressivists' authentic voice pedagogy. Women's studies students report that they write with integrity in women's studies, which is qualitatively different from the way they write in other classes.

However, such a conclusion conceals the array of rhetorical choices these students have learned to negotiate with such facility. Students' writing choices give reason to reconsider constructivist dismissal of "expressivist" and "cultural feminist" views of writing and reason to strategically reappropriate articulations of pedagogy that allow time and space for young women to "assert a voice" as personally, academically, and politically beneficial to them. Students are not voicing a textually true self that lives hidden beneath the surface of their expression. Writing in women's studies gives young women opportunities to take on multiple rhetorical identities for multiple rhetorical purposes. Writing allows them to speak without being spoken to, and it alters traditional dispositions of female power in the classroom.

Emotional and Therapeutic Literacies

Emotional expression is an effect of writing in women's studies. Writing allows students to express how they feel about particular issues and experiences. Expressing their ideas about things helps them to feel better. Additionally, students name therapeutic solace as an effect of writing. However, little evidence of therapeutic discourses appears in the students' writing. Writing serves as a self-help tool for gaining a sense of understanding and peace in dealing with situations that cause students psychological pain. Writing helps students deal with trauma and depression or both. Students frequently link emotional expression and finding therapeutic solace to "asserting a voice." Writing helps them explore how they feel and helps them identify warrants underlying positions and arguments they consequently build.

Expressivists consider rhetorics of emotion in their discussions of authentic voice pedagogy. Elbow (*Writing with Power*) believes that the search for voice means exploring feelings: "angry feelings, perhaps depressed feelings," which then may become a catalyst to the sorts of reflective thinking and writing that result in "growth or development" (284). Elbow indicates that it is not just personal emotional growth that comes about through writing to voice anger, hurt, or betrayal, but intellectual development as well (Gradin 98–99). Although Elbow does not advocate raw emotions and feelings as good writing within the confines of acceptable academic writing, he does advocate instead that "expression is at its best when an overflow of powerful emotion is recalled and recreated through language later, not at the moment of the overflow" (Gradin 99). These views have led to constructivist criticism of the expressivist emphasis on emotional expression and exploration as a mere reflection of the inner self, which is meaningful only to the individual and, therefore, representative of "radical individualism."

As a result, finding one's voice has more frequently been translated by constructivists as an expectation that "authentic" writing is the result of writing with "passion." Regardless of whether the student is engaged in writing "strong narrative—in good sequential order, lots of detail and elaboration, a clear, supportable conclusion" (Wells 325–326) or "the various forms and functions of academic writing" in which students learn "conventional forms and better analytical skills" (Bridwell-Bowles 47), the expectation is that students should write with "passion," not emotion.

Distinctions between writing with passion and writing with emotion are difficult to determine. Bridwell-Bowles discusses passionate writing in the context of inviting students "to participate in transformation, to write with passion about subjects that are complex, politically charged, politically correct, or even politically incorrect" (47). Wells discusses "passion" as the rhetorical construction of a responsive public where the desire to learn and the willingness to argue engage the deepest energies transacting between writer and reader (329). Apparently "writing with passion" is acceptable within a constructivist framework, but emotional expression is not. Additionally, writing for therapeutic solace invokes a psychoanalytic paradigm that traditionally has exploited and punished women (e.g., Freud, Gilman, GRRLS's volatile negative reaction to a mental health organization's involvement in the 1996 annual conference of the National Women's Studies Association). Yet young women in women's studies at Aspen Grove express the value of writing in terms of mental health healing and self-help, both therapeutic concerns.

Because emotional expression and finding therapeutic solace through writing are not explicitly discussed in current constructivist work, neoromantic expressivist notions of a social-expressivist pedagogy have attempted to reclaim the strategic usefulness, particularly to writing women, of authentic voice pedagogy, which includes emotional expression and writing as therapy (Gradin). Sherie Gradin's book *Romancing Rhetorics* demonstrates the usefulness of establishing an intellectual tradition for expressivism within a constructivist feminist perspective. Gradin is a feminist neoexpressivist who illustrates how expressivism is historically related to romanticism. She interprets this connection in a positive light.

Gradin uses the history of romanticism to relate expressivism to postmodern constructivist views and argues that reclaiming a romantic heritage enriches contemporary composition theories. She critiques constructivist (mis)readings (Berlin "Rhetoric and Ideology" *Rhetoric and Reality*; Faigley "Competing Theories of Process") of expressivist intentions, which fail to notice the underlying socially constructed assumptions about the writer and potential value of writing to women, in particular. Theoretically well grounded, Gradin moves thinking forward and constructs a version of social expressivism, which "blurs the categorical lines between social theories and theories of individualism" (xv). She finds feminist value in the expressivist concern for voice, emotive processes, and lived experience. She argues that reclaiming expressivism is "anything but retrograde," although others in the field are disturbed enough about neoexpressivism that they are taking up intellectual arms against the "upstart of expressivist talk" (Winterowd).

Gradin demonstrates how the personal and intellectual are yoked in expressivism because Elbow, in particular, "chooses not to separate writers and students into non-holistic elements. Writers are complex beings within which emotional, psychological, spiritual, analytical, and intellectual developments are related" (Gradin 99). As a result of her rereading of expressivism, Gradin suggests a rhetorical pedagogy, which she names social expressivist, that rests within the romantic enterprise but which is based on the opposite of radical individualism. For Gradin, the subject (the self) is not a single definable entity that stands alone, as Berlin ("Rhetoric and Ideology") argues. "The romantic subject is defined only through the connections to other objects, subjects, and, unless in the throes of a mystical experience, through language" (Gradin 101).

Gradin invokes her own personal experience using journal writing as therapy and peer group response to complete the writing of her dissertation as the only empirical evidence she proffers to defend further exploration of expressive writing from a constructivist feminist perspective. At a point when she was feeling discouraged from reading and writing and from academic pursuits in general, she wrote a personal essay for a composition course that was organized on expressivist principles. She writes that her academic difficulties were exacerbated by a history of childhood sexual and physical abuse. She writes an essay in an effort to speak back to the abusers in her life:

> Had I not been given the place to voice these things in language at that point in my college career, had I not been afforded this kind of self-expression, I would not have continued school. I would have remained silenced and voiceless in all ways—including academic ways. (142)

Gradin concludes that finding a personal voice is the start to finding the many kinds of voices and identities needed to survive academically:

> The work that the academy accepts as worthwhile requires the striking of particular kinds of poses, selves, and voices. If women professionals are to have the kinds of academic selves that generate publication, action, respect, and finally, tenure within the university, we, as women, must somehow learn to compose different voices from those our culture at large has designated as acceptable or typical for us. Likewise, if our women students are to find success within the university, they must learn a myriad of voices. (142–143)

Gradin's work parallels in interesting ways the findings about writing in women's studies. Gradin suggests that a "personal" voice is one among many that a writer can invoke to become aware of the power that full participation in a discourse community might represent. Additionally, she suggests that writers take on multiple identities and that the "expressive" voice can shift and alter with the many identities a writer might try on at will. Because her work is theoretically rather than empirically based, the findings of this study add a performative gloss to Gradin's romancing rhetorics. These positions together may begin to amass new support for conclusions drawn by other feminist compositionists who have been critiqued for essentializing the female writer. When opportunities can be created for female students to say what they otherwise might not say and to be listened to and acknowledged by others who admit to struggling with similar issues, even if their methods of intervention and resolution diverge, then, as the female students report in this study, they find ways to connect what they know with what others know. They feel a sense of power where they used to feel powerless.

Women's studies students attribute both personal growth and intellectual development to the emotional expression and therapeutic solace they experience through writing. Their claims support both Elbow's and Gradin's conclusions that "personal," "authentic," and "emotive" writing is necessary to growth of self, mind, and power:

> First, it's writing about how you feel and figuring out what you feel. It's absolutely necessary to take this class if you're a woman. If you're in high school. It teaches you to respect your life, I think. Just your thoughts and feelings—and you're actually even more aware of everything that is going around. It makes you feel like you have power to, you know, it gives you power to do anything you want. To say anything you want. (Margaret, personal interview, May 24, 1995)

Women's studies students realize that splitting the emotive from the analytical has had negative consequences for them. They express how they feel, and consequently they begin to understand things that confuse them or that are invisible to them. Figuring things out allows them to say what they think and to do what they want.

Expression of anger is the most commonly named emotional effect of writing in women's studies. Students use writing primarily as a format to vent anger and frustration over issues raised by the content or in reaction to an event in their everyday lives. The students' writing changes their approach to the reading material or their experience and opens up avenues to vent their anger at the issues raised by academic content:

> I think the way I approach the reading material has changed. I have become more

aware of the things surrounding me by writing and it's easier to express my anger [when I am reading] the articles (Meridian, writing evaluation).

Women's studies students frequently mention that writing gives them an opportunity to vent feelings of anger and frustration in situations in which they otherwise feel unable to speak. They claim that they have learned this strategy writing in women's studies where they can vent their feelings and write whatever they want without fear of retaliation. As students situate their personal experience narratives in the larger cultural context, they can respond from a position of power in which they reject the dominant cultural narrative.

For example, Solo tells about a time when she was in a class and the teacher was discussing current events:

> [Writing is a tool I can use] you know, like that day when I got really frustrated when that teacher was talking about rape, about girls asking for it when they get raped.... I went into the library and just wrote about it because it just made me so mad. And then I gave it to Tabouli and I said "Read, read, read..." because I was so frustrated over it. I like being able to say and also to write it because it is easier I think for people to read something you've written than for them to listen to you go through it and to listen to your thinking process—cause it is a lot easier on paper. (Solo, personal interview, May 8, 1995)

Solo did not think she could argue about rape with the teacher, even though she was deeply angered. She was afraid to contradict the teacher's position because it might jeopardize her grade in the class.

Solo instead chose to write and to share with Tabouli, a woman's studies classmate. Tabouli told me about Solo's writing after class one day:"She was really pissed off and I told her she had a right to be. You know how she can get when she is really mad." Later, Solo wrote about the incident in her writing response log, and both Emma and I responded to her. Writing allowed her to say what she wanted to say, and she felt that she had reclaimed some of the power that she felt the social studies teacher had taken away.

She said to me, "I was 'empowered' by this writing to you and Emma and Tabouli. Next time Mr. X won't get away with shit like that. At least I don't plan to keep quiet about it the next time." She concludes that the next time a teacher does something like this (and she is sure there will be a next time) that she can articulate a rebuttal because she has vented her anger in writing. Solo finds the agency that resides in the power of making connections with others and of building alliances that foster responsible action.

Students use writing to say emotionally charged things to their peers that they struggle to express face-to-face. In some instances, students use writing for interpersonal communication. Margaret talks about times when she gets mad at her boyfriend and vents her anger through writing:

> If I am just really mad at my boyfriend, I just write it out and I just tell him off on paper. You know. Not that I am not going to tell him off in person. It's like, I just need to talk to him, not tell him off, but like at the moment, if I am in class and I need to get all these things out, I just write it. And then I crumple it up. Sometimes I write a letter, you know, addressed to him and it's like I am going to give it to him, and you know I don't. But I will talk to him later. (Margaret, personal interview, May 11, 1995)

In other instances, students use writing as a precursor to forwarding a position in a public forum, such as the classroom or face-to-face interpersonal communication:

> Writing made it easier to comment on something that I didn't want the whole class to know.... I am speaking more of my mind. I was taught never to interrupt people and to always keep quiet so at first I had a hard time talking in an open discussion at all. So when we wrote, it made it easier [to be able to speak later]. (Candy, writing evaluation)

Occasionally the emotional expression writers experience through writing is less an issue of letting emotions out and more an issue of connecting with emotions from which they have dissociated:

> My writing has become more personal. I am not detached from my emotions in the writing. They reflect my emotion of the moment, compared to how they used to sound thought out to fit a social norm. (Sharon, writing evaluation)

Students commonly identify this holistic connection as providing a feeling of safety. Oftentimes they connect safety with "honest" and "authentic" expressions. Feelings of safety are fostered through the vehicle of writing in women's studies:

> In English we write about the book we are reading and about grammar. In women's studies we write about our feelings. We can express how we feel. I have

noticed that I can express myself more and tell how I really feel. (Unsigned)

Safety is a result of having one's ideas accepted as inherently valuable rather than as having to fit with some expected norm to receive positive evaluation.

The students claim that emotive writing in women's studies has therapeutic value, as shown in the following writing evaluation:

> The writing assignments have brought up a lot of things in my mind. Some of the memories are very painful and some are OK. They helped me get a lot of frustrations out that have been locked inside of me for many years. I feel that I am more at peace with myself because of it. (Lois, writing evaluation)

Writing allows students the opportunity to recall and deal with issues that they may have forgotten or repressed. They gain a stronger, more appreciative sense of themselves through the writing process. Students characterize this partly as a process of self-discovery and building self-esteem—learning through writing to know what they think, know, and believe and partly as a process of self-appreciation—learning through writing to see themselves as worthy, important, and valuable human beings:

> Writing forces me to organize ideas and thoughts. It challenges me to trust someone and let them read it. It's allowed me to write in a different way than I write in my journal (facts, events go in there, plus pure emotions). Writing in women's studies about the rapes and my bisexuality has made me feel more free to not hide these things. They can't silence me anymore. (Louise, writing evaluation)

Writing allows these students to separate the trauma in their lives from themselves and find a sense of self-acceptance and peace.

As Louise explains, writing about the times she was raped helped her to gain a sense of peace in dealing with the psychological pain, which resulted after the trauma. Margaret explains that writing helped her to overcome her problem with severe bulimia because the writing allowed her to stop "hiding behind the lie." LeTisha explains how writing gave her release from years of depression:

> The strongest example I have for using writing to make a possible difference for me was [using it] to recover from depression. I have been depressed ever since the sixth grade, which I have battled on my own. To be confused at a young age or even elderly is hard, but when there is the feeling of your world closing you in, like

> elevator doors, writing is the only way out.... [Writing] has helped me a great deal.
> If I did not write, that elevator door may have shut and gone 12 feet under.
> (LeTisha, writing evaluation)

Writing allows students first to articulate and then to process psychologically the experiences and perceptions of themselves that have psychically damaged them. They say that they begin to heal. "I mean even if I don't share it with anyone, I feel better about things after writing" (Trisha). Being able to express their emotions through writing helped them move out of a "stuck" place and into a course of action:

> Writing was like everything else in class. It's helped me be able to express my emotions and feelings a little better. And more articulately. It was like, "Hey. I am feeling this way right now. OK..." Now I know what to do about it. (Thomas, personal interview, May 25, 1995)

Writing about their feelings helps them to understand what they feel.

Students are clear that the topics addressed in women's studies boost self-esteem and give them the confidence to speak and write what is on their minds. Furthermore, writing gives them an occasion to see themselves as a work in progress and not as the failed product of someone else's pathological analysis. The problems that young women confront through writing give them the opportunity to try on alternate, more powerful subjectivities that displace the confusion, depression, and anger in which the dominant discourse about adolescent girls inscribes them. Writing as a mechanism of therapeutic solace acts out their resistance to female positioning in mainstream culture.

The writing and the content cannot be separated from the context in which they co-occur. By using writing as a tool to explore the complex ideas and environments encountered in women's studies and to affirm positions they feel and that others feel, students feel better about their self-perception and have more confidence in themselves. They feel more connected to others in class. In turn, this translates into better achievement in school. Several of the students remark that their feelings of confidence have multiplied as a result of writing and women's studies. This spills over into other experiences and activities in their lives. Writing about gender issues builds self-understanding, and self-understanding about gender issues of concern builds confidence for these students. Writing helps them to disagree with the discourses that frame their lives.

Rarely does a student have an emotional outburst or emotionally charged response in class discussion. What is more likely to occur in class is an anecdotal report, which is accompanied by an emotional declaration:

> In my junior high the awards for girls were things like "best smiler," "best clothes," "cutest." The boys got "best in science" and "best in math." At first, I thought it was neat that I got the award for best smile, but then I realized that I was better in math and science than the guys that won the awards and it made me angry. (Sheila, field observation notes)

On very rare occasions, a student may be so moved by a particular idea that an emotional outburst occurs. During these infrequent occasions, a student cries in class or lashes out verbally in anger.

Different from classroom discourse, students' expressions of emotions range the gamut in their writing. Whereas students' emotional expressions in class are more likely to occur as metacognitive statements about "things that make me angry, frustrated, happy, etc.," students generally feel at ease to write and express a full range of emotions. Language indicative of emotional discourses is vividly invoked throughout the writing samples. For example:

> I'm sick of having these memories (of being raped) around, but as my therapist tells me, they'll always be there whether consciously or not. It horrifies me to see how many other people go through this stuff, yet I still feel like a freak for having this done to me. Yet it wasn't really done to me or against me, because to them I wasn't a person, just a thing, as all women seem to be viewed in our society. This above statement explains to me why rape is so common. We're all just things, tools for men to get their feelings and anger out on. Just there to use. FUCK THEM. (Louise, masculinity/femininity history writing assignment)

Louise uses emotionally charged words and phrases, which express feelings that she feels unable to express publicly. She writes "I'm *sick* of... it *horrifies* me... I feel like a *freak*...we're all just *things, tools* for men... just there *to use. FUCK THEM.*" Louise's diction uses harsh words that depict a full range of reactions to the degrading experience of rape. "It makes me so mad that I can't get mad." However, writing allows her the space and the opportunity to vent her despair, her anger, and her frustration. It also allows her to have the last word, to reclaim and reconstruct a self apart from the experience. She writes in a moment of distanced reflection that this experience wasn't really about her personally: "Yet it wasn't really done to me or against me, because to them I wasn't a person, just a thing, as all women seem to be viewed in our society. This above statement explains to me why rape is so common."

She constructs an amazingly credible and cool position, which argues that rape happens because women as a class get used by men as a class. Louise assumes many faces by appealing to the logical structure of argumentation, "This above statement explains to me..." She also appeals to the pathetic[1] structure of emotional reaction. She avenges the rawness of feeling. By the end of the course, Louise exclaims, "I learned in women's studies that I am OK" (Louise, field observation notes).

Louise makes space for a theory of agency that arises in constant innovation of a self she wishes to perform. Louise's textual venting is akin to those of many other students who use a number of emotional discourses in their writing to work through issues, ideas, and experiences from which they have disassociated in order to maintain culturally acceptable female norms. Louise's text represents the wavelike ebb and flow of a discourse that moves in and out of position. She is the angry victim and the cool analyst. She is at once in charge and out of control. Louise's text explodes the myth of a stable, unified self and explores how identity might be multiply constructed out of a myriad of experiences. Through writing, she continually tries on, consumes, and exchanges these identities at will.

LeTisha invokes the discourse of psychoanalysis to describe the effects writing has on her emotional well-being:

> I became deeply depressed at the age of twelve and it lasted up until last year. I wrote to express my anger, pain, love, joy, hate, and any other emotion a human can experience.... I've learned most about myself through my writings, it is my therapy to myself to help me come to terms with me [*sic*] feelings.... My writings [*sic*] have mostly come from anger I have towards my family and peers. Also towards myself. I question my actions in my writings and analyze them best as I can. (LeTisha, writing autobiography assignment)

Her diction employs a number of psychoanalytic terms and phrases: "depression," "becoming deeply depressed," "learned most about myself," "my therapy," "come to terms with my feelings," "come from anger," and "analyze them best I can." She accomplishes this without the help of clinical counseling. LeTisha demonstrates the ways in which writing helped her to heal the psychological dissonance she claims to have experienced.

Elbow discusses the rhetorical distinction the writer learns to negotiate between developing a "real" voice and producing pragmatically successful writing—polished pieces that work for specific audiences and situations (cited in Gradin 98), stating: "Deep personal outrage, for example, may be the only authentic tone of voice you can use in writing to a particular person, yet that voice is neither appropriate nor useful for the actual document you have to write" (Elbow *Writing with Power* 307). Gradin implies that the "real" Elbow refers to is not an essential self that underlies the rhetorical performance. Writers at once are socially constructed and multiple selves, the complex of many voices and identities negotiated and performed to enact a rhetorical "real" that fits the purpose of the occasion. Women's studies helps writers to enter a conversation at a point where they feel comfortable and to find their ways across complex rhetorical landscapes. Writing seems to provide an extraordinary vehicle for these adolescent female students to connect "personal," "authentic," and "emotive" voices with the intellectual environments of the classroom, echoing shades of Emig's distinctions about writing as a "unique" mode of learning ("Writing as a Mode of Learning"). This seems particularly significant to these young women because of the oppressive and disconnected conditions in which they typically find themselves in school. In general, the discursive silencing of girls systemically performed by the school does not will students the power to speak critically about inequities, passions, emotions. Writing becomes a vehicle to counteract girls' silence.

As so many have pointed out (e.g., Alvine and Cullum; Barbieri; Belenky et al.; Gilligan, Lyons, and Hanmer; Martin "Becoming Educated"), the educational journey is particularly damaging to female students because it splits reason from emotion. The students at Aspen Grove have lived with the damage on their skin. They have learned that to speak against that which is authorized by the school can earn one punitive consequences, which range from grading outcomes such as Solo named and feared, to harassment and humiliation, to suspension and expulsion. Students learn quickly not to speak what they think, feel, and believe in school. As a result, interrupting the silencing discourse of school, which is a primary purpose of women's studies at Aspen Grove, requires a great deal of disruptive interference on the part of the teacher. It takes the students time to realize that Emma is providing space for such cacophony to erupt. Writing becomes a tool with which they negotiate the terrain from silence to speech.

Writing opens the space for interruption, disruption, and interference. It gives these students opportunities to name and to speak and to pave the way for change.

Educational philosopher Jane Roland Martin (*Reclaiming*) has called for rethinking education so that it might encompass more female-friendly strategies—enabling emotion and feeling to become as much a part of the educational process as analysis, critical thinking, and self-sufficiency (192–193). Writing in women's studies provides female students with such a favorable educational climate—a location and an opportunity for integrating all the selves that women desire, connecting reason with emotion, thought with action, self with experience. The context constructed by writing and teaching in women's studies makes possible such integration.

Relational Literacies

Women's studies students articulate awareness of conversations that construct relational performances, which hold meaning among students, the teacher, and the researcher. Students say that writing is a social transaction requiring writer, text, and reader, which constructs the central focus of these relational connections:.

> We wrote journals so that you began to understand us, and to make sure that we were actually growing, learning, and understanding the concepts. The essays about ourselves were very knowledgeable for you and ourselves. You were able to get to know us, and in return we were able to get to know ourselves. (Sheila, writing evaluation)

Writing constructs more equal relations among the teacher, the students, and the researcher. Students realize that agency resides in the power of building connections and alliances with others.

A number of feminists including Janet Emig (*Composing Processes*) indicate that student-teacher relationships are at the heart of learning, particularly for female students (Alvine and Cullum; Barbieri; Belenky et al.; Gilligan, Lyons, and Hanmer). Building relational connections and alliances is a constructivist effect of writing in women's studies, which students favorably identify. Alliances and relational connections generally are constructed as a result of the classroom "readarounds" described in

Chapter 3. During readarounds textually mediated conversations occur student-to-student in the presence of the teacher and researcher. Relational connections occur because students perceive interconnections among content, pedagogy, and research intervention in women's studies class. Relational connections also occur because dialogue is constructed textually between students and the researcher.

The significance of these constructed conversations is not singularly in their pedagogical value as relation-building tools. Susan Miller describes conditions that enable the disenfranchised to construct a temporarily empowered platform from which to speak and write transformative versions of a life. Miller describes written language as self-referential, coherent, independent of its source (*Rescuing the Subject* 11–15). When written texts come "through" the writer and perform concretely inscribed assertions about what it means to be a gendered student writer in a system that privileges one sex over the other, the disenfranchised move temporarily from the wings into the spotlight. Students' texts perform as representations of gender action and performance enacted in the lives of these adolescent girls. Readarounds create a theatrical spectacle of multiply-authored selves who perform center stage. Students recognize the textual opportunity to reconfigure and transform their experiences. Readers move in and out of synch with the written texts of their bodies and momentarily transact gender reformulations. Writers take on roles that mimic and oppose the dominant gender discourse. They write themselves into a larger conversation through any role they desire. In these moments, gender is made visible as "a persistent impersonation" passing as the real (Butler *Gender Trouble*).

Student to Student

Women's studies students specify relational connections with other students as an effect of writing in women's studies. Generally, readarounds provide the space in which these connections occur. Readarounds create a space for open discussion around the ideas in student written texts:

> When you took the quotes out of our writing and we all read them out loud—I think the writing really does help because not everyone is going to come out and say what they think. So it gives you a better idea of what everyone is thinking.... We could understand where we were all coming from.... It made it safe because everyone else was doing the same thing. We were all writing about the same

things, the same topics, but our own different experiences specifically. (LeTisha, personal interview, May 17, 1995)

Readarounds provide the opportunity for every class member's voice to be heard and to count.

Readarounds build an atmosphere where every idea is received equally, thus creating a sense of collectivity and solidarity in the class. Students see possibilities both for similar and for different gender performances revealed in the texts of their peers. They are able to consider the multiple texts enacted by other gendered performers and contemplate the many identities that they potentially may enact:

> When we did readaround things...people could see what you were thinking and you can see how people react and you could see what other people were saying. It was like you can relate to them. And that helps you in the class because it feels more together, you know, and you can know what other people are saying. And it helps your situation because you don't think that you're the only one who feels that way.... (Trisha, personal interview, May 11, 1995)

Readarounds construct a conversational context that enlarges the borders of the written discussions.

Readarounds provide students with opportunities to confront the alienating isolation that occurs when one questions cultural norms especially as they come into range in a high school women's studies class. The students report that being able to read what their peers are thinking and writing about gender issues of common concern helps them to realize that they share similar views and experiences. Even when students disagree or hotly contest an issue of concern, they find a sense of connection with others through readarounds because students realize that they are all thinking about similar gender issues even though they might perform their gender in radically different ways. Prior to the shared reading of all their texts, students tend to experience a sense of isolation from those same others. They believe: "I am the only one who is thinking about this stuff" (Lesley, personal interview, May 23, 1993).

For example, during one semester, nearly half of the students in the class reported that they had been raped.[2] Students reported the rapes in their reading response logs during the section on women and violence. I was the only one who was aware of the frequency with which these students had experienced acts of personal violence. Walker and I decided together to construct a readaround conversation in class from response log excerpts.

After reading, students wrote again. The students' second set of responses indicated horror, relief, surprise, and reassurance. The most frequent proposition was, "I thought it was my fault—that I was the only one this had happened to." Through the shared knowledge that came with the realization that rape was not uncommon among the members of their group, students found a new way of knowing and acting. JoAnna explained how she had decided to take martial arts classes and how that had helped her become strong. She started volunteering at the rape crisis center so that she could talk to others who might be able to use her help. LeTisha got out of a relationship in which she had been forced to have sex. Thomas confessed to having pushed his former girlfriend too far—he realized that what he had done could be considered rape. He wanted forgiveness from the group. Seeing through new eyes, students gained power from sharing experiences in which they had felt powerless. They planned altered courses of future action, which included reporting the incident to the police, getting professional help, talking with the crisis line volunteers, and moving out of abusive relationships.

Readarounds build trust and respect among class members. Students realize that what they have to say is important and that their ideas will be received in a trusting and nonjudgmental atmosphere:

> I realized that people respect what you say about certain things and even if you disagree on something, it's not thoughtless. You respect the opinions and that's what made me feel like I could trust you guys and everyone in here. On paper I felt like I could trust you all. Because you were kind of the leaders of this whole experience. It felt safe in here. (Margaret, personal interview, May 24, 1995)

Students are challenged to realize that safety in the classroom is not the result of consensus among classmates but the result of feelings of trust that are built when all written ideas are received in an uncensored context. No one's voice is interrupted or hushed. The result is that the students feel safe and accepted and bound together by the common experience of the class. Students are able to see themselves in relation to radically variable perceptions of adolescent girls (and boys) in school. Writing in women's studies provides space on center stage for them to view and consider alternatives.

Readarounds also provide students with opportunities to construct shared meanings and understandings about gender issues of concern in their culture. Solo explains this phenomenon of group-think:

> When I see what other people are thinking, it just helps me think. I can see whether I disagree or agree with others' ideas and then I can talk better and I can write better after I have thought about what other people are thinking. It helps me to know what I think when I see what other people are thinking. It helps me clarify my thoughts, so then I can write it because before that, I really don't know.... I think it's good to be able to know people who weren't speaking out had the same opinion or had thought the same things as you. It is good to be able to see what other people were thinking and that you weren't alone with your thoughts. (Solo, personal interview, May 8, 1995)

When everyone's ideas are made public, the students have thoughts other than their own to connect and reason with. The conversation enlarges and becomes more meaningful both individually and collectively. Multiple selves and voices are explored. Students share the experience of multiple textual selves performed.

Teacher to Student

Women's studies students describe building relational connections with Walker through writing in women's studies. Generally, their comments are conflated with the overall atmosphere of the women's studies classroom and must be distinguished as such rather than as a direct effect of conversations that occur strictly through writing. Walker has very little interaction with the students through writing. However, the students are aware that Walker values both the writing and my contributions to the class. They braid these connections tightly together:

> We trusted you.... I think you trust teachers when they trust you. I mean like some teachers you can trust just cuz you know they're going to—a lot of it is they don't do anything that would be opposite and they don't necessarily do stuff that abuses trust or supporting, but they just never do anything that encourages trust either. Like you guys would tell stories about what had happened to you and everything and we just trusted that we could talk to you about what had happened to us. (Solo, personal interview, May 24, 1995)

The students gain an overarching sense of constructing relational conversations between Walker and themselves, but it is embedded in the context of the overall environment created in the classroom, not just with writing.

At times, Walker shares her own written texts with the students to motivate further discussion about an issue of concern. Students find these experiences of textual exchange with Walker to be relation-constructing events that create an open atmosphere of possibility in the class. When Walker shares writing, it generally is viewed as part of the more global impressions the students have of writing, of women's studies, and of Walker as their teacher. For example:

> You and her never talked down to us. I can't stand to be talked down to....You sat here on your computer and you had your own opinions and you had your own things to add in and Emma did too. And I remember when you read that poem that you wrote about fishing. "OK," I thought. That was so great and Emma read a poem that she had written also. It just opened up. I mean that really did it for me when you read that poem cuz it felt like you were comfortable with us and so for me it made me feel like I can say whatever I want after that. Or I could write whatever I want. It is not many teachers that would open up to their students. (LeTisha, personal interview, May 23, 1995)

The students plait together the many impressions they have of Walker within the open conversational space she constructs in the classroom through both verbal and written interactions. Walker creates an environment for students to discuss and write freely and to perform their gender differently if they wish.

Generally, students see a distinction between the researcher role and Walker's role in women's studies. They realize that women's studies is a joint effort, but that Walker and I both have our own roles:

> I have Emma in other classes and I see her more as a teacher. In this class she is a lot more relaxed, though. But I can tell that she still is doing the teacher stuff and that she is pressured into it. She is a relaxed teacher most of the time, but it's not a set schedule in women's studies. She'll go whatever way we want to go. And so I think you get a lot more into the personal stuff because you respond to our journal. And you are not in charge of the class. She is up in the front and you sit off to the side. I just think you think about our writing more because that's YOUR job. She is in charge of everything that is going on, but I think she really wants us to get the idea cuz she wants us to learn. But she can't concentrate on the writing as much as you. Or as much as she wants. (Trisha, personal interview, May 18, 1995)

Students understand that the conversations that occur between Walker and them in the context of class discussion and the conversations that occur between them and me in the context of their writing are separate but equal and connected parts of the entire women's studies conversation as a whole.

Researcher to Student

Students unanimously identify building relational connections through conversations constructed textually between the researcher and them as an effect of writing in women's studies. I attempted to construct these conversations intentionally in keeping with my pedagogical underpinnings for teaching writing in this context. I intended to construct dialogue with the students about issues of gender concern. I wanted both to deconstruct status quo assumptions that appeared in the writing and to challenge students to explore multiple other gender choices. Several students characterize the feedback as providing a sense of acknowledgment:

> Feedback I received on my writing made me feel good.... It was like this is cool—she can relate to it—so it means I like expressed my ideas well enough that somebody else could understand what I was trying to say, which is always helpful to me because everybody is always telling me: "Come down to my level. I don't get it." It was like obviously there are some people who can understand me. (Thomas, personal interview, May 25, 1995)

Students frequently mention that our exchanges demonstrate that someone is listening and can understand their points. They feel validated that their writing holds meaning for me. In other classes, teachers either write the obligatory "good job" (Trisha) or "you need to work on your punctuation" (Sharon) or, as in Thomas's case, teachers have indicated that they are confused by what their students write.

My textual interactions with many of the students are not a matter of simple acceptance. I pushed hard on them in our exchanges. However, students understand that our exchanges, though critical, demanding, and thought-provoking, cut to the heart of contradictions that arise for them in a women's studies class peopled primarily with "other" female bodies. They knew that I was willing to accept them even when I was unwilling to leave unchallenged some of their pronouncements and conclusions.

Many of the students indicate that relational connections are built as a result of shared trust, which comes from effacing the boundaries that generally circumscribe adult-student interactions in school. These relationships exist between us through written dialogue:

> When you would write back and stuff, you'd tell us the truth, your own personal experiences. You would say like, "I think you're right about this" and that helps you know you have a connection. To know that someone else is reading what you're writing and listening to you. It breaks down barriers. I think, "I can actually talk to this person." You talk about it and it helps to know that even with the age difference....I mean even somebody older has the same feelings and they think that what I am saying is not just some screwed-up teenager thing. Like some high school kid. It just feels good to have somebody write back to you, you know, actually more than a *"good"* with a few lines under it. (Trisha, personal interview, May 18, 1995)

When students feel that their opinions are validated, they are inclined to write more and think harder about the written exchanges that occur:

> In fact I felt like I had to write a lot because I wanted you to know what I was thinking. Cause you had responded to me and so I thought that I owed you that much. When I first got my journals back and you had written a lot of stuff and I knew that it wasn't just like you were grading papers or whatever. From the first, I realized that I could do it more and you wouldn't throw it back in my face. You took us seriously. It showed you actually cared about my development.... Not that I just relied on your responses. It's more that you cared. You wanted to read it. It's more than just an assignment. Even if it's not just the writing, you want me to think about it more than after class is over. Most teachers just give you assignment after assignment and they don't care if you learn it, remember it. So the class is a bust. But with you it's an ongoing thing. (Trisha, personal interview, May 18, 1995)

The relationship speaks to them of mutual trust and respect. They are quick to note that they are not writing or thinking about these things as a result of trying to impress me or because they believe it will help their grades. They generally assert that our exchanges hold meaning for them because "I listen and take them seriously."

Students mention how relationships build over time. They trace the development of relationships between themselves and me across conversations throughout the course. Generally, students say that I follow their lead rather than try to take them somewhere they are not intending to go. This enables their learning and helps them consider other possible courses of thought and action:

At the beginning of the semester, my responses are really detached. And I feel like your responses are like "Oh." Detached from me, as a result. She's detached and she's not really learning any information or anything, so you are like, "Oh. That was nice. Thanks a lot." You know? And then I start talking about how I feel and how I want to make changes and I start to apply things to my life like with my parents getting divorced and my family being so crazy. My dad is an alcoholic and my mom is psychotic and my sister is like she has lost it. She has this boyfriend and she's lost her identity in him. And I start writing about that stuff and I talk about how I feel and so because I question more, you have more comments. You can offer more response and more help.... (Sharon, personal interview, May 12, 1995)

Students say they feel "empowered" by this pedagogical strategy because they realize that it constitutes their journey to temporary self-understanding. It is interactive and not top-down, a result of having someone try to explain or teach it to them. Learning occurs through writing and therefore belongs to them personally; they value it for its long-term rather than course-confined effects.

Women's studies students have a sense of the sanctity of the relational experience that is constructed vis-à-vis writing and the way it contributes to their learning. The shared transactions that occur in women's studies are distinct from any other relational connections they have experienced in school, as the following quote demonstrates:

I looked forward to reading what you had to say in each one because I was opening up certain issues to someone that was interested in what I had to say and that wanted to hear that. Because I would try to talk to my parents or my boyfriend and they would be just like, "Oh...OK...Cool." But you just—it's a neat experience to talk to someone who is really listening. And who cares and can respond to me. If you had questions about something I said, you wanted more, you know? That was how you communicated that you cared about what I thought.

If I were to open up to my friends—you know they're my friends and I trust them with my stuff, but the way the whole high school situation is—I couldn't trust them even if they were my best friends.... There's so much talking going on. It's not even gossip—well I guess it is gossip. But I just knew that you guys knew all the background about every issue and I knew you wouldn't go and run and tell somebody and I knew that you would take what I had to say to heart and understand it and write to it. This whole class is about that. I knew you would take me seriously. You would respect my opinions, what I think. And give me your opinions about issues. And I knew that I could trust you because of all our open discussions about everything. (Margaret, personal interview, May 24, 1995)

Although we often disagree in many exchanges, students conclude that someone is listening to them, that someone accepts and respects their ideas, and that someone is challenging them to think critically about the issues raised in these textual exchanges. They find such exchanges meaningful sources of learning and relatively distinct from other exchanges that commonly occur with adults in school. It matters to these students who is listening and how what they have to say is heard. Our exchanges perform a pedagogical ritual (McLaren) of teacher-to-student feedback that reconfigures the typical sanitized conversations these girls have with adults in school.

At stake in the conversational links built among the participants of women's studies at Aspen Grove is an understanding of gender performativity enacted within the constraints imposed by the school, a compulsory system. Because girls' experiences in schools tend to be neither comfortable nor safe, writing in women's studies hopes to alter the punitive and oppressive mechanisms of the system. As students' texts move to the center of this classroom and construct conversations among teacher, students, and researcher, the roles identified for female students in school are put out of synch with the texts girls are culturally and institutionally expected to perform. When the status quo is disrupted with other versions of femininity, other subversive and transformative discursive possibilities emerge for girls. Students use the occasion of writing in women's studies to textually parody identities and cross-dress in other gendered possibilities, as Butler suggests (*Gender Trouble*, "Gender Trouble," *Bodies that Matter*). In that way, women's studies students reframe girls' discursive anatomy and revise the scripts and performances of gendered positions, which historically have positioned females in schools in subordinate roles. Writing about issues of relevance in a context that centers girls' texts enables multiple other performance possibilities to appear. Students report that they have experienced safety, trust, connection, and at least cognitive movement toward an understanding of other possible castings of "female," "feminine," and "student" in the school environment.

Literacies of Performative Transformation

I use the term *performative* borrowing from philosopher J. L. Austin

(*How to Do Things with Words*), who describes performatives as a class of linguistic utterances. According to Austin, a performative is a class of utterances, which are institutionally bound and connect speech and action. "The term 'performative'...indicates that the issuing of the utterance is the performing of an action—it is not normally thought of as just saying something" (6–7). The utterance puts into effect the institutional relations that it names. Performatives as a class of utterances carry no semantic value outside the institutional acts they are "said" to perform. Performatives cannot be strictly "true" or "false" but instead are either "felicitous" or "infelicitous" based on who utters the performative and where and how they utter it.

Austin's singular example of a performative utterance is the declaration, "I pronounce you husband and wife" by authorized clergy or civil servant. That utterance is institutionally bound and cannot be philosophically argued as either true or false. "I pronounce you husband and wife" and other utterances that carry culturally instituted regulation (e.g., "You are expelled" uttered by the principal of the school; "You failed this class and cannot graduate" uttered by the 12th-grade English teacher) is deemed "felicitous" only when it is spoken by a particular person vested with specific institutional authority in a specific ceremony or ritual event (e.g., expulsion or notification of failure). Under the regulations of the cultural institution that ordains the truth consequences of the utterance and sets the conditions for the ceremony or ritual event to take place, an utterance is deemed felicitous only when the person conducting the ceremony (or ritual event) has the institutional authority to enact the legal and cultural sanctions ascribed to the performance of the utterance.

Therefore, "I pronounce you husband and wife" or "I expel you" or "I fail you and you cannot graduate" are utterances that cannot carry felicitous linguistic relevance unless it occurs under the auspices of conventional conditions. It constitutes a felicitous linguistic function only when performed within the arena of culturally and legally bound regulatory conventions governing the performance. The utterance is not viewed as separate from the marriage or expulsion or failure text it produces. For example, if Jeri's brother taunts, "You are going to fail English class and not graduate if you do not get off the telephone and do your homework," it does not carry the institutional or performative weight that the same statement would uttered by Jeri's English teacher. Ultimately, in determining the linguistic consequences of a performative utterance, it becomes impossible to separate out its performative effects from the political and cultural intersections in which the statements that enact the marriage or expulsion or failure to graduate are legally produced and institutionally maintained.

Judith Butler borrows from Austin to identify ways in which substantive effects of gender are performatively produced and compelled by compulsory practices of gender utterances: "There can be no gender identity behind the expressions of gender; that identity is performatively constituted by the very 'expressions' that are said to be its results" (*Gender Trouble* 25). The proclamation, "It's a girl!" carries with it a full spectrum of expectations that are enacted upon the body of that text. The range of gender understandings and performances by "girl" or "boy" bodies are constrained by culturally sanctioned norms. Discourse preempts the possibilities of other imaginable gender configurations within culture. What is read as a typical gender identity becomes the "law" of that identity. Stylized repetition of discursive enactments of "boyness" and "girlness" both identify the culturally sanctioned performance and allow the audience to read it within the constraints of "normal" cultural interpretation.

Austin sees performatives and Butler sees genders as properties of language that interpret cultural "reality" as it works within culturally instituted conventions, which is how I appropriate the usage here. This is not to say that either language or a declaration of gender identity makes it so, however. It is to say that language defines and limits the enactments of "real" institutional and cultural performances and cannot be separated from them. Language and gender identifications are the media through which we understand culturally gendered performances.

Girls in school are discursively constituted to enact gender performatives in an institutional space that is bound by uncomfortable, unsafe, inequitable, and performatively oppressive conventions. Girls are expected to be polite, quiet, dutiful students who do not get too much in the way. The purpose of women's studies at Aspen Grove is to interrupt the discourse of oppression that traps high school girls in subordinate, silent, and inhospitable roles and to give students tools for thinking their ways out of the repressive trap.

Writing is one tool that creates a discursive script, which interrupts, disrupts, and reconfigures normative performances of "female" and "student" in the compulsory institution of the high school. Because these performative utterances occur under the auspices of a culturally sanctioned institution, when a student writes a script that interrupts the status quo of institutional norms discursively designated for girls, her text sets about a performative enactment of transformation that she identifies or wishes to make in her life. Writing creates the discursive space of possibility for interruption, disruption, and reconfiguration. This is not to say that writing alone accomplishes the transformation. Without construction of a discourse of possibility, it is unlikely that any possible life transformations could occur. Writing helps to create the location and opportunity for performative consideration of transformation.

Women's studies students' performative utterances appear generally as (a) *reflective revisions*, utterances whereby a writer declares a revised sense of self; (b) *experiential edits*, utterances whereby a writer constructs enabling conditions for change—for reconsidering personal responses and actions to specific stimuli and events; and (c) *transformative performatives*, utterances whereby a writer scripts a sense of future self—writes a life she wishes to perform. *Transformative performatives* generally appear in two ways. Some transformative performatives explain a transformation that either has occurred in the writer's life or of which she has become aware during women's studies. Other transformative performatives set courses for the writer's future action. Instances of *transformative performatives* suggest that writing may be part of a process in which young women alter their vision of the sociocultural possibilities available to them.

Deciding whether students' transformative utterances are "true" or "false" or "real" is incommensurate with Austin's and Butler's views of the nature of performatives. Rather than truthful or authentic, Austin would consider the utterance "felicitous" or "infelicitous." Because the student utters before a person authorized by the school (teacher/researcher), students' performative utterances are received as felicitous performatives. A student's self-report of transformation must be seen as passing as a "real" enactment of her understanding of gendered performance. As students utter experiential edits, reflective revisions, and transformative performatives in their writing, they disrupt the status quo in a compulsory system that perniciously maintains a regulatory function of keeping female students in a subordinate slot. Their transformative utterances are deemed "felicitous" and potentially disruptive within this context.

Experiential Edits

In some instances, students declare that a scripted sense of self leads to actual changes in lived experience. Students assert that they used to behave in certain ways, but now, with the help of writing, they behave differently. *Experiential editing* is the term I use to categorize responses that fit this pattern. An experiential edit is an utterance in which a student asserts that writing has created an enabling condition for change—for reconsidering personal responses to specific events. When editing experience, students assert that writing allows them to adjust their actions from former patterns of behavior, which they currently find oppressing, to "edited" patterns of behavior, which they claim are more empowering:

> I am more assertive as a result of writing in women's studies. I try not to act like I am a dumb girl, you know. And then, like if I don't want to do something, I don't. I don't feel obligated to do something just because ...to make the social connections, or whatever. It's not worth it. You know? I finally figured out that if I don't want to do something, I don't have to and if they're mad at me they can just, they get over it in ten minutes because I get over it, you know? ...It's self-empowerment, whatever, you know? I feel like I am important enough that I can stand up for myself. (Trisha, personal interview, May 18, 1995)

Trisha believes that writing in women's studies has helped her change in substantive ways. She views her former self as passive and conforming to female stereotypes. She views her edited self as more assertive, more independent, and more self-empowered.

Margaret describes her former self as struggling to deal with being dismissed from the varsity cheerleading squad as a result of an eating disorder:

> When I started [women's studies], I was trying to work stuff out from not making the cheerleading squad because of my eating disorder. I had a lot on my mind and I didn't really have much to say. And since women's studies, I have totally tuned into what I want and what I feel and before it was kind of just like, I mean I didn't actually not know, but I didn't do anything about it. Writing has given me like the motivation to see myself.... I am making my life more what I want it to be. I can say more what I want and what I like. (Margaret, personal interview, May 24, 1995)

Margaret attributes writing with providing the impetus to analyze her patterns of behavior and consequently to edit her experience in ways that are more appealing to her. She claims that she is more self-assured and outwardly vocal in expressing her desires as a result of writing and reading in women's studies.

Reflective Revisions

In other instances, students declare that writing serves to script a revised sense of self. Writing provides women's studies students with an opportunity to reflect on their patterns of behavior and to identify contradictions between what they say they think, feel, and believe and what they actually do, which contradicts their thoughts, feelings, and beliefs. *Reflective revisions* is the term I use to categorize responses that fit this pattern. A reflective revision uses writing to review and analyze things students have said and done in the past and to determine what they would say and do differently in the future. Students identify incongruities through writing and, with these realizations, they claim to align their behavior with their ideological positions:

> I remember I don't know exactly what happened [but there was] something I wrote this one day and then something happened and I made a hasty reaction. And right after I had done that, I got into thinking about it and I was like, "I just wrote about that." In last period, you know. And why in the heck did I do that? I'd remembered what I wrote and I could have acted better than I did. Because when something is written down and it's probably just your psyche, like a psychological thing, but if it's written on paper, then it's a fact. It's not just, "I think this, it's like this is what I know," you know? And so you behave that way.

> It's like if you put it in writing, it's kind of like a contract with yourself. You can make like a handshake contract and you can break whatever part and there's nothing to hold you to it except your own conscience and you can rationalize that out. And when you put it on paper though, it's like it's there. Somewhere there is going to be that paper and if you don't do what you said you were going to do or something like that, then somebody can eventually come out and say, "You didn't do that. You are a liar." And that makes you feel really bad. (Thomas, personal interview, May 25, 1995)

Writing helps students realize that they may be doing things that challenge their perceptions of themselves. Writing forces the issue. They see it as a contract with themselves, by which they compel themselves to refocus and recommit to their intentions.

Writing serves a temporal function that slows the writer's thoughts down long enough to allow critical analysis and reflective revision to occur:

> I think just, it [writing] actually makes you take the time and look at yourself. I mean there are a lot of people who go through [women's studies] and never analyze how they are and how to figure out what they want and stuff, so the writing makes you stop and think about it. It makes you think about how you want to do some of these things. (Solo, personal interview, May 8, 1995)

Writing serves a reflective function, which helps the writer to analyze and to revise her experience.

The distinctions between experiential edits and reflective revisions are subtle, and often the superimposed line between the categories blurs. Experiential edits generally refer to changes students claim the writing in women's studies has enabled them to make in their performed behavior. Reflective revisions generally refer to the processes of distancing and analyzing that occur through writing, which allow the writer to view the distinctions between their beliefs and their experiences. Consequently, the writing allows writers to propose suggested revisions to either their ideology or their lives accordingly.

Transformative Performatives

In the most complex writing transaction of the three, students declare that writing has served to script a sense of future self. Writing provides them with an opportunity to write a life they wish to perform. I use the term *transformative performative* to characterize responses in this category. In some instances, students also note that experiential edits set a transformative script in action. In the case of *transformative performatives,* students perform a desired self as they write about changes they would like to make in their lives:

> I feel like when I started women's studies class, it was a difficult time for me. I was kind of unsure about everything and it was kind of a hard time in my life. But now I use [what I have learned in women's studies]. Even with my boyfriend I am using it, you know? Cuz I know, I know that no one should be treated like a possession.... And I can relate to the specific things I learned in this class. In the reader and in the writing. It makes me feel a lot clearer... and that I can do something about it. I can have like my own voice and I can choose what's best for me.
>
> I think that the biggest issue was my body image and dealing with that—the

cheerleading and the eating disorder—and I think the article on anorexia, bulimia... it had a section about the warning signs and everything. I looked at that and it made me more aware of what society has done to me. Not even about the whole food issue, just about trying to feel important in society. And I just felt like it made me feel that I was really fat. It's about trying to live up to what society wants me to be. And it's impossible to live up to what they want you to be because it's not you.

Being able to talk to you (through the writing), and you and Emma helping me talk to Charis [a counselor who works with students with eating disorders] really helped with that. I stopped doing that [vomiting]. I think that made me realize that I have to stop. And that was a big issue for me....

I knew more people, more women were going through this, and uh, most women. Trying to measure up to the image society wants, and they were being hurt by it. I realized it wasn't all that personal. There was someone I could talk to about it. Or these were stereotypes and it wasn't just me. I changed what I was doing. (Margaret, personal interview, May 24, 1995)

Students trace their transformation through the course of women's studies and beyond. They explain that they understand earlier patterns of behavior—in Margaret's case: cheerleading, bulimia, being with a possessive boyfriend—can be understood differently through the context of the reading and writing accomplished in women's studies. Students are able to detach the behavior from themselves and see it as a socialized response. They are able to declare a will to change as a result and to set a future course of action that transforms the self they have been in the past.

Writing gives students the opportunity to assess critically what they are saying and doing and how they need to behave differently if they want to accomplish the things they say they want to accomplish:

[The writing in women's studies] is like, well OK, I am writing. This is how I define myself. I say I want to be independent. I want to do things on my own. I don't want to like have to have a boyfriend to do it, like what I really want. I want to really find myself and learn about stuff and I don't want to feel like I am just a product of society, but like I wasn't doing anything about it. I was like trying to define myself as that, but I wouldn't do anything to change myself like to actually physically not be that way until I like wrote down, "This is what I want to be." Then I said, "Look at you. Look at you. You don't do anything. You just hang out and kind of don't do anything to get yourself going where you want to be." And it's like, it made me look at myself and say, "OK. Get motivated." Like…"Apply to college. Figure out what you want to do. Just kind of get a direction." You know? Yeah. Like, you know, I applied to college. I feel more independent.

It's like I don't want to see myself fall into the same patterns as my stepmom and my mom did cause my mom was always like, "I never wanted to end up with a family," and blah blah blah. "I was gonna be a lawyer or model or a this or a that." And she's gonna be like 50 soon, and she never got any of that accomplished. And I didn't want to say, like this is what I am going to do and then just end up married some day with all these kids and realize, "HEY, that's not what I wanted to do." You know? So the writing kind of makes me have a reality check and say unless you go get these things done, you're going to end up that way.

I think there's like for this kind of writing, it made me look at myself and I think if you are more in tune with yourself, you will do what you want to do and you think about things and you know who you are through the writing and you can learn a lot easier. You know that's you…cause if more people wrote and were more in tune with themselves, it would make things a lot easier for them wanting to be who they want as people. Inside and stuff. (Sharon, personal interview, May 23, 1995)

Writing helps students by forcing them to recognize the transformative nature of their written assertions and to analyze what they need to do to enact that performance. They set a course of future action that performs a transformed sense of self. Writing also interrupts the gendered status quo as students analyze and examine others' experiences. Students do not want to mess up their chances to enact a different gendered self than others before them have performed. Through writing they are able to analyze their behavior and their ideologies and set performative scripts for behaving differently. In Sharon's case, she decides to move away from home, to apply to college and to finish school regardless of the pressure that she gets from her parents and grandparents to meet a nice boy and get married when she finishes high school (Sharon, writing response log).

The examples of transformation claimed in performative utterances range from the trivial to the traumatic in terms of larger societal values. However, as Walker points out during one interview,

A teenage crisis is a teenage crisis. Whatever it is, it is their value of life. For some teenagers, that may be that they are raped by their father. For others, it's that they don't know which guy to go with to the Junior Prom. Or they have a zit on their chin. It's not the level of the crisis in terms of societal values. Where in their life—THAT is the crisis, and a crisis is a CRISIS, whatever it is. And so, when you create a safe space, you get what is really going on at whatever level that it's really going on. And for Sonia it may be, "I am bothered by this objectification." And for Louise it may be this horrendous series of abuses. But you are going to get what is real for them.… It can be anything in the mix. And it is anything in the mix. (personal interview, June 26, 1995)

Walker and I marvel at the range of issues of concern, as shown in the following quote:

> The reading on "Femininity" got me thinking for the class period, but also for hours afterward. I realized things that I do myself to stifle progress. Take Saturday night. I was out on a date with a guy. It was girl's pref, our first date. I was driving. When we went to get into the car, he offered to get my door. I REALLY hate this. I didn't want him to get my door, and I started to say so, but stopped before a single word crossed my lips. I didn't want to offend him, or make him think I was some "femi-Nazi" (as my mother so lovingly refers to them). And besides, it was our first date, and I really liked him. I'm so quick to say that I am who I am and if people don't like it, screw 'em. But part of who I am is the fact that I hate guys getting doors for me, like I'm some frail thing without the strength to do it for myself, and I couldn't say that to him for fear that he might not like me, or think I'm not "feminine." (Tonja, writing response log)

In her writing, Tonja questions the convention that women are weaker, that men should help women by doing things like opening car doors for them, that women should not assert opinions that contradict standard gender performances if they want to be acceptable to other members of their culture—in Tonja's case, both her mother and her date. This is an important issue to her even though others, especially (male?) adults, might find it of less critical significance. However, Tonja interrupts the conventional gender narrative by writing out of the silence she admits to constructing around her. Her admonition serves to interrupt the regulatory practices of gender coherence by acknowledging contradictions between Tonja's beliefs about herself, the "femininity" conventions she has been taught, and the gendered performances she gives. Writing enables her to pause on these contradictions and interrupts the discursive subordination of "female" by giving textual substance to multiple other performance options that may be considered.

Tonja's reflective revision is significant, but no less so than Thomas's transformative performative, which might seem more traumatic from an adult perspective. Thomas's story of his transformative realization, which he (or she) admits occurs through writing, in comparison establishes the wide-ranging nature of students' performative scripts:

> Writing in women's studies helped me personally by reinforcing the idea that I was

supposed to be a woman. But somewhere in my genetic sequencing something went wrong.... I still have this shocking realization once in a while that—"You are not a woman and you don't necessarily know how women think and feel".... My female self helps me—it's incredibly helpful because one of the things that I really have is being able to look at a situation from a hundred different points of view. It really helps being able to say, "OK, which is better for this particular situation? Being male, a strong leader? Or being bossy and stuff?" Or just saying, "OK. We'll let them do it their way—how they want to do it and hope it works out." (Thomas, masculinity/femininity history writing assignment)

Writing helps Thomas realize that his outside body does not fit his inside identity. He concludes that he should be in a "woman" rather than in a "man." Writing helps him realize that there are multiple performance options available to him. He is transformed because he can choose. He sees this rhetorically and can make a performance that best suits the audience, the purpose, and the situation.

Examples of transformation provide representative demonstrations of students' awareness of ways writing might serve within a framework of feminist performance theory and a social context of discussions of gender in a high school women's studies class to deconstruct notions of gender stability as well as interrupt conventional assumptions about gender-appropriate behavior. Students see themselves writing to organize their lives and to script out performances they desire to act out. They see themselves writing action plots and creating dialogue that provides them with stage directions, which write and revise the experiences of their present and future lives. The writing acts as performative, felicitous utterances proclaiming scripted courses of action that the students intend to follow.

Literacies of Teaching

Emma Walker generally agrees with students' characterizations of writing in women's studies. However, there is a subtle but critical difference between the ways the students describe the effects of writing and the way Walker describes the effects of writing in women's studies. Although Walker and the students use similar language to identify the effects of writing, the meanings ascribed to their descriptions vary significantly. The students describe the effects of writing in terms of the processes through which they learn about themselves; Walker describes the effects of writing in terms of educational outcomes and pedagogical benefits she identifies as important.

Teaching and Learning

Naming the effects of writing as a significant tool that enables learning is central to both Emma Walker and her students. However, Walker's descriptions are more constructivist than expressivist in nature. For example, Walker discusses the organizing and clarifying function of writing, whereas a representative response from a student characterizes writing to learn about herself.

> I think the writing encourages students to not only read it, but to think about it. And they come back to class with more questions, more comments, and the level of what is going on is definitely more sophisticated than without the writing. (Walker, personal interview, June 26, 1995)

> I think that writing is really useful. It gives people a way of thinking through and understanding what they are dealing with. I know that it has really helped me to sort through my views.... If I had come into this class and I had no idea of any of these things, there have been times that I have been very confused. The writing has always helped me figure things out. (Trisha, personal interview, May 11, 1995)

Walker focuses on the academic benefits of writing named as "thinking," "questioning," and "discussing," which lead to greater understanding of the material and more sophisticated discussions in class. Trisha, representative of most of the students, sees writing from the perspective of how it benefits her individually in sorting out her personal views on issues raised by the content. Walker, on the one hand, is concerned both with the larger context of helping students to develop thinking skills that will enable them to succeed in many arenas in school and beyond. Ultimately, however, she wishes that they will become more critical about the nature of their gendered subjectivity in the wider context of their experiences and help in the project of social transformation. On the other hand, the students are simply pleased with the ways in which writing helps them to sort out their personal views on issues that they see are of relevant concern to them.

Walker and the students discuss the critical learning processes enabled by writing similarly, but their objects of concern are different. The students primarily think of learning in women's studies as a process of self-discovery and the practical application of the women's studies content in their daily lives. Although the content becomes the catalyst for the students' self-discovery, the primary object of their study and concern is themselves, not the content. Walker primarily thinks of learning as the process of coming to know the women's studies content and becoming acquainted with the intellectual and theoretical tools she thinks will enable social transformation. Of much less concern to Walker is the specific ways in which the students may actually apply women's studies to their lives.

The phenomenon of finding coparticipants in one setting adopting crosswise uses for the same language is discussed by Mary Louise Pratt in "Arts of the Contact Zone." As Pratt explains, the idea of the contact zone is intended in part to contrast with ideas of community that underlie much of the thinking about language, communication, and culture that gets done in the academy. In keeping with autonomous, fraternal models of community, analyses of language use commonly assume that principles of cooperation and shared understanding are normally in effect. Descriptions of interactions between people in conversation, classrooms, and medical and bureaucratic settings readily take it for granted that the situation is governed by a single set of rules or norms shared by all participants. It is assumed that all participants are engaged in the same game and that the game is the same for all players. Pratt discusses how meaning is negotiated and how participants manipulate the rules of the game to achieve the ends they most desire. Although Walker and the women's studies' students are not at odds with each other—they see writing as accomplishing learning—but learning that is defined differently for each and is meeting different sets of needs for each.

The distinction between the students' perspectives on the effects of writing in women's studies and Walker's perspective of those effects is subtle and begs elaboration. The students overwhelmingly identify effects of writing in terms that are commonly characterized as arising from an expressivist stance: self-discovery, asserting a voice, emotional expression, therapeutic solace. In this fashion, students call primary attention to traditionally expressivist notions about learning and the individual and personal benefits that arise from the learning and self-discovery that occur through writing. Emma Walker acknowledges that personal benefits occur for students—the students' expressive characterizations of writing "ring true," from her perspective (Walker, personal interview, June 26, 1995).

However, Walker foregrounds the global, cultural, educational, and pedagogical benefits of writing in women's studies. Walker describes effects of writing in language that more typically reflect constructivist purposes.

Educational Outcomes: The Personal Is Political

Walker never separates the personal from the political, and her complication of these issues vexes simple distinctions that composition studies has drawn between expressivist and constructivist perspectives:

> Writing not only plays an important role, it plays an essential role in accomplishing the personal and academic goals of the class. What I learned from the writing is that while Gilligan talks about that wall that they hit at about 12 or 13—that it's a reality and many young women are silenced—most of them. They may never speak in class. They may NEVER speak in class. I mean we had students who never opened their mouths, but their resistance and their thought process comes out in their journals. And we know in education, that that is what we call a passive learner...and I knew there were passive learners, but I would bet money that there are far more passive learners among women than men. (Walker, personal interview, June 26, 1995)

Whereas the students refer to effects of writing as "finding or asserting a voice," an issue of concern to an individual agent, Walker notices the effects of writing on gendering issues of broader cultural concern.

Prior to incorporating writing in women's studies, Walker thought generically about passive and active learner behaviors typically attributed to psychological positions on learning. She assumed quiet students were "passive learners." When Walker examined the ways in which students asserted a voice and argued well-grounded positions in women's studies writing, she glimpsed the very active thinking and learning processes in which students were already engaged. She was unaware that students were actively responding to the ideas presented in women's studies before writing was incorporated.

Through writing, Walker is able to connect Gilligan's developmental theory on female silencing with theoretical positions on active and passive learner behaviors. She realizes that female students' passive behavior is culturally acquired and not a biologically determined cognitive consequence, as she had previously thought. In other words, she used to think that quiet students were either "shy," "withdrawn," or "just not getting it." As Walker tracks for the first time the students' intellectual and emotional engagement with the content that occurs through their writing, she becomes aware that her previous above-mentioned perceptions about quiet students are unfounded. Writing enables Walker to understand her teaching and the students' learning from a performance point of view. She thereby is better able to realize the academic and personal goals that she has established for the class.

Walker's descriptions of writing acknowledge the conceptual issues of focus in the women's studies curriculum, which enable both the students' personal growth and their political development. As students engage the women's studies content critically through writing, the conclusions they draw become self-determining consequences that ultimately guide their personal growth and development as they learn to speak out of silence—a highly politicized act (Walker, personal interview, April 17, 1996). Even so, Walker does not direct students' personal growth into politicized arenas even though she views political action as an important outcome of women's studies.

Walker organizes content in a consciously politicized fashion and teaches so that students can bring highly politically charged content to a personal level. However, the specific ways that students confront conceptual questions and ultimately work through them in their personal lives are not her concern. Walker designs the questions that open the door to political organization of the personal, but she does not articulate answers at which she wishes the students to arrive (Walker, personal interview, April 20, 1996).

Although Walker does not isolate the personal from the political, most of the students have not yet learned to grapple with more than the personal effects of writing in women's studies. Even so, Walker always frames students' personal growth in a global political context, which is organized around contemporary cultural expectations for women.

> There is the academic stuff that is important, ...but we had a course where they could deal with the personal stuff that came up in class as it inevitably does every term....I see women's studies as a place that really does do what Rod (the principal) intended it to do, which was to just validate, particularly young women, validate their confidence and it gives them the tools to look at things from a different perspective and name what bothers them and gives them specific tools—actually, I think it becomes intensely personal....What they walk away with is personal. (Walker, personal interview, June 26, 1995)

Walker is concerned with how women's studies students negotiate their individual gendered subjectivity in/against/among Western cultural assumptions about being female in society.

Providing a catalyst for personal development of her students is not the focus of her teaching, but it becomes a benefit of engaging content at a political level. She encourages students to look through the lens of content and find a focus on their personal issues. How they ultimately resolve their issues is their concern (Walker, personal interview, April 20, 1996).

Walker believes that writing is a tool that helps bring into focus the personal and political issues that have been raised by the curriculum she has designed.

> What you walk away with is personal and a lot of that has to do with breaks in your life, what you already know, what you're willing to examine, your own real-life experience, and I think what you gain—I think it becomes really unique—I think, for instance, with Rachel, who comes from a Jewish family that feels very "other" in our state, it gave her some way of relating to otherness. Some similar understanding of others, which we know. It made her be able to name it and find a space besides the typical place. You see, you have to hope that they will see the different perspective of what being the other really does in relation to class, religion, race, you know. From my perspective, it's the consciousness raising that is the most important reward of women's studies. (Walker, personal interview, June 16, 1996)

Here, Walker refers to Simone de Beauvoir's articulation of the positioning of woman as "other than male," which constructs woman's subordinate position in modern Western thought. For Rachel, the benefit is making sense of her subordinate positioning as a Jew in the predominantly Mormon culture in which she lives, where she is called "Gentile." According to Walker, political revelation of this concept for Rachel resides in its personal relevance to her experience.

Walker characterizes writing in women's studies along several lines simultaneously. She points to the ways that it promotes critical and analytical thinking and satisfies institutional accountability goals that her school and district value, while promoting broader educational and pedagogical goals for transformative social action. In this way, Walker achieves the institutional validation she needs to keep women's studies going, while subverting the ongoing institutionalization of gender discrimination that typically oppresses female students in school. Writing in women's studies, although described in expressivistic terms by the students and occasionally glossed expressively by Walker, accomplishes the goals that constructivists claim for writing. Walker speaks of the effects of writing fundamentally in language reminiscent of James Berlin's version of a social-rhetorical writing curriculum as providing students with opportunities to become "agents of social change rather than victims" (Berlin, "Rhetoric and Ideology" 491).

Literacies of Achievement and Transferal

Walker glosses her characterizations of the effects of writing in women's studies with several academic performance benefits. Students learn to write more fluently, which enables them to write with greater grammatical savvy, which results in stronger academic writing. Walker identifies several students who had been limping along in other classes. She says they become better able to write essays and research papers required in academic work. Better able to meet the required demands of their classes, students shift their attitudes toward writing and schoolwork. Students enthusiastically transfer writing knowledge and thinking ability developed in women's studies to their other academic classes:

> Solo would write—when she first wrote in AP, she could hardly write in complete sentences. And then when she wrote for her journal in women's studies, she just wrote. She could write just beautifully. In women's studies, in terms of writing and the thought processes, it just flowed. Then she's in AP European history and [the writing she did in women's studies] helps her with her formal writing and her writing improved enormously over a year. So, I mean, even though it's not intended to be a writing program to teach her to write, it does that.... And the level of writing improves, as does the level of thinking, the level of questioning in classroom discourse.

> ...I think it helped in a lot of cases. Kate, even though she wrote beautifully in her journals, had great difficulty writing academically. And her English teacher would say, "You know, that writing in women's studies is really helping her." Rachel—I had her simultaneously in AP European when she was taking women's studies—and her writing improved markedly, as well. Just their ability to express themselves gets better as a result of what we were doing. (Walker, personal interview, June 26, 1995)

Walker attributes tremendous academic value to the writing work that is done in women's studies. As women's studies students progress as writers and transfer what they have learned to their work in other classes, they achieve distinctly in other academic work. This helps fulfill the social goals Walker has for students in women's studies because she sees education as the great equalizer—as the door to full participation in the culture. If students succeed in school, they expand their opportunities for choosing multiple other possible life options. Without education, Walker believes that her students greatly limit their opportunities for achieving economic and social parity.

Building Relational Pedagogy: Making Visible the Invisible

Walker identifies several pedagogical benefits of writing in women's studies. Writing improves her teaching and helps her accomplish her educational goals. Writing allows students to perform at their own level. Writing conceptually engages students at varying levels of ability and achievement. Written exchanges are not used to evaluate students on the basis of institutional norms. Therefore, students feel validated by conversations that occur. Walker and I do not grade student writing, so students write without fear. "I think we have a much broader range of students in the class now than we did three years ago, but the writing allows them [to achieve whatever] their level. What they end up doing is just blowing my mind" (Walker, personal interview, July 17, 1995). Walker is impressed with the personal and academic growth and development, which occurs through writing.

Walker realizes that writing helps to construct a sense of safety in the classroom in three important ways. First, writing exchanges help to establish that Walker and I are interested in students' growth, development, and possibility. Written dialogue provides students with a sense that we can be trusted. As a result, students are more likely to let down their defenses and discuss how they are relating to concepts addressed. Knowledge is defined and mediated through all members of the group. Walker finds that this is essential for accomplishing her objectives:

> The only way the interaction will shift is when we build a safe environment. We are testing the waters and since the young women are—you know, as Gilligan is saying—their interest is in protecting the web, and they check that out. They're not going to get to that level of trust with us until they know that it's safe. And what you are really doing [with the writing] is creating a safe space.... It's not that they gotta be more real or more authentic, you want a safe space in which they can

> speak and write their lives. And not be judged. And some of them become willing
> to take that risk. (Walker, personal interview, July 17, 1995)

Students realize we are not going to judge them for how they say what they say—that we will take them seriously and respond to them honestly—that they can trust us and risk telling us all the possible ways they think. When students feel free to speak and write their lives in an atmosphere that is willing to suspend judgment, they can move conceptually in greater leaps and bounds than they do when lecture-recitation and discussion are the primary instructional methods.

Second, writing creates a sense of safety in the classroom overall. Students are much more wary of judgment by their peers than judgment by their teachers (Walker, personal interview, March 17, 1995). When students' own writing is used in readarounds as a central text in class, Walker sees the benefit for accomplishing her educational and pedagogical goals:

> The readarounds were very valuable to them in terms of creating that safe space. Because once they realized that they weren't alone, they weren't the only one that is feeling this. Because they think they are the only one. And then there is that moment of recognition that there are 30 people who have written the same stuff I wrote. It opens up the space. The writing helps them. (Walker, personal interview, June 26, 1995)

The collectivity established through readarounds is essential for accomplishing class goals and becomes a pedagogical benefit for Walker. As students are given the platform to speak through readarounds, they realize they are not alone in their gendered experiences nor in their responses to those experiences. As a result, Walker notices that they rise to new levels of engagement with the conceptual frameworks of the class.

Third, Walker finds that writing creates spaces for students to speak about issues of concern privately with a trusted adult or anonymously with peers through readarounds. It helps her provide professional assistance for students when necessary. Students connect through writing with individuals and organizations that provide counseling, therapy, crisis management, shelter, and so on. Students discover that someone is willing to engage them seriously and professionally. They feel safe and Walker's pedagogical goals are achieved:

> Louise didn't have to say that stuff aloud. She could write down what has

happened to her and then we can validate it. Then we could say, yes this did
happen to you, and we can understand it and yes you're OK and yes you have a
place where you can talk about it at school instead of at the therapist who you see
once a week or once a month or whatever it is. That has to be important to a kid
that age. If there is a safe space in school where it's OK. We believe you. We
absolutely believe you. (Walker, personal interview, June 26, 1995)

Students find a place in school where they can come to rest. Written
exchanges meet their needs momentarily; they temporarily can worry less
about their bodily and psychological safety and engage the conceptual issues
introduced in class.

Students critically assess their locations and view their experiences
through conceptually altered lenses when they write in women's studies.
Often, Walker claims, they set themselves on wholly new trajectories:

When you have it in the form of writing in front of you, you have the lovely
luxury of being able to trace your own thoughts on paper—what happens to all of
us, I think—we tend to when the circle starts changing...what ends up happening is
you can see it change. You don't get caught up in the same circle. You begin to get
out as you get on the top. It makes it really clear to the students because it is in
black and white, concrete—in front of them—in their own words—their
observations, what they say they would like to change, who they say they are and
for some reason, it seems to—and I have had a lot of students say...that writing
helps them form an identity that's different or more evolved. They begin to see
the next stage that they want to be for themselves.... They begin to understand
that they are moving in a direction that makes them a stronger person. That makes
them a more independent person. And that is usually very attractive to them and
they want to be that. Then by the time they get to there, they go, "Oh. Well, I see
that I could do...," you know. And then they begin to see the next step and the
next step. It's almost a Hegelian dialectic, I think, that occurs for them, for want
of a better model I guess. And the writing seems to make that more traceable for
them, more apparent to them (Walker, personal interview, June 26, 1995)

Through writing, students construct a sense of self and script lives they
desire to perform.

Walker understands in greater depth than ever before the things that
students are thinking about and the problems they are trying to solve. Her
revelations help her to frame the content of women's studies in greater
focus with the students' personal concerns. Madeline Grumet has argued in
referring to the teacherly "other" that "the personal is a performance, an
appearance contrived for the public, and that these masks enable us to

perform the play of pedagogy" ("*Scholae Personae*" 37). Walker's teacherly self is enacted in her performance of a personal presence that students' follow because they desire it, not because it represents a pedagogical imperative of self-disclosure or private relationships on Walker's part.

For example, based on her reading of Gilligan, Walker embeds a need to build meaningful relational connections, through language, that meld personal relationships with students within the educational and pedagogical goals for the class, rather than simply as a matter of connecting with students on a personal level:

> And more than anything else, as a teacher I learn so much more from the journals in particular than I do from discussion. Because every kid ends up participating. Every student gets a say...and I learn what they are dealing with, stuff I would never get to know otherwise. (Walker, personal interview, July 17, 1995)

Walker performs her teaching in the vernacular of intimacy—inviting students to reveal ways in which women's studies content veils their *scholae personae* so that she might better understand the students' academic performances.

Writing allows the teacher and researcher to engage the students in personal conversations that push them to think critically about the concepts presented in the curriculum, not just to disclose narratives of personal experience:

> When they write, you know more about the students either way—academically and personally—than you would never know otherwise.... It's a very important tool in women's studies because what it allows you to do, you know, in the dialogue in the journal is to push, you know, to converse with them. We learn so much about them and eventually even with the girls who are the most shy, when called upon, they will say something because you have conversed with them or there is a real thought process going on. And they have internalized things that you've said that even if you don't see anything coming out in discussions—or it doesn't come out in role playing or group work, but it does in the writing. So writing is really important. (Walker, personal interview, June 26, 1995)

Writing allows Walker and me to sustain the students in ongoing, in-depth conversations that not only provide us with a relational view into the students' thinking on certain issues but also allow us to build connections with students that construct the opportunity for such exchanges to occur.

Walker realizes from her study of Carol Gilligan's work with adolescents that these relational connections are key in accomplishing the goals of the course, and they happen most acutely in the writing exchanges. However, she is ultimately in this relational space offering connection, not friendship or a glimpse into her personal worlds. This is not a moment of private exchange, as the following statement demonstrates:

> I think that the one part that Gilligan got right...was that magic moment in her own research where she had the sense that if the young women were really going to share their lives and their thoughts with her that meant you had to have an authentic relationship and what that meant was you had to abandon the quantitative objectivity. You had to get down in the trench with them. You had to be able to say, "This has happened in my life. Let me give you this example from my own experience." And when we started doing that—that's when the level of interaction shifts. (Walker, personal interview, June 26, 1995)

Walker suggests a reformulation of privatized notions about individualistic mentoring connections; a performance of relations that students must interpret as an extension of the private into the public arena of the classroom. They must see adults enacting such a performance before they reciprocate with their own staging of an embodied text that meets the rhetorical demands of writing in women's studies. Walker cannot meet her pedagogical goals or achieve the educational aims of women's studies without this transaction. So writing helps her perform the relational while keeping the personal unseen in another text.

Walker's performance of a pedagogy of the "personal" to further her educational and pedagogical aims is not chicanery. She does not violate time-honored notions about the teacher-student relationship. What Walker offers to students is a range of personae with which the students are variously invited to interact to meet the needs they identify as most salient in their lives. What Walker offers is relational, however, not personal, and the distance between the two is both cavernous and insistent.

Susan Miller narrates an interaction between herself and her students on the last day of a writing class—an event that was read by Miller and by her students both as an answer to a question about the upcoming final exam and as an off-color joke. Miller tells how a female student had asked whether she preferred large or small blue books for writing exams. Before Miller could answer, an ex-Marine now security police male student next to her announced, "You know that size doesn't make any difference—only the point." And another woman's voice retorted, "You wish! That's what they always want to think. You wish it were true, but it's not." Miller responded, "I hesitate to share this now, but I prefer large ones." She analyzes this interaction by writing:

> There is an institutional imperative—exam, a prescription for its writing, and a certain amount of responding anxiety, expressed as the first student's question. But there is also, undeniably, a visibly different text of the "personal," written by the students as interactions with each other in which they overcome anxiety by making a dirty joke, without regard for my comfort. That I was (precisely) their straight man, not their "teacher," is abundantly clear, as is their difference from me and from the institution's interests at this moment. We were, then, "relational," not "personal" with each other in this public space. My privatized interests, like their "individuality," were suspended, finally turned to laughter at a personal matter I am reluctant to share. (Miller *"In Loco Parentis"* 164)

Miller's example suggests that what can be said about pedagogy and the personal from this analysis is "more elastic than those (analyses) that create the so-called empowering mode of individualistic teaching" (Miller *"In Loco Parentis"* 163).

In other words, I am suggesting that Walker's choices to enact the personal in service of the pedagogical do not reinstate what Miller refers to as the personal mentoring relationship "we so insistently but ambivalently portray as offering a space where we can continue to imagine privatized relationships in decidedly public spaces" (*"In Loco Parentis"* 163). Walker's extensions to the personal are moments that parody the personal and thereby utter performative texts, which reconfigure girls' understandings of the discursive gender performances available to them. Walker's performances of the personal give her students multiple options for a teacherly/womanly identity, which they may interpret as the body of the real, but which is performatively a cross-dressing of the body they desire in their teacher (Butler *Bodies that Matter*).

Walker sees her role as enacting the imaginary grounds of privilege from which teachers are authorized to speak and to influence the young. Although the school expects her to cite the law and reproduce subjects that fulfill the femininity constraints inscribed by institutional authority, Walker's project is to subvert that law and create space for a more possible future. Here, as with Emig and her student subjects Lynn and Victoria (*Composing Processes*), both Walker's and her students' texts disavow much, closet much, and present the body of their writing as cross-dressed representations of texts that are outfitted to fit both the rhetorical, the institutional, and the gender occasion. Whereas Lynn and Victoria's high school teachers could not read their texts as alternative possibilities, Emma Walker knows exactly what writing enables her to accomplish. She shows us through the door and introduces us to the "subject" of composition again.

As Janet Emig (*Composing Processes*) surmised so many years earlier, the findings of this study indicate that the literacy effects of writing are circumspectly dependent on the student-teacher, and, in this case, also the student-researcher relationship; the relative meaningfulness of the content of the class to the students; and the social context in which the writing occurs. In other words, literacies of writing are dependent in this case on the pedagogical, developmental, and political contexts, which co-occur through writing, teaching, and women's studies curriculum. Although literacy exchanges among the teacher, the researcher, and the students in this study often occur in hotly contested spaces, students conclude that in order for school-sponsored writing to have an effect, the adult(s) authorized to teach/research in the school(s) need(s) to listen to them, to accept and respect their ideas, and to challenge them to think differently about the issues raised in literate exchange. In women's studies at Aspen Grove, these students find such literacy exchanges between the adult females in the class and each other both meaningful sources of learning and relatively distinct from other exchanges, which commonly occur with adults and with their peers in school.

In this chapter, I have presented the overall findings of my study of literacies of writing and teaching in the women's studies class at Aspen Grove High School. Although most of the students report a positive valuing of women's studies and of writing in women's studies, two atypical cases—those of Alisa and JoAnna, who responded in distinctly different ways—put quite a different spin on the overall findings of the study. The cases of Alisa and JoAnna complicate notions of writing as a tool for unsilencing young women's writing literacies in women's studies class.

Notes

---

1. This is not the commonplace sense of the term; *pathetic* here is derived from the Aristotelian *pathos*—meaning making an emotional appeal.

2. Walker reported in January 2001 that this class of students was the only one she has had in more than ten years of women studies in which such a large percentage of students reported having been raped. This class (thankfully) has remained somewhat anomalous in this respect (personal interview, January 4, 2001).

Lies and Silences

A Presence of Absence in the Women's Studies Classroom

Keeping secrets often means telling lies.

—Joan Beck

Lying is done with words and also with silence.

—Adrienne Rich

Silence can be a plan rigorously executed. Do not confuse it as any kind of absence.

—Adrienne Rich

Women's disquieting relationships with silence have a long and embodied history in feminist studies. One orchestration of silence is constituted by the blotting out, erasure, and devaluing of women's political, textual, literary, and historic past (Olson; Rich, *On Lies*; Spender, *Women of Ideas*). Feminist social and literary historians report that "the entire history of women's ongoing struggle for self-determination has been muffled in silence over and over" (Rich *On Lies* 11) and that women's writing has continuously been exiled to a realm beyond sound and significance (Broe and Ingram).

Another studied symphony of silence is sounded in women's relationship to public forms of speech, such as in the classroom, from the podium, and before the people. In addition to the problem of women's limited access historically to public forums, feminist scholars demonstrate that women taught early that "tones of confidence, challenge, anger, or assertiveness are unstrident and unfeminine" (Rich, "Taking Women Students Seriously" 243) continuously struggle in their efforts to speak publicly even when they have opportunities to speak granted to them (Belenky et al.; Brown and Gilligan; Gilligan *In a Different Voice*; Gilligan, Lyons, and Hanmer; Pipher).

Yet another chord of silence is strummed interpersonally. Feminist psychologists discuss the ways in which women harbor secrets from friends, from relatives, from themselves as if not telling would somehow "render untrue their experiences of struggle" in relationships, with loneliness and isolation, with domestic violence, abuse, and rape; with finances; with children; with their disappointments; with their worries about health; and with their revelations about sexual passions and desires. These unspoken secrets signify "a terror of words, a fear of talk" (Fine).

Still other sounds of silence echo in the linguistic proscriptions of English discourse, which hinder, hurt, and bind women to the lives we might imagine and will ourselves to live. Feminist discourse theorists report that many women remain mostly unconscious of how the structure of the English language, its vocabulary and organization, forces us to repeat the structures that deny us stature and agency in the world and of the role of language in shaping our oppression (Penelope xiv). As a result, women find it difficult to think outside of the categorical imperatives available to us through language, such as "mother," "housewife," "daughter," "whore," "girlfriend," "teacher," "nurse," "secretary" (Kramarae; Lakoff; Penelope; Spender *Man-Made Language*); and even as we learn the courage and the necessity of speaking for ourselves, and acting out resistant roles, our thoughts still conform to the structures that perpetuate female subordination (e.g., Holland and Eisenhart).

The silencing of female sexual subjectivity has been extensively examined by French feminists Luce Irigaray and Helene Cíxous, who have argued that expressions of female voice, body, and sexuality are essentially inaudible when the dominant language and ways of viewing are male. Inside the hegemony of what Lacan has called "The Law of the Father," female desire and pleasure can gain expression only in terrain already charted by males. This discursive silencing has wide-reaching ramifications in the lived experiences of flesh-and-blood girls and women. One example of the effects such instances of silencing have on female bodies has been discussed by Michelle Fine ("Sexuality, Schooling"), who has investigated the regulation of female sexuality in school. Fine reports an absence and prohibition of discussions of female heterosexual and homosexual desire in girls' sex education and other sanctioned curricula. Additionally, she describes the presence of two prevalent discourses of female sexuality as "violence" or "victimization," which teach young women that they must learn to say NO for fear of pregnancy, transmission of disease, or possibility of abuse and rape. Such discursive silencing of female sexuality prevents young women in schools from developing any sense of subjective sexual agency.

This brief overview indicates that stories of women's silences and female silencing are indeed multiple and well documented. In response, many feminist literary and historical scholars have attempted to recuperate the writing of women whose works have been silenced by recovering lost and unpublished manuscripts and by reviving historically vilified texts (Gilbert and Gubar; Lerner; Rossi; Walker "Afterword" "On Refusing to Be Humbled"; Washington). Additionally, a number of feminist rhetorical scholars have attempted to unsilence "womanly rhetorical capacity" (Murphy) by rhetorically reconfiguring the lives and written works of forgotten and marginalized women from the Sophists (Jarratt) and Aspasia (Glenn) to Mary Wollstonecraft (Barlowe), Sojourner Truth (Lipscomb), and Ida B. Wells (Royster) to Louise Rosenblatt (Hallin) and Julia Kristeva (Clark). Although written language has served as a power to relegate women to the silence of the margins, these feminists argue that writing can also be constitutive power—the power to place women's voices among those that would be heard. Other rhetorical scholars have examined the relationship between power and writing, but they have done little to look at women's specific situations and experiences vis-à-vis writing. In this chapter, I take the materialist feminist perspective laid out in Chapter 2 to explain the rhetorical performance in an earsplitting delivery of silence—specifically identified as the absence of written language—silence as a symbolic presence to be analyzed and considered relative to the textual performances of young women writing in women's studies at Aspen Grove High School.

These cases trouble notions of unsilencing that I have forwarded and yet find fault lines in notions of female silencing that depict silence as absence—a negative or null set, a devaluation that subordinates the bodies, minds, and spirits of women. Several African-American feminist scholars including bell hooks (*Talking Back*) and Alice Walker (Walker "On Refusing to Be Humbled") have written about silence as a strategic subversive feminist mechanism—that women's silence can be intentional and useful and that women can choose when and where they wish to speak because while many women have found their own voices, they also know when it is better not to use them (Washington). These feminists argue in essence that silence does not have to constitute negative rhetorical action, but can in fact be a powerfully present and positive move that enables both self-definition and self-determination. In this view, silence becomes purposeful rhetoric, a vital feature of discourse (Belanoff; Gere).

Engagement and Resistance

Most students in women's studies use writing to speak beyond the historical silences identified by feminist scholars in numerous disciplines. Women's studies students write to engage ideas presented in women's studies content, to assert a voice and find access to discursive strategies of argumentation. Writing in women's studies, for the most part, alters lives. As students proffer experiential edits, reflective revisions and transformative performatives, they find the confidence and conviction to build different lives from the material of their writing.

Writing, however, is also used as a tool for resistance in the course. Some students use writing to resist women's studies. Resistance generally occurs in one of two ways: either a student refuses to write at all or a student writes to work through their resistance to ideas presented. Walker views instances of resistance in an educative light:

> They weren't prepared a lot of times…. But there wasn't consistent resistance. It was piecemeal, and I perceive a certain amount of that is healthy because it's not like this operates down and across the board. I think your experiences when you are seventeen—there is that part of it that doesn't work at all and part of it works well. And I think that is dependent on their life experiences. (Walker, personal interview, June 26, 1995)

Walker assesses resistance as partial and temporary. Writing gives students a place to stew or to hide. She thinks students will reengage when they are ready, and they might not be ready until they are 30:

> I think one of the hardest things about teaching women's studies… is—to seventeen-year-olds—is that their life experiences are incredibly limited for most of them. What breaks down for them [are]…the roles portrayed for them in church or

with their parents that haven't worked. They have seen that break down. [And so you get someone]...who puts on a front to the work in which she appears to be the perfect, happy girl but she talks to me and her friends about being terribly depressed and suicidal. That comes out in her writing, too. And she portrays a great deal of distancing and resistance and that sort of thing, but it isn't that she doesn't notice the incongruity. She wants to keep it out there. And the writing lets her. And when she's ready—she kind of hangs around and asks enough questions until I finally trip across what it is she really wants to talk about.... But she doesn't dare move too far afield. She is stretching as far as she is really capable of going, so I am feeling all right. (Walker, personal interview, June 26, 1995)

When students resist, they may demonstrate great facility with writing but little engagement with the concepts presented in women's studies. They use writing to resist what they are not ready to accept about themselves or their culture. They also may resist writing because they secret a number of unsettled personal issues that contradict the seamless standpoint they want desperately to project. Writing about concepts presented in women's studies would require confronting their dichotomous positions or revealing their contradictory persona(s) for public scrutiny. As a result, they do not write with any level of engagement or they do not write at all. Walker does not get anxious because she senses what is going on. She assumes that each student will "get it" when she is ready to "get it," and meanwhile if she does not write with any degree of serious reflection, it is OK.

Alisa and JoAnna: Two Case Studies of Persistent Resistance

The Case of Alisa

Alisa is a sophomore at Aspen Grove High School. She is young in comparison with most of the other women's studies students. By media standards, she is a lovely and attractive young woman—white, tall, long-legged, blond, green-eyed, thin, and voluptuous. Alisa is also Mormon. Her mother, a British citizen, moved to the United States before Alisa was born. Her mother had converted to Mormonism after receiving home visits from Mormon missionaries in her native London. She moved to the United States at their urging so that she might meet a Mormon husband and be married "for eternity" in a Latter-day Saints temple.

Alisa's parents have been married and divorced to each other on two different occasions, and they each have married and divorced another person, as well. She moves between both parents and prefers her dad to her mom. Alisa is very concerned about making relationships "work" with men in her life. She is upset with her mother for "not working harder" at her marriages. Alisa talks about how she cuts herself when boyfriends get upset with her. She mutilates the skin on the underside of her forearms with a Swiss Army® knife as a way of dealing with their anger and disapproval. "When I cut through the flesh on my arms, I can stay calm and happy. I know that I can keep the peace with them [boyfriends], " she writes. Alisa says she will be the one to show her parents that marriage can work because she will work hard enough at it.

At the time Alisa was enrolled in women's studies, her mother was in an abusive relationship. Alisa spoke privately with Walker about this; Walker gave her information about the YWCA Battered Women's Shelter. At Alisa's urging, her mother attended women's studies class with her one day. Alisa said she wanted to get her mom out of the relationship with the abusive boyfriend, but her mom was "too chicken" to leave.

The most common response Alisa makes to readings in women's studies is "I didn't like this article. I found no point in reading it." In my initial responses to Alisa, I asked her to explain why she did not like the readings. Responding to my request for elaboration, she explains that the articles go against her sensibilities of what will be true in her experience. Her writing frequently valorizes the normative trope of femininity. She wants to go to college and to have a fun and exciting career until she gets married. Then Alisa proposes to have a happy marriage, and lots of children with whom she can stay home and mother, while her happy husband supports the perfect family. She believes in "prince charming" and eagerly awaits the day that he will sweep her off her feet. Alisa's desires stand in stark contrast to her actual life experiences.

For example, in one assignment Walker tells students she would like them to write a paper that responds to Carol Gilligan's stage theory of girls' development, which they have read the night before:

> This is what Gilligan's book says is the process, it's the crisis point for girls' identity. Go back through your life, think about the "nice girl" thing, the "disassociate" thing, the "hitting the wall" thing. How are you in your own life? How are you going to solve the dilemma of wanting genuine relationships when you voice over your feelings in relationships? How do you expect to have a

genuine relationship when you have all learned how to do that? Go back through this process and explain how it happened to you. And then write, this is what I think about how I can solve it. (Walker, field observation notes)

Alisa's response is given below, in Figure 5.1.

Figure 5.1: Alisa's Response to the Dilemma Posed by Gilligan's Analysis

---

The Dilema [*sic*] of wanting a genuine relationship if you voice over your feelings!

In a relationship, you need to find out as much as you can about that person, especially if you plan to marry that special someone and have a genuine relationship. Most couples we find think that they know almost everything about their mate or companion, but what else we find is that they most likely have at sometimes voiced over their feelings. This is usually leads to contension [*sic*] and at some points, divorce. Let me help you to understand why things like this would occur. It all starts in the beginning where the boy likes the girl and the girl likes the boy. And because of this, neither one of them wants to lose each other; and if something bothers them, or if they have a question about each other, most likely they will let it drop. After they go out with each other for a while and start to feel pretty comfortable around each other they will start to ask the questions that they've always wanted to know, and start to tell each other what bothers them. Pretty soon they find things out that maybe they don't like and have a hard time dealing with. So then problems occur and there's nothing you can do about it; except talk it out and hope for the best.

My solution however would [be] to be patient and understanding, and to talk with one another and don't let things drop, and ask questions and listen to each other, talk problems out and most important still be nice and honest and be open and let your real feelings show early in the relationship and you shall have a most great and loving and genuine relationship!

Walker wants evidence from the writing that students are making connections between Gilligan's explanations of female development and their own personal experiences. She is also trying to set up a situation in which students might begin to deconstruct gender roles and look discursively at multiple other possibilities as a result of learning from Gilligan that the task of female socialization is to voice over your feelings (Walker, personal interview, October 5, 1995).

On the surface, it appears that Alisa has fulfilled the requirements of Emma's assignment and in Emig's view ("Writing as a Mode of Learning"), Alisa has learned; she has made meaning from the materials of her experience. First, she hands in a paper, which is all that is required to get full credit. Second, she addresses the topic in an authoritative manner—projecting a voice of expertise and confidence gained from experiential knowledge. This is accomplished in two ways. First, she examines the oppositions set up by the "dilemma" in a generally thoughtful way, "Most couples we find think that they know" all they need to know about their potential mate, but what happens when "what else we find is that they most likely have at sometimes voiced over their feelings." Second, Alisa assumes an authoritatively pedantic mode by using the second person nominative pronoun "you" as subject and an imperatively functioning sentence purpose, "Let me help you to understand why things like this would occur." With that transition, she attempts to teach her reader how to solve the dilemma that "they" and "you" might have in establishing genuine relationships. Both these discursive moves—assuming the voice of authority and examining complicating caveats—are generally valued conventions of scholastic writing. In a standard secondary classroom, Alisa has written a text that most of her teachers would value highly.

However, Walker explains to students that work in women's studies is different from other schoolwork. She says, "Trust me. The hard work you will have to do in women's studies is internal" (field observation notes). With the "Dilemma of Genuine Relationships" assignment, Walker hopes that students begin to understand the "real" (material) dilemma that they face as feminine socialized subjects. She hopes that examination of the dilemma will help them to deconstruct their gendering, to think about possible escapes and about multiple other possible gendering options. Alisa's paper indicates no evidence of accomplishing any of these "internal" objectives.

Alisa's text performs the discursive conventions generally valued in scholastic writing in secondary schools. However, Alisa's text does quite a bit more than that. Her text also performs expected gender formations described by Gilligan, which Walker hopes students will deconstruct. Alisa writes that her solution "would be to be patient and understanding, to ask questions and listen to each other, talk problems out and most important still be nice and honest...." Although Walker did not specify it in her articulation of the assignment, Alisa defines relationship strictly from a romanticized heterosexual perspective. Alisa's text is a performance of the "tyranny of the nice girl." Her solution scripts the ways "nice girls" should behave in a relationship, and ways that performing the "nice girl" script will be rewarded—one has a "most great and loving and genuine relationship!" (Alisa, the Dilemma of Genuine Relationships freewrite). Alisa unproblematically reifies Gilligan's description of the voicing over or silencing that females do in relationships, how girls take themselves out of relationships for the sake of the relationship. This is not what Walker was hoping for; Alisa's silencing of the issues represents a complete disavowal of the ways in which traditional gender formations are problematic for females.

Alisa has been told that her job in women's studies is to make internal connections. Her text consistently performs resistance to this task. There is no evidence of connection to the experiences she has lived in the "Dilemma" text or in any others that she writes. The two places in which she gives her readers a glimpse of the writer behind the text are first, with her use of the authorial voice "Let me help you understand...", and second, "My solution, however, would be..." Although invoking an appeal to the writer's instantiated authority, she asserts a voice of expertise from personal knowledge, but she gives no evidence that would enable the reader to see hers as a credible position simply on the basis of her authority. It is as if what is not present is saying, "I have no intention of letting you in on how I know this, just take my word for it." In this sense, Alisa's text similarly scripts a defensive performance. It is as though what she has and has not written is saying, "This is how this dilemma can be solved for 'you' and 'they.' It has worked for me, I am one who knows, but I am not willing to tell you how I know."

I do not mean to suggest that Alisa is writing a fiction that covers over an undeniable truth that exists intact underneath. Judith Butler suggests that imaginary practices of identification with authoritative versions of femininity and romance seek recourse to the constituting authority that precedes its imaginary structure (*Bodies that Matter* 109). The priority and the authority of the "right" versions of femininity and romance are constituted through this recursive turn. Alisa invokes the law of femininity to effectively bring into being the very prior authority to which it defers. Citation of the femininity law is not representative of a true authority that rests underneath on the body of Alisa's text or experience. Rather, her instantiation of that subordinated position is a fiction produced in the course of its instancings. In this sense, then, the instance produces the fiction of the priority of these sexed positions. It does exactly what Alisa wants it to do; it produces the effect of the citation itself and "it invokes the heterosexual norm through the exclusion of contestatory possibilities" (Butler *Bodies that Matter* 109). Alisa subverts the intended process of women's studies by citing and sanctifying feminine norms she craves.

Viewed within a larger context of Alisa's experience is what Alisa does not write in her text about the dilemma of genuine relationships. Certainly, given the context of her experience, Alisa has the knowledge to speak from a position of contrapuntal authority on the topic of dilemma that might split open the incessant coherence of a fiction of "prince charming" and "happily ever after." Alisa effectually silences her knowledge by refusing to write about or examine her experiences with and/or in relationship. Alisa instead gives a pathetic drag performance—cross-dressing in the gestures and acts of a "most wonderful and genuine relationship." She hyperbolically mimes a performance that defers to the authority of traditional gender roles. Her text impersonates the "and they both lived happily ever after" script and invokes a system of pervasive disavowal, in which she becomes the "girl in relationship" that she has "never" loved and "never" grieved (Butler *Bodies that Matter* 236–238).

Alisa refuses to know what she knows. She experiences a provisional failure of memory. She enacts a performance of a fictional body and a life, which she wishes for herself but which does not exist. She has witnessed other gender options in the incoherent fragmentation of her experience. Alisa might otherwise assist a radical resignification of the symbolic domain using authoritatively as evidence her experiences with polite silence, cutting her self to stay calm and happy when boyfriends indicate their displeasure, witnessing her mother's abuse and inability to get out of relationship, and through the painful ritual of her parents' serial divorces. Alisa might deviate "the citational chain toward a more possible future and...expand the very meaning of what counts as a valued and valuable body in this world" (Butler *Bodies that Matter* 22). However, Alisa resists the project set before her in women's studies and retreats to the fictional safety of masculinist domination and compulsory heterosexual love and romance.

Although making a typical and valued scholastic move, Alisa's resistant performances are disappointing given Walker's postmodern agenda. Nonetheless, if Alisa's had been the only resistant text we received in response to the Gilligan dilemma assignment, we might easily have forgotten about it. However, a number of other students perform similar texts of resistance in the first round of written responses. Walker and I are discouraged reading students' papers. We want students to consider a feminist rewriting of the trope of femininity, not hold it up as desirable and possible truth. Because we think that women are particularly disadvantaged by self-silencing in relationships, we persist in trying to rupture students' picture-perfect versions of solution to the dilemma of genuine relationships.

In an attempt to trouble the seeming coherence of students' projections, I bring additional information into the conversation. Since they had interpreted "genuine relationships" to mean heterosexual romantic relationships, I read an "Op Ed" syndicated column on a date rape case heard by the California Supreme Court. "For Sexes, Early Communication Helps" considers a "clear" case of miscommunication, which occurred between a college man and woman. The details regarding the rape case are curious enough to warrant inconclusive opinions:

> It seems the female student, during a romantic evening, invited the male student to her room and while he was there, the two became increasingly amorous…. Everything went fine for a time. The two cuddled nude under the covers. However, when the cuddling led to sexual intercourse, the woman was upset and that led to her charges of rape. (Frymer)

After reading, I asked students to contemplate how "telling the truth," "maintaining a happy countenance," and "compromising" might get complicated when interlocutors make very different foundational assumptions about acceptable standards of behavior or interpret meaning of behaviors in very different ways. I asked students to think about their nearly unilateral assertions that being "open and honest, patient and nice" will solve the dilemma of genuine (heterosexual, romantic) relationships given the information of this case.

I asked them to freewrite for 10 minutes and respond again to solving the dilemma of genuine relationships in light of this additional information.

A sampling of responses follows:

> I think that the miscommunication between the man and woman began when they got nude to cuddle. You don't need to get undressed to cuddle with someone. Right there I think shows that the woman is giving some sort of permission to him saying that it's OK to have sex. I think that they both should have, up-front, been open and honest about what they expected or wanted from the other person. To me, that's honest communication. I think that what one person is thinking may not be the same thing someone else is thinking. That's where openness comes in. (LeTisha)

> My response to this problem is couples should have more communication in their relationships. But since communication is sometimes not always there between a man and a woman, I think that women and men should use body language to show that you're interested or not at all. Actually, it comes down to just saying "no" on either side, whether you're male or female. (Sheila)

> My response to that problem is women need to be more considerate towards men's feelings and men need to be less pushy. Women need to not ask so many questions, but men need to be willing to answer the questions asked. I'm not one to take sides, so if I had to come up with a solution, I would have to say that knowing what one another is like, what they're thinking, and how they feel is the key to a lasting relationship. Overall, knowing each other physically, mentally, and emotionally through open communication is a vital element. (Sharon)

> Total communication is a good thought, but you cannot always go with that thought since there really is no such thing as total communication. Although you always tell your "spouse" your feelings and the truth, there is always going to be a gap between both of you. To have a good strong relationship both people need to have a knowing of the other person, the world around them, and communication. No one succeeds when they first try. (Candy)

The students' texts perform many of the moves that Alisa's initial response did. The writers assume the voice of authority but keep the content at a distance. They do not discuss any alternative perspectives, which might perform engagement at a personal, experiential level.

Nonetheless, when students were writing second responses, Walker and I unwittingly interrupted their level of engagement in an unexpected way. This interruption gave us new insight into the subversion and resistances these students' texts were performing. During the time students were writing, Walker and I were whispering quietly at the front of the room. I had brought a poem that I had written about my own experiences in a heterosexual romantic relationship with solving "the dilemma of genuine

relationships when you have been trained to voice over your feelings."
Walker read it silently to herself as students wrote. We both started to laugh
when she finished reading. We had a brief, whispered conversation about
issues raised by the poem while students were writing. At the time, I
noticed that students seemed more interested in our conversation than in
writing. Some responded with whispers to each other; others looked and
raised their eyebrows. When writing time was up, Thomas said, "You need
to share your funny stories" (field observation notes).

Walker caught me off guard by telling me that I had to read my poem
to the class. I was not prepared for this. The poem captures some fairly
intimate details of a personal relationship and deconstructs the dilemma of
women's silencing. Although completely appropriate to the task we were
asking of students, I was reluctant to read this poem—to share details of my
experiences outside the women's studies classroom. However, Walker
insisted. She was not going to let me off the hook. I read the poem.

August, Snake River:
The One That Gets Away

Waiting for trout risings,
we watch
the Snake slither
beneath the raft. Hooking
has been slow today. And yesterday.
And last week. Hissing tempers
mount in these dying
days of summer.

Presenting perfectly
toward the willowed bank,
the biggest hog in the river
swallows your hopper tease.
You finesse this fish play,
baiting your pleasure,
fish fear.

Handing over the arced rod,
you challenge me
to land this catch. Trout panic

jerks the taut line. My useless fingers
contract. The fish runs,
reel singing.
I grab it. Silence its voice.
My first fish
bolts into open river.

I hold an erect fly rod
in my limp hand.
Presenting perfectly,
your fork-tongued strike
hits its mark,
"Don't you know that whine
is the sweetest song a fisher hears? Why
do you think guys buy those reels?
So everyone will look when the fish runs.

"Never touch a singing reel.
When a fish wants to run,
Let it run. You have to be responsive to its needs,
give it what it wants. Tease it a little,
play with its desires.
If it wants to go,
let it go.

"Repeat that
100 times: 'If a fish wants to go,
let it go.' Tire it out,
then reel it in. Be sure
to throw it back.
Breathing."

(Catch and release:
I know, I know, I know.
I get it.)

"100 times: If a fish wants to go,
let it go. Shit,
I'm not mad that you lost the fish…
That was our last hopper."

I dip water from the Snake to
cool my cheeks. "If a
fish wants to go,
let it go. If a fish wants to go,
let it go. If a fish wants…
Let it…."

Later I cast
Where only pelicans and
Herons see.

Under stars, you apologize
for rough play, and I
give in to passion. After,
you sleep. I dream about
fish. You have to be responsive to their needs,
give in to what they want. Tease them a little.
Play with their desires.
If they want to go,
let them go. Let them go.
Let them go. Let them.

I wonder,
"Do trout
Trade sex as love to fill the void?"

If a fish
Wants…   Trout panic.

Let it go.
Catch and release.   Be sure

to throw it back breathing.

I know, I know, I know.

I let it get away.

The Snake slips
Silently into night.

A very lively discussion followed. Close to the end of class, I asked students to freewrite one more time. A sample of their responses follows:

> I don't think you can experience a good relationship unless you know what a bad one is. If all you think you've seen is a good relationship, what are you going to do if the relationship you're in doesn't go as you figured it would? My sister is with a guy that could do anything wrong and yet still talk my sister into getting back with him. The hardest thing in my life is going to be able to trust some guy. I feel sometimes like getting into a relationship to let my mom and sister see the changes that I would go through. I've seen a lot of bad to believe in good too easily. (Maria)

> I think that you are right. You are making me think a lot about my past relationships and I'm realizing that I basically did whatever they wanted. I went into the relationships "blindfolded" because I always thought he was the one, but in all actuality, he was nothing but a jerk and I got hurt in the end. I'm now seeing someone who doesn't seem like the rest because we are getting to know each other and dating first before we get into an actual relationship. He wants to get to know me better and we are friends. I think that's how you should start, is being friends. I'm going to look more carefully into relationships now that I have more insight on certain situations. (Sheila)

> I just got out of a relationship where the boy always tried to change me. First, it started with shaving my legs. I said okay. And every once in a while, I would give in, then it just led on to other things. And the more I gave in, the more I lost myself. Before this relationship, I knew pretty much who I was. Now, I'm trying to find that person. It's hard, but I'm making progress. I used to feel empty, stupid, etc. Now, I still feel empty, but everyday I try to find what I want and not care what everyone thinks. I don't want really to get into another relationship, because I'm scared of losing myself totally. Sometimes, it is just so damn confusing. (Tabouli)

After reading these texts, we discussed the differences Walker and I noticed between the students' first responses and their final responses to the "dilemma." I asked students to talk to me about what appears as a more "honest," integrated performance, about moments of personal confession. The students unguardedly explained that "it's the writing in school thing. Teachers ask you to write things all the time and you don't know what they are going to be used for. I think it makes a big difference knowing what we can expect from you. When you tell us the truth, we can tell the truth" (Jeanne, field observation notes). "I am constantly making things up for teachers; why would I tell them the truth? I make stuff up for teachers all the time. I am not going to tell them what's really on my mind. It's different when I can trust them, know that they are going to be honest with me" (Tabouli, field observation notes).

It appeared to Walker, the students, and me that these responses moved to a whole different level of performance. Students generally shifted from second- and third-person imperative mode into first-person narration and reflexive analysis. We read their responses as more "honest," more reflexive, puzzling, questioning, temporary, and unfinished in comparison with the pert, finished proclamations in the first papers. It is seductive, given our goals, to interpret this as a moment of "Aha! We finally have accomplished our purposes. Students are puzzling with these issues and seeing the incoherence of gender socialization. They are connecting with the chaos and disruption of their experience. They are showing us what they know." However, that view serves further to instantiate an essentialism that we are trying to deconstruct.

There seems to be evidence in the texts that students are engaging at a personal experiential level and beginning to deconstruct traditional gender roles and to look for multiple other options. However, to conclude that what they wrote in their first responses was less "true" and "weaker" evidence of learning than what they wrote in their final responses would be misleading. Butler is clear that there is no "real" or "true" gender identification—there is only that which is performed and that which is not performed:

> Sartre would…have called this act "a style of being," Foucault, "a stylistics of existence."…Beauvoir…"styles of the flesh." These styles all never fully self-styled, for styles have a history, and those histories condition and limit the possibilities. Consider gender…as *a corporeal style*, an "act,"…which is both intentional and performative, where *"performative"* suggests a dramatic and contingent construction of meaning. (Butler *Gender Trouble* 139)

What we experienced is just another performance of yet another discursive script, the script we desire to read. These texts might be read as a stylistic performance of "following the scholastic conventions set by the teacher." I wrote and read a text that performed a first-person narration and reflexive analysis. So did they. Although students' texts seem to reveal a more complicated view of "the body of the performer and the gender that is being performed," it only seems more "true" because as readers, we see less distinction between the "body" and the "performance" we desire.

The interpretations that Walker and I give these textual performances are an attempt to cohere our feminist agenda. We read these texts as "passing for the real" because that is how we want to read them. Certainly, we must assume that there is student refusal and resistance of our deconstructive agenda cross-dressing as coherence and learning, which is evidenced in Alisa's final response:

> My parents have been divorced 4 times and I am only 16. I believe I know myself and I think you should walk into a relationship expecting the very best but just prepare yourself mentally for any possibilities of a problem or dissappointment [*sic*]—but don't search for the problems—just let things happen and work for the best! My parents have not, however, and I always tell them that one day I'm going to show them how it's done. I also believe that I would do anything for my husband, if he did what I asked him to only do. And if he didn't I wouldn't do what he wanted me to because if I did even though he didn't do things for me, then that would just set me up for heartache & anger and things would be worse—*we have to compromise and cooperate.* (Alisa, Gilligan third freewrite)

Although Alisa brings her experiences into textual discussion, a move we read as acknowledgment that other versions exist beyond the dominant story of abiding heterosexual love and romance, she still insists that the performance of the "nice girl" will get her that "happily ever after" relationship she desires. She mimes the teacherly text and subverts our agenda by tricking us into seeing her narrative reflection as "passing for the real." Alisa resists our press to subvert the citational authority of the law. She persists in refusal and resistance even with several admittedly coercive attempts on our part to push her to see other readings for her life experiences.

Writing about the gender roles dramatized and made visible through deconstructive writing assignments seems to help students to deconstruct their own gender roles and see the availability of possible escapes from female subordination in patriarchy; yet Alisa certainly provides evidence to the contrary. Writing about gender issues seems at times to serve the deconstructive purposes of a postmodern feminist agenda such as Walker's. However, the pattern of Alisa's responses indicates that she is one student who needs to hold to normative narratives. The theory and style she invokes in order to cope with her day-to-day experiences are the stereotypic trope of femininity, not our feminist revision.

My responses to Alisa indicate confusion about the contradictions between what she believes to be possible and the experiences she has lived. I desperately want her to accept my feminist-styled version of reality rather than punctuate hers. I want her to think critically about the self-sacrifice she enacts when cutting her skin as a method to stay politely silent in relationships. However, Alisa is not ready to see what I see. As a result of questions I ask Alisa, she tells me that I made her feel that she was a "bad writer." She reports in her final reading response log, "In women's studies I learned that I couldn't write. My other teachers say I am a good writer, but in here you always ask questions that make it seem like I can't write. I really want to write well." Pushing students to view experiences and ideas they are reluctant to accept and causing doubt about a student's ability to write certainly is not my intent; however, at least in this case, and perhaps in others of which I am unaware, it is nonetheless the undesired effect.

At the end of the semester, Walker is less concerned about these failures than am I. She reminds me that Mark Twain said, "There is nothing so useless as an untested virtue." In time, these students will remember what they were unable to learn during the course of women's studies. "When it is relevant to their experience, they will be reminded of these lessons" (Walker, personal interview, June 26, 1995) and see their way through to how they might need to perform their gender differently. When students come to recognize the "loss of the sense of 'the normal,' when 'the normal,' 'the original' is revealed to be a copy, and an inevitably failed one, an ideal that no one can embody" (Butler *Gender Trouble* 138–139), then "the possibilities of gender transformation" will be found "precisely in the arbitrary relation between such acts, in the possibility of a failure to repeat, a de-formity, or a parodic repetition that exposes the phantasmatic effect of abiding identity as a politically tenuous construction" (Butler *Gender Trouble* 141). The students will both "construct and receive a context" in which the "performance of subversive confusions" can be fostered (Butler *Gender Trouble* 139).

The Case of JoAnna

JoAnna is a senior. She enrolled in women's studies for two consecutive semesters during her senior year. She was the only student who self-identified as a "feminist" on the first day of both the autumn and the spring class. In each class, JoAnna was distinctly ahead of other students in understanding feminist issues and in articulating her own feminist critical consciousness. JoAnna talked frequently in class and generally made comments that were quite insightful. Nonetheless, JoAnna only completed one out-of-class writing assignment and five in-class writing assignments during the entire year. She wrote significantly less than any of the other students.

JoAnna grew up in New England. She moved to the Intermountain West in the eighth grade when her parents divorced. JoAnna, like Alisa, is Mormon. She lived with her mother and older brother until her brother went on a Mormon mission during the summer before her senior year. During her senior year, JoAnna lived with her mom. She and her mother "are very close." JoAnna, somewhat atypical from other students in women's studies, speaks only with the highest regard for her mother.

JoAnna is a strikingly attractive young woman. She is about 5'5" tall. She is white and has a deep olive complexion, brown hair, brown eyes, and a sculpted Romanesque nose. Other students, both male and female, look at her and say, "JoAnna has a body to die for" (field observation notes). JoAnna is strong and athletic. She turns heads when she walks down the hallways at school. Her closest friends are members of the cheerleading squad, but JoAnna is not interested in "that cheerleading bullshit" (personal interview, May 24, 1995). JoAnna is extremely intelligent and mature beyond her years.

JoAnna is also a victim of violence. A man unknown to her attempted to rape her at knifepoint one afternoon during her sophomore year as she was walking to a friend's house after school. She recounts:

> I was walking over to one of my friend's houses after school. This guy pulled over in his car to ask for directions, and then he jumped out and started to rape and attack me. He was doing his stuff on me. He had a knife. I got all cut up. Somehow I got away. I don't really remember how I did it. I didn't go home though. At least, I knew enough not to go home. (JoAnna, field observation notes)

JoAnna was able to get away from her attacker but received several threatening telephone calls following the failed rape. She knew her attacker was still watching for another chance to get her. The police were unable to do anything about it and questioned the veracity of JoAnna's report:

> They said that I had to be hurt more badly than I was to go after him. I was cut up

and bleeding, but I didn't need any stitches, so it wasn't bad enough for the police to do anything about it. They took my statement, but that was all. (JoAnna, field observation notes)

JoAnna began taking martial arts lessons following the attempted rape. By her senior year, she held a black belt in karate. She says that the experience, although frightening, changed her life for the better. She thinks she is stronger and more confident and she "won't take shit from anyone" (field observation notes).

During both semesters of women's studies, JoAnna was far ahead of other students in making connections between the content and her experience. She showed intellectual aggressiveness and did not hesitate to argue with peers or with Walker or I when we failed to see things from the "feminist" perspective upon which JoAnna insisted. The fact that she wrote little more than a few paragraphs during two full semesters of women's studies troubled me. I asked her about it, and she told me that she was sorry: "Don't take it personally. I just can't get into anything that seems related to traditional school work" (JoAnna, personal interview, May 25, 1995).

At fall parent-teacher conference, JoAnna's mother spoke with Walker about her concerns for JoAnna's well-being. A Mormon bishop had come to their house to tell JoAnna's mother that JoAnna was sexually involved with her karate teacher, a 28-year-old married Mormon man, a father of four. JoAnna was being blamed for breaking up a happy Mormon family. JoAnna adamantly denied the affair to her mother. JoAnna's mother was hoping Walker might be able to help. JoAnna never discussed this alleged affair with Walker or me, although we both opened doors for a discussion to occur on several different occasions.

We had ample opportunity because one of JoAnna's close friends, Nikki, who was also in women's studies, had told Walker and me that she was romantically involved with a married man. Nikki reported that he had forced her to have sex with him. Nikki was quite upset, but she did not want to report it as rape "because she loved him."[1] JoAnna provided a great deal of support to Nikki during this time and both of them talked with us on several occasions about Nikki's situation. Walker and I thought that JoAnna might also take this occasion to talk with us if indeed she, too, was involved with a married man, but JoAnna never said a word about it. Given JoAnna's conversations with Nikki and us, her adamancy about feminist issues, her absolutely convincing statements about plans "to go to college, become an FBI agent, not get married until she was in her late twenties, and general suspicion about men's intentions where women are concerned" (JoAnna, field observation notes), Walker and I determined that the idea of JoAnna having an affair with an older, married man was "ridiculous." We slipped into assuming that the Mormon bishop was mistaken and "out of line."

Walker and I spent a great deal of time with JoAnna both during and after school hours trying to help her catch up with incomplete schoolwork, the result of increasing absenteeism. Throughout the year, however, JoAnna had a terrible time with truancy. Consequently, she did not pass most of her classes her senior year, and she failed to graduate with her class. When it became evident that she did not have enough credits to graduate, JoAnna was devastated. I tutored JoAnna so she could take and pass the Graduation Equivalency Diploma [GED]. I called up a number of professional favors to get permission for her to test for the equivalency diploma prior to her 18th birthday; if she passed, school district officials promised that they would give her the Aspen Grove diploma, as well. I had no doubt that JoAnna could pass the test with ease. However, she never showed up for the testing appointments we made. JoAnna never took the GED, as far as I know. I have not had contact with her since.

A year and a half hence, Walker received a call from the karate teacher. He had divorced his wife and planned to propose marriage to JoAnna "over the loudspeaker at Nordstrom in the mall, so as to really surprise her." He had a diamond engagement ring and wanted Walker to be there because "JoAnna thinks so highly of you. I know she won't say 'No' if you are there." Walker politely declined.

A few days later, JoAnna dropped by to see Walker at school. She showed off her ring and told Walker that she had been sexually involved with this man since shortly after she began martial arts classes with him when she was 15. Walker reported that JoAnna told her, "I know you told us that your one rule is not to get married before we finish college, but I love him and look forward to being a stepmother to his five children, aged two months to eight years." (Walker, personal interview, October 15, 1996). JoAnna also told Walker that he was going to help her get the GED and that she had a good job working for him in his insurance business. Walker said that she tried to be upbeat and supportive of JoAnna's choices and that she only lost her temper for a brief moment during their conversation: "You've been involved with him since you were fifteen and he has a two-month-old child??? JoAnna, do the math!" (Walker, personal interview, October 15, 1996). Walker did not attend the wedding, and she has not heard anything from JoAnna since. Walker told me that "apparently, JoAnna needs this relationship. I am sure I will see her again when she learns what it's like to take care of someone else's kids" (Walker, personal interview, October 15, 1996).

Even though Walker was somewhat skeptical and disappointed by this turn of events in JoAnna's life, she does not pass judgment nor attempt to press her expectations onto JoAnna. Walker's understanding of the seductive distractions that shift and move ways of performative knowing among her students helps her to take such disruptions to her feminist appeals in stride. If Walker were to enforce the "demands, taboos, sanctions, injunctions, prohibitions, impossible idealizations, and threats" (Butler *Bodies that Matter* 106) that already keep in place the normative fiction of femininity converse with feminism, she would cite the organizational law that keeps the spiritless female in place. In keeping with her assumption that each student will "get it" when she is ready to "get it," Walker backs off from these distractions and lets them go. She knows that JoAnna will need someone to whom she can come back when the time comes. Walker will be available.

JoAnna's case is most difficult for us to imagine. Perhaps our incessant desire to reproduce the feminist subject that JoAnna herself constructed with her performative utterances in class became the literacy event that provoked JoAnna's resistance to the writing. Were she to write, she would invariably have had to reveal an embodiment of her feminist confusions or write lines of lies upon the text of her own body. Her desire for Walker's approval, and perhaps for mine as well, turned her to an escape from words that might otherwise expose her other seemingly contrapuntal desire to bask in the gaze of a powerful male whom she professes both "to fear, to love, and to need" (JoAnna, personal interview, May 24, 1995).

I think the deconstructive lesson I ultimately learn from JoAnna as a subject is how she defies essentializing positionality and pushes me to reconsider my politics in a different light. I discover that I am guilty of losing at my own game. My quarrel with feminist compositionists all along has been that they dismiss as essentializing empirical work that examines the female writer. As I press JoAnna to embody the feminist trope, which I desire, I promote an essentialized feminism, one that fixes and constrains the feminist subject to a particularized postulation of "true" feminist identity, one that cannot see enabling possibilities in the path that JoAnna chooses to travel. However, the fact of JoAnna's sophisticated feminist positionality in every other case eventually forces me to examine my foundationalist presumptions that limit feminisms to a binary polarity—that one cannot stand both inside feminisms and inside a patriarchal and, to my view, in an apparently unequal heterosexual relationship. The internal paradox of my assessments of JoAnna's case fix and constrain my students, the very subjects that I hope to represent and liberate because through this lens I turn them away from view (the game I accuse postmodern feminist compositionists of playing). With an essentialized view of a feminist politics of transformation, I write JoAnna, my most radical subject, to the silence of the margins.

However, all is not lost. Although it is certainly problematic to suggest that JoAnna's choices constitute a transformative feminist agenda for adolescent girls, JoAnna's case gives me reason for pause. I am forced to examine the exclusionary possibilities of an essentialized identity politics of any kind. There are thousands of ways to be feminist. Butler is again helpful on this point. Butler writes that the political task is "not to celebrate each and every new possibility qua possibility," but to redescribe existent possibilities, which have been designated as culturally unintelligible and impossible:

> If identities are no longer fixed as the premises of a political syllogism, and politics
> no longer understood as a set of practices derived from the alleged interests that
> belong to a set of ready-made subjects, a new configuration of politics would
> surely emerge from the ruins of the old. (Butler *Gender Trouble* 148)

Many other configurations might proliferate or become articulable within the discourses that establish intelligible cultural life, confounding the very binary of sex, gender, and their derivatives. In this way the "fundamental unnaturalness" of a system that allows only two sexes is exposed and undermined (Butler *Gender Trouble* 149).

If I become willing for a moment to reconfigure what I clearly see as an impossible tension between JoAnna's professed feminist articulations and her desire also to be held in the gaze of sexualized objectification, then I might expose the "fundamental unnaturalness" of cultural configurations that place the sexuality of a legally underage girl and a married father of four in opposition with feminist literacy practices. Certainly, in desire for multiple possibilities for transformation, I must be willing to reconsider the abject spectacle. Is it not possible to both hope for and to find wholeness, equality, and freedom within a politics of contemptible sexual desire redescribed as providing fulfillment, liberation, opportunity, pleasure, assurance? Might not JoAnna be practicing feminisms strategically?

The critical tasks of performance theory that make possible this translation are first to locate subversive strategies of gendered parody, mimesis, and irony to describe the ways in which sexed bodies "cross-dress" or stereotypically role play other sexed bodies. The next task is to affirm the local possibilities of intervention through such performances. Finally, the analyst is able to present the immanent possibility of contesting notions of a real or ideal through such performances (Butler *Gender Trouble* 147). These strategies allow us to redescribe JoAnna's case.

JoAnna is stereotypically role playing an "I am a feminist" script. She cross-dresses as a young Mormon woman, a victim of attempted rape, who is stronger and wiser for the experience. These performances provide possibilities for local intervention; we affirm that JoAnna is strategically miming feminist possibilities, which intervene and disrupt patriarchy. As evidence, JoAnna cites the confidence and strength she has gained through the "lessons" of her martial arts mentor without a hint of irony because she senses it means the rupture of patriarchy. JoAnna disrupts notions of a real or abiding feminism that exists intact underneath the display. In a somewhat spectacular move, JoAnna removes herself from the role of victim to the role of powerful agent enacting cultural change, even if that change occurs within a small circle of players. Patriarchy is momentarily dispersed and subverted in JoAnna's move through devastation to recovery. JoAnna writes herself in from silence to center stage.

There is undeniably no comfort in suggesting a politics of transformation enacted in the material facts of JoAnna's case. I name this bizarre possibility as a means to horrify myself and you, the reader, just long enough to recover a redefined feminist politics from the ruin of the old with a conversion of expressive to performative notions of gender identity. JoAnna's refusal to write upon her body the utterances that she speaks is a performative strategy, which moves her to a place of power rather than a place of abjection. We can no longer simply accept a reading of JoAnna's case as the trope of the other woman, the vixen, the victim, the disadvantaged, or the whore. She is completely in charge and pursuing her desires strategically.

Joanna's silence is not an expression of a body underneath that she disavows. It is a refusal to be written into a place that disallows the body of her desire. She writes upon her body the text she names and wins her prize. JoAnna refuses the problematic text of female adolescence. She is accepted by approving adults for her in-class feminist proclamations. The classmates whom she disdains identify her as separate from them—as "independent and strong." JoAnna wagers on the support of two adult women whom she respects and receives countless hours of their time and assistance in return. She gains confidence and physical strength and earns a black belt in karate. She escapes the legacy of dropping out of high school by attaching to a relatively wealthy man who will support her in getting her GED and will pay her college tuition when she decides to apply. She legitimates herself within the Mormon culture; she agrees to marry and becomes a "mother figure." Where is the power now?[2]

In this line of reasoning, a rewriting of the null set of silence is possible. JoAnna constructs a definite presence of absence in the writing classroom. As a result, compositionists might see other readings for students like JoAnna—disenfranchised subjects who remain silent during school-sponsored writing, yet who in effect write a more empowering subjectivity upon the text of the body. Through sustained social performances of writing that provide opportunities to question the very notions of an essential sex and a true or abiding masculinity or femininity or feminism, the writing subject's performative character and the performative possibilities that writing provides for proliferating other possible identity configurations are available. The critical strategies are to locate the possibilities for intervention in various performances of textual mimesis, irony, cross-dressing, hyperbole, and silence and to contest normative versions by exposing multiplicity.

In attempting to examine Alisa's and JoAnna's very audible silences through a performative lens, I find myself thinking about the regulation of female sexuality in school, about the absence and prohibition of discussions about female heterosexual and homosexual desire in girls' sex education, and other sanctioned curricula.[3] I also find myself thinking about the presence of a discourse that teaches young women that sexuality as violence or as victimization means that they must learn to say "NO" for fear of pregnancy, transmission of disease, or possibility of abuse and rape. However, as Michelle Fine points out, adolescent girls rarely reflect simply on sexuality. Their sense of sexuality is informed by a number of influences: peers, culture, religion, violence, history, passion, authority, rebellion, body, past and future, gender, and racial relations of power. Adolescent women assume dual consciousness—at once taken with the excitement of actual/anticipated sexuality and consumed with anxiety and worry. Too few safe spaces exist for adolescent women's exploration of sexual subjectivities; however, there are far too many dangerous spots for their exploitation (Fine "Sexuality, Schooling" 81–82).

As we might see from the cases of JoAnna and Alisa, desire unspoken speaks loudly in spite of the regulation and maintenance of its silencing in schools. In the case of JoAnna, we have a student who won the time and heart of her teachers through appropriating the discourse of feminisms, while she was simultaneously protecting a taboo sexual underlife. In the case of Alisa, we have a student who constructs versions of a romantic underlife that belies and silences her day-to-day experiences. There is definitely more to JoAnna's and Alisa's silence on these issues than apathy or resistance. I struggle with the notions of authorship that such a reading implies. I am certainly not interested in reenacting expressivist notions of personal revelation as the genuine or authentic textual space whereby "womanly rhetorical capacity" becomes visible and available. However, if Gilligan's claim is accurate—that a transformative pedagogy for teaching girls is to be found through relational connection between grown women and young women—then feminist teachers need to create a pedagogical space in classrooms where adolescent female desire can be unsilenced and explored.

The choices that women make in order to survive or to appear good in the eyes of others are often at the expense of women's relationships with one another. Certainly the experiences and voice of the karate teacher's first wife and his children and of Mormon doctrine on "marriage for eternity" are silenced in my translation. Nevertheless, if women can stay in the gaze of girls so that girls do not have to look and not see, if women can be seen by girls as speaking and knowing subjects, if women can sustain girls' gaze and respond to girls' voices, then perhaps, as Virginia Woolf envisioned, the opportunity will come and the dead poet who is Shakespeare's sister will put on the body which she has so often laid down and find it possible to live and write her poetry (*A Room of One's Own* 113) Perhaps students like Alisa and JoAnna will have opportunity to write beyond the pale of silent resistance and find more progressive ways to understand and communicate their experiences and their desires.

Notes

1. This is not a study of female sexuality; however, we did learn much more than we wanted to know about our students' sexual lives. We were amazed at how remarkably unconcerned our students were with the moral implications of their actions and at how much stock they put in "I love you," even when the men they were involved with were married.   Sharon Thompson has completed a brilliant study of adolescent female sexuality, which I review in Chapter 6 in relation to the experiences of women's studies students at AGHS.

2. Clearly, the very real lives of the karate teacher's first wife and five children presumably have been disrupted and hurt by JoAnna's involvement with this older man. It is difficult to suspend judgment against JoAnna in order to differently analyze the potential politics of transformation I forward here. In order to make the analysis of my case, I also remain deafeningly silent on the sexism and patriarchy so completely in evidence in the facts of one younger beautiful woman "taking" another woman's and family's "man." Is transformation possible when other lives are damaged in the process? Only in the ludic play of textual analysis. In material reality, I hardly think so.

3. Abstinence is the sanctioned curriculum on sex education in the schools. We live in a culture that uses sex to sell nearly everything. The overwhelming prevalence of sexually stimulating images, sexual innuendoes, and sexual activity and intercourse on television and in film certainly present a mixed message to adolescents who are otherwise taught at school to "Just say NO."   Approaching sex education by telling students that abstinence is the safest route ignores completely that students are sexually active at younger and younger ages. Additionally, it denies students educational opportunities to discuss healthy sexuality with informed adults and their peers. Given that students like JoAnna and Nikki engage in sex with older married men, that students like Alisa cut

themselves to maintain loving relationships with boys, and that nearly every student in the case study sample admitted to being sexually active, discussions in school about what it takes to develop healthy loving sexual relationships seems more than warranted. It is essential to healthy adolescent development.

Writing in Women's Studies

A Subversive Drag Performance

What would happen if one woman told the truth about her life?

The world would split open.

—Muriel Rukeyser

What would happen if the whole world became literate? Answer: not so very much, for the world is by and large structured in such a way that it is capable of absorbing the impact. But if the world consisted of literate, autonomous, critical, constructive people, capable of translating ideas into action, individually or collectively—the world would change.

—Johann Galtung

Women's studies at the high school is anomalous. It does not exist with any degree of frequency to be considered part of the typical culture in most public American secondary schools. Indeed, in an embedded portion of the annual conference of the National Women's Studies Association (NWSA) at Skidmore College in June 1996, NWSA considered for the first time the case of women's studies and adolescent girls with any degree of depth. A casual review of information presented at this conference reveals that perhaps only a handful of women's studies classes are in action or under development in public and private high schools around the United States. Emma Walker's appears to be the longest-running and most well-developed course of its kind.

As a result, it is reasonably cautious to assume that there is no institutional "common sense" on the subject of women's studies at the high school level. No discursive preexistence to describe, contrast, mitigate, subvert, transform, resist. What occurs in women's studies at Aspen Grove High School is always in the process of making and remaking itself. What is found there is a marginal borderland in which the literacies, secrets, lies, dreams, and lives of adolescent girls at Aspen Grove are taken on, changed, hidden, rewritten, altered, and discarded at will. Although it is an institutionally authorized location, what is produced in Emma Walker's classroom becomes a subversive discursive stage on which girls are able to write, revise, script, costume, block, rehearse, speak, and perform "in drag" lives transformed out/right (Butler *Gender Trouble, Bodies that Matter*). This is theater of the absurd.

As well, the intersections among writing, the curriculum, and teaching in Emma Walker's women's studies classroom creates a unique pastiche of fantasy, a kind of carnivalesque sideshow. The effects named for writing in women's studies at Aspen Grove must be appropriately localized and historicized—they can never be unstitched from the effects named for Emma Walker's women's studies curriculum and pedagogy. Writing, the women's studies curriculum, and Emma's Walker's pedagogy are inextricably intertwined. Therefore, any claims made about writing and the female "subject" of composition must be understood in relation to their appearance within the borders of Emma Walker's classroom during the period of this investigation.

As a result, it might be conventionally tempting to dismiss the findings of this study as ungeneralizable. However, to do so would be to banish to the margins what is found there. To do so would be to ignore what might be learned about the adolescent female writer from this investigation. To do so would be, as Susan Bordo suggests, to let institutions off the hook too soon for their hardened defense against social transformation. In Chapter 2, I discussed Susan Miller's urge to return compositionists to examinations of the "subject" of composition, the writer and her writing—studies accomplished in specifically designated locations that might address the multiple identities that student writers must occupy in order to be successful. The findings of this study offer one such tentative view of the subversive drag performance that is writing in women's studies at Aspen Grove.

Girls Writing Lives

Schooling continues to perpetuate a legacy of sexism that disadvantages female students. If we are to create conditions that allow girls in school to speak above a history of silent and disenfranchised voices, we have to begin to recognize the enormity of conditions from which we attempt to unsilence their lives. Many of the students enrolled in women's studies at Aspen Grove mutely carry with them to school every day the embodied knowledge of rape; incest; pregnancy and abortion; sexually transmitted disease; anorexia; bulimia; bisexual, transgendered, lesbian, and gay identifications in a largely heterosexual world; the trauma of sibling and parental suicide; the secrecy of taboo romantic sexual liaisons; the scars of physical and sexual abuse; marks of self-mutilation; the internal damage caused by misuse of alcohol and drugs. Not to mention what we do not know about our students or about the students at Aspen Grove that we have never met.

Nevertheless, whether aware of or oblivious to what these girls carry with them, parents, teachers, and the school expect these high school students at the least to attend class regularly, refrain from disciplinary infractions, and perform well enough academically to graduate. Many must accomplish much more than the minimum. They must excel academically, socially, athletically, as leaders in extracurricular organizations or as cheerleaders and drill team members. Additionally, Mormon girls are expected to demonstrate moral piety; to refrain from alcohol and illegal drug use; and to protect virginity. These girls day after day dutifully sit in classes, study the world history of war and conquest, learn how to solve algebraic equations, conduct chemistry experiments, swim laps and write five-paragraph themes about the use of symbolism in *Romeo and Juliet*. Rarely are their lives discussed.

It is no wonder they dissociate; just do the work and don't think about it. How else can they survive?

Women's studies gives adolescent women a location and opportunity to (re)connect their lives to their academic studies. During the course of any given class, Emma Walker teaches women's history; rhetorical, visual, and discourse analysis; interpersonal communication strategies; literary theories and content; and strategies for living on one's own and managing a household. Walker knows the lives of her students. She listens to and learns from them. She uses what she learns to provoke new understandings about everything the class reads and writes. She names the oppression these students face in multiple repressive and oppressive cultural systems. She forces an examination of the uncomfortable truths about society and calls her students to action.

The women's studies readings themselves suggest the power of connection and relevance to students' experiences. Selected readings open readers' eyes to the significance of meaning connected not only to their own lives, but to the lives of others. Writing in women's studies supports and is supported by reading. Writing is shared in communitarian experience.

Reading and writing in women's studies are acts of performative interpretation. Students have relevant experiential knowledge to share, which illuminates the ideas found in texts; academic knowledge is extended as it is linked to other kinds of knowledge. The social, interactive dialogue between teacher and students, researcher and students, and among students is pedagogically valued as knowledge performed outright.

Walker's women's studies class exhibits a stunning example of ways to interrupt the legacy of sexism in the schools. Emma Walker's women's studies class demonstrates careful use of the tensions between individual and community, between the world of the text and the world outside it, between Emma Walker as a teacher and as a human being, between belief in and doubting the possibility of the system. Reading and writing in women's studies give young women opportunity to speak and write the truth of their lives and to find those truths valued as performative sources of legitimate knowledge.

Reading and writing in women's studies give adolescent women a forum for integrating what they know with what the school wants them to know. As girls write their lives in relation with the lives of other women they read about or encounter in class discussions and readarounds, they begin to see the point of developing literacies that help them question the lies and silences of their lives. Women's studies at Aspen Grove provides a brilliant example of ways in which schools might enfranchise female students.

Girls Writing in Drag: The Significance of Writing in Women's Studies

Writing in Emma Walker's women's studies class at Aspen Grove contests the institutional norm established for adolescent girls in school. Women's studies writing occupies a subversive discursive location that reconfigures what is "normally" found for girls in schools. By writing in a women's studies class, girls are able to remove the cloak of silence and passivity "normally" worn by girls in school. They become able to cross-dress as "successful" student subjects in a high school classroom.

Through writing, these girls learn to think critically and analytically about themselves. They "speak" with conviction. They argue well-supported positions. They construct a stance. They express emotions and find therapeutic solace. They build relational connections with their peers and their teachers. They create transformative performative scripts, which propose changed courses of action for their lives.

Women's studies students act up. They act out. They write convincing texts that reframe them as student subjects. They create textual outbursts that displace the discursive position of silence "normally" held by girls in high school.

In *Bodies that Matter,* Judith Butler asks:

> If performativity is construed as that power of discourse to produce effects through reiteration, how are we to understand the limits of such production, the constraints under which such production occurs? Are these social and political limits on the resignifiability of gender...or is it a variable boundary set and reset by specific political investments? (20)

Butler asks this question to assist a radical resignification of the symbolic domain. By this, she wishes to check the sociopolitical boundaries that might reconfigure discursive exigencies, which define gendered ways of behaving, interacting, valuing, thinking, believing, speaking, reading, and writing in the world. Through repeated deviations from the gendered "norm," Butler hopes for a more possible future—to expand the very meaning of what counts as a valued and valuable body in this world (22).

For deviations to be effective, discursive practice—performative "acts" that both (re)name, (re)enact, and (re)make "gender"—must be repeated in both regular and sanctioned practice. The power of discourse to produce that which it names is linked with the question of performativity. As a result, the performative is one domain in which discourse acts as power—as ways of behaving, interacting, valuing, thinking, believing, speaking, reading, and writing in the world. There is no power construed as a "subject" that acts, but only a reiterated acting that is power in its persistence. Gendered subjectivity is identified through normative repetitive acts. These form a combined "nexus of power" and discourse "that repeats the discursive gestures of power," citing the "law," which applies to behavior marked by discursive repetition.

The repeated citation of the law gives the performative its binding or conferring power. When deviant performative acts in the form of (re)making, (re)naming, and (re)enacting female student behavior appear and appear repeatedly as discursive practice under the auspices of a legally authorized sanction, such as within the confines of a public school classroom, they break the citational chain of discursive power that performatively authorizes the citing of the patriarchal law. Repeated deviations from the "norm" open a space for different discursive organizations of "female student."

Writing in women's studies at Aspen Grove breaks the citational chain, which legitimates ways of being passively and silently female in public American high schools. Writing in women's studies at Aspen Grove works to resignify gendered ways of writing and learning because it occurs in the institutionally sanctioned space of a public high school classroom. Writing in women's studies, girls are free to write exploratory and disruptive notions about being female in and out of school. They are permitted and encouraged to do so. In writing, girls construct performative transformations of selves they envision themselves being/becoming. Girls see themselves as works in progress, acting out their resistance to mainstream expectations for adolescent girls in their culture. Writing allows them to take on multiple identities, to speak without being spoken to, to alter traditional dispositions of power. Girls are constantly innovating and performing gender and sexual identities across a spectrum of articulations. They speak up, they speak out, they create a chaotic nuisance that distracts the state of normalcy. A radical postmodern feminist subject is mimed and performed.

Girls writing in women's studies dress in "drag." Girls enact a parody of "passing as the real" female student/writer. Their writing performances take on conventionally accepted norms while uttering outrageous declarations. Writing in women's studies allows girls to try on the "failure to repeat their gender" as their culture would have them do, while learning to write conventionally accepted forms of standard written English. Here they find an opportunity and a location to expose their "deformity as failed girls" and to laugh heartily as they begin to understand ways to produce writing that fits commonly valued academic forms and conventions. This is a very good practical joke on patriarchy.

Writing in women's studies becomes the moment that Judith Butler describes as creating the "possibilities of (gender) transformation." Parodic repetitions of other possible gender performances expose "the phantasmatic effect of abiding identity as a politically tenuous construction," which can be taken on and taken off at will (*Gender Trouble* 140–141). Writing in women's studies provides the discursive occasion for a temporary resistance, a momentary resignification, and a potential self-subversion of the law of femininity as it constrains the acts, practices, and subjectivities of female students in schools (*Bodies that Matter* 109). It also gives girls the tools to beat the masters at their own games. Women's studies students learn that writing helps them to know what they know and to learn new ideas and content that they desire to understand. Girls realize that the capability to produce writing that ably manipulates the standard conventions of written English helps them—the "subjects" of composition—to gain the "goods" that the society they are in views as valuable. Writers in women's studies artfully learn the power of mimicry, of parody, of sarcasm, of textual drag, of active silence as tools that serve to subvert female subordination in the cultural hierarchy.

I am reminded of Sharon's ironic parody of culturally inscribed laws governing femininity (Chapter 4). She writes that notions of femininity are a "double whammy on the brainwashed things." With a thick sarcastic tone, Sharon grieves that girls "are never taught to grow up—just that they are baby machines, to sit around, grow fat, and have cute brats." Through writing in women's studies she is able to "fail to repeat her gender—to expose her deformity as a failed girl." She is able to laugh derisively in the face of the failure, an act that cross-dresses her for success. A young woman who rarely speaks in class, Sharon writes fluently with strength of purpose and persuasive conviction. In the final scene, having performed an ugly parody of housewifery and motherhood, she concludes: "How many girls do you think, if they weren't taught to think this way, would really want to stay home with children?"

Although no direct causal link can wisely be made, it is interesting to be reminded that following writing in women's studies, Sharon rejects her parents' and her grandparents' bid "to look for someone nice to marry" after high school graduation. She instead enrolls in the local community college and transfers to a large state university across the country the following year. She tells me in our final interview, "Hey, this is what I want to be, and I want to attain that goal and nothing is going to stand in my way. And I'm not just gonna like go, 'Oh well, I want to do this and then blow it off and just like be a flake about it'" (Sharon, personal interview, May 23, 1995). For a brief but powerful moment, Sharon has subverted the laws of femininity governing female students in school. She has created for herself a more possible future.

However, the notion of discursive resignification, discursive cross-dressing is not linked directly to the notion of gender parody or impersonation. The writer in women's studies does not put on a "mask" or "persona" to cover over the "one" who precedes that putting on, who is something other than its gender from the start." Neither does this suggest that "this miming, this impersonating precedes and forms the 'one' operating as its formative precondition rather than its dispensable artifice" (Butler *Bodies that Matter* 230). "If drag is performative, that does not mean that all performativity is to be understood as drag" (231).

What it does suggest is that writing in women's studies as a subversive drag performance constitutes an artificial yet aggressive resignifying effort to negotiate cross-gendered identification, as Sharon has. Writing in women's studies allows resignification of both "female" and of "student" precisely because it provides both the location and the opportunity to reconfigure meanings of "female student" in the high school. As girls write in women's studies, they perform the student self they have reclaimed—learning at the center, with an outspoken voice and a strong position, in possession of the full range of human emotions, in relational connection with both curriculum and pedagogy, self-directing transformative courses of lived action. They act out a performed identification that reiterates a gendered idealization even in its "radical uninhabitability" (Butler *Bodies that Matter* 231). They become the self "they never loved and never grieved."

The notion of both writing-as-drag and gender-as-drag is significantly related to the problem of unacknowledged loss—the self one is, who one cannot be; the self one wants to be, but who is another. To the extent that "gender is an assignment, which is never quite carried out according to expectation, its subjectivities never quite inhabit the ideal s/he is compelled to approximate," so writing is also an assignment, which discursively represents an ideal the writer's subjectivities may never quite inhabit:

> Gender performance allegorizes a loss it cannot grieve, allegorizes the incorporative fantasy of melancholia whereby an object is phantasmatically taken in or on as a way of refusing to let go. (Butler *Bodies that Matter* 234–235)

This is why students who write in women's studies are so deeply transformed by the reconfiguring of the gender assignment through the writing assignment. They travel through hell to get there. The practice by which both (re)gendering and writing in women's studies occurs—the explicit embodying and resistance of norms—is the overt rejection of a compulsory practice, a forcible (re)production within the constraints of compulsory systems of gendering and schooling. Writers are able to discursively resignify the self they never loved and never grieved. In so doing, they create tranformative possiblities and claim a more powerful self.

As Butler indicates, the possibility of an enabling social and political resignification occurs when there is occupation or reterritorialization of a site that has been used to abject a population. What occurs through writing in the women's studies classroom at Aspen Grove High School is political affirmation from and through the very institution that in prior enactments had as its aim the erasure of precisely such an affirmation. Girls in a public school reterritorialize their typical location of oppression by writing a different script. The opportunity for resignification in a location that previously oppressed the signifier calls for a rethinking of gender performativity in schools, creating the enabling cultural condition through which all willing first becomes possible.

Such a theory of agency is especially disarming in light of the gendered selves many of these girls (and boys) are expected to perform as members of a Mormon community. Gender subjectivity is rigidly regulated among members of the Mormon Church. Young men and women are expected to perform very specialized roles. Mormonism is a patriarchal religion: women in this subculture are expected to defer to men in every aspect of their lives.

They are expected to marry young—as virgins, have many children, keep a spotless and attractive home, and strive to raise their children as perfect and faithful Mormons. Men are expected to hold the priesthood, and protect and provide for their families.[1] Failing to perform those roles right carries punitive consequences that may last "throughout eternity."

The peer culture is heavily invested in making certain that young Mormon men and women perform their gender roles right. Sex role expectations outlined by Mormon culture structure masculinity and femininity patterns of response in the Aspen Grove community vis-à-vis form and anti-form, whether the students are members of the Church or not. The parody of these roles that many of the students write and rewrite in women's studies makes their performances all the more serious and hilarious. When Sharon sarcastically mimics the pain of the young (Mormon) wife who ended up in poverty because she "failed to perform her gender right"—leaving her alone with four young children to support and with no education or employable skills that might sustain her—she is constructing an alternative subjectivity that explodes the Mormon belief in a stable, unified femininity. She is laughing in the face of the authority, which names her. Sharon takes on a role that opposes the dominant discourse. She reclaims the loss of self and upends the patriarchal version by which she has been inscribed.

Alisa and JoAnna split the difference. Their performances, one of textual silence and resistance and the other of resistance through textual silence, represent the chaotic tensions that threaten to pull apart their lives. The dominant discourse is too powerful and too seductive. For beautiful Mormon women, the promise of security and a life lived "happily ever after" is too great. For Mormon girls like Alisa and JoAnna, to take on multiple selves, to speak without being spoken to, to alter traditional dispositions of power prove too much. They resist the feminist alternative because it threatens to rupture and explode the foundational assumptions that lend coherence to their lives, coherence that they desire deeply because of its absence in their experience. They insist on affirming the veracity of the fiction of the status quo.

As materialist feminists, although we are disappointed by these contrary moves, Walker and I acknowledge that we have no right to deny our students' desires to gain the "goods" that their culture views as right and necessary. Writing about feminist issues of concern in a women's studies class ultimately offers slippery glimpses of another possible future—but does not serve to transform the subjectivities of the writers in every possible case. Among students who appear less recalcitrant than Alisa and JoAnna but who may resist as well, the parodic shifts and tendencies displayed in their writing may simply serve as temporary moments of adolescent rebellion, a phenomenon Mormons do not welcome but forgive as long as the youngster enters back into the fold at the appropriate time (for men this is when they go on their mission; for women it is when they marry).

In some cases, women's studies ultimately protects and preserves the dominant discourse by allowing a momentary transgression without grave material consequences in effect. However, women's studies cannot be considered to fail as a result. The jury is still out on cases like Alisa's and JoAnna's. The power these girls have invoked to write their own futures through their experiences in women's studies has vested them with transformative possibilities. What they ultimately conclude may constitute a radical feminist version of adolescent empowerment.

As a result of the study, a theory of agency has resided in the assertion that a powerful subjectivity results from connecting with others and from building alliances. Walker was raised in a Mormon household. I have been married and have raised children. We are both white and middle class. For the students, we represent bodies that they desire. We can teach these students outrageous feminist ideas because they can still leave the sanctity of the class knowing that the two adults who present the possibility for constructing alternative subjectivities do not seem to have strayed too far from the normative trope the students envision for themselves. Certainly, we would have to expect a different outcome if, for instance, I was an African-American lesbian or if Walker was an outspoken radical atheist or if one of us was a gay male and the other was a prostitute or *Cosmopolitan* cover girl. We would certainly expect a different outcome if the foundations for building relational connections with the students were limited and constrained by more radical embodied discontinuites between the adult leaders of the group and the students.

The tenor of the class might be significantly different, for example, if homosexuality was permitted as a discourse in the classroom and more of the gay, lesbian, bisexual, and transgendered students were "out," or if the teacher or researcher or both could speak out about their politics of advocacy for inclusion of sexuality issues and sex education in the curriculum. It would be impossible to imagine similar effects for writing if the class, race, sexuality, or religious identifications of the teacher(s) were less congruent with those of the students.

However, this is not to say that the body underneath the teacher and the body underneath the students must match in order to promote an equitable sharing of classroom authority. It is simply to suggest that acting out resistance to mainstream culture would certainly take on different forms and anti-forms if the "subjects" involved were differently located. Students might not be willing to perform transformatively at all if they felt unable to build a sense of trust and connection with the teacher; and the failure to connect might be more possible under different sets of circumstances. Nonetheless, construction of relational connections so pivotal to the success of transformative performative writing in a women's studies class can otherwise be enabled.

Reframing Views of Process: Making Female Students Visible in the Writing Classroom

The contemporary fields of composition studies and rhetoric are built on a foundation constructed by Janet Emig and others in the late 1960s and early 1970s. In the explosive developments that have established the discipline since then, the female writer has been hidden from view even though, as I discuss in Chapter 2, she is prominently present and accounted for in Emig's (*Composing Processes*) foundational work. Struggles to achieve disciplinary status have, as Susan Miller suggests, "superseded interpretive analyses of how students write, of what they write, or of how well they succeed in doing so depending on their specific instruction" (*Textual Carnivals* 200). What is needed, Miller offers, is a return to the subject of composition—the writer and her writing.

As Emig implied and Gilligan affirmed in her work, it matters to these students who is "listening" and how "what they have to say" is heard. These claims raise rhetorical issues regarding the nature of student writing, the nature of school audiences, the performance of student subjectivity, and the potential for student transformation in the writing class. They raise questions about the ways in which writing continues to be taught and practiced in secondary school. They also raise questions about the predilections of compositionists, who have questioned the political appropriateness of early process orientations to composing and composition teaching. The students in this study value equally the pragmatic literacies of writing in characteristically "expressive" and "constructivist" terms. Data suggest that delineations between these categories cannot be simply determined. Indeed, data suggest that theoretical boundaries that have been drawn around "competing views" (Faigley "Competing Theories") of process are not so neatly identified, at least in the case of female writers who are writing in a high school women's studies class.

The findings of this study suggest that the boundaries that have been drawn among competing views of process as distinctly essentialist or constructivist in nature are both artificial and unhelpful to female students who are composing. The conventional wisdom on theories about writers and writing processes that emanate from disciplinary debates advantage a patriarchal organization of knowledge in composition and rhetoric and overpower a more equitable, gender-sensitive view. When female students are given "frequent, inescapable opportunities for composing" (Emig *Composing Processes* 100) through writing invitations that are simultaneously aware of expressive, cognitive process, and social rhetorical/feminist components, they are able to accomplish moments of discursive, interpretive, and performative transformation. Inviting students to speak out and speak back to normative expressions of femininity and masculinity allows them to perform several alternative options that have the potential to transform social practice.

Margaret, for example, reads about and studies the portrayal of females in the media, about the feminine masquerade, and the manipulation of the female gaze. Through writing, she begins to come to terms with her bulimia and consequent loss of a position on the Aspen Grove cheerleading team. She takes notes in her response log entries and begins to respond to facts she picks up from the reading. She tentatively explores the connections she is making between what she reads and her own experience. When she writes her formal paper, "A Masculinity/Femininity History," she explores her upbringing and the effects media have had on her image of herself. In her final freewrites, she argues a position against the dominant portrayal of women in the media. She links her position to high incidents of eating disorders among young women. Margaret develops a persuasive argument and provides adequate evidence to support her case. In the process, she proposes a changed course of action for her own life. She steps between the cracks, shifting at will among her sense of identities.

Students like Margaret can write a great deal, and they can write well because they have a deep personal investment in the issues and ideas they write about. They try on alternate subjectivities, which they can put on or disrobe at any moment. Women's studies writers participate critically in the discourses that shape their lives by taking on a variety of roles and demonstrating opposition to the discursive positions that "normally" direct female and male lives.

Throughout the process, the audience receives the students' writing with the seriousness it warrants; however, they receive it as a work in progress that can shift and turn at any given moment. Deconstructive challenges to writers' thinking are delivered with respectful appraisal and encourage moves in any direction. Reader/writer relations develop in an atmosphere of trust and amicable exchange because of the solidarity that begins with consciousness raising and remains an ideal. Feedback to the writing encourages a politics of critique. The writer and the reader face each other on level ground. Meaning is open to further interpretation. Non-belief allows for the learning of something new. The reader and writer seek recognition for their diverse lives. There is no means to a proposed end. New conditions obtain. These are plurality and multiplicity and simultaneity of condition. Meaning is non-essentialized; a new conception of plurality and change is possible. Outburst, revisions, identity play, and silence are welcomed and challenged. Written text is not viewed for its potential as a finished product, but for its potential in mediating the moment.

Writing proceeds from invitations to engage a topic or an idea performatively, to begin from a personal standpoint and to play with a full range of social, political, and feminist possibilities. The writing is not used to gauge what students can recall or what they comprehend. The writing is not used to judge a student's facility with academic conventions, but to give students opportunities to wrestle with issues that give local and historical depth to the postmodern moment. When students situate their personal experience narratives in the larger sociocultural context, they are able to take on multiple identities that act out their resistance to mainstream culture. They innovate, alter identities as they wish, and become aware of the window on full participation in discourse communities that their writing represents.

In converting expressive notions of process to performative notions of process, as Butler directs, compositionists might recuperate the "subjective" losses the field has sustained. Compositionists might learn to see the reflexive/expressive writing that Emig calls for neither as a precursor to a more desirable finished product nor as an artifact that represents the authentic voice and essential identity of the writer underneath. Compositionists might see performative texts that enact "postmodern qualities of antiform, play, chance, anarchy, and silence" (Faigley *Fragments*) as process for its own sake. In such visions, compositionists might then with writing create possibilities for proliferating "subject" configurations outside the restricting frames of the status quo.

The reappropriation of process-oriented strategies as a constructivist form gives compositionists the means by which all students can participate as momentarily empowered subjects. Students do not write to replicate discursive forms that reproduce the society as it is. They use recuperated processes to reinscribe their personal narratives as works in progress, which produce chaotic, unfinished, piecemeal, sporadic texts that exemplify the pulsating movements of discourse that intermingle with constant innovation of identity. The outcome of the composition course shifts from gatekeeping function, which serves the interests of the institution, to acts of student empowerment, which fulfill the democratic and egalitarian aims of the field.

The effects of writing in women's studies at Aspen Grove are the result of the profound simplicity of language play. Some feminist compositionists have explored female rhetorics from the standpoint of female-friendly genres. They have presumed following cultural and feminist positions that narrative and journal writing are more female-friendly than argument, for example. However, the girls in this study are not at all hesitant to take up a range of genres from narrative and journal to argument as long as they are able to write across a range of invitations—and respond in any way to the exigencies of text. They play with, resist, reconfigure, parody, mimic, and retextualize the personal, intellectual, and political connections that they make through writing. The combination of subversive discursive events that are women's studies at Aspen Grove accomplish a textual revolution because of their lack of coherence and finality, not in spite of it.

Here compositionists may wish to examine parallels between the recent history of feminist critical and theoretical development and developments in our own field. The practical work of feminists has been sidetracked by debates surrounding essentialist and constructivist views of the female subject. Likewise, the practical work of compositionists has been sidetracked by debates regarding disciplinary status, which pivot around essentialist and constructivist views of the "subject" of composition.

Compositionists need to act as though the disciplinarity of composition is established and to acknowledge that the "goods" the society views as necessary have been obtained. Doctoral degrees are granted in composition and rhetoric at several institutions. Several professional journals dealing with composition and rhetoric are published. Compositionists have tenure at leading research institutions and their operating budgets far exceed those of their "higher status" colleagues in English literary studies because compositionists teach nearly everyone who enters the university. Compositionists have earned the right and the responsibility to move past the discipline wars and the field's collective femininization. Compositionists have earned the right to recuperate process-oriented strategies as postmodern forms. Making this move invariably will allow compositionists to promote texts that raise postmodern cacophony and invite *all* toward a more possible goal of widespread written literacy.

Pragmatically, meaning in the context of the institutions that feminists and compositionists both are trying to transform, the most powerful strategies against liberal humanist notions of the singular rational human and writing subject have been those that demystify both "human" and "writer" and their claims to "neutral" perspective. Demystification, making visible the invisible, has been accomplished *through* identifying general categories of social and writerly identity in the so-called essentializing work. This strategic essentialism has given both content and force to the notions of social interest, historical location, and cultural perspective identified in constructivist work. Where liberal and cultural feminist work have accomplished the primary task of demystification in feminisms, descriptions of expressive and cognitive process approaches to writing have demystified the work of the writer in composition studies.

Some feminists have questioned whether abandoning the strongest analyses along liberal and cultural lines—for example, classic feminist explorations of the consequences of female-dominated infant care or of male biases in our disciplines and professions—would be to reject the foundation undergirding feminist understandings of history and culture. There is in this healthy skepticism a parallel warning to be sounded for compositionists.

Certainly, questioning the suggestion that all (female) writers write out of a univocal, fixed conception of social identity and location is necessary if compositionists are to provide opportunities for all (female) writers to engage a writing subject who is able to participate with facility in a variety of literate discourses. However, while engaged in inquiry, it seems folly to abandon what compositionists have learned about writers' processes from expressive and cognitive process investigations because sociopolitical identities are not foregrounded in the original research. This resembles the proverbial act of throwing the baby out with the bathwater. It is also to cover over what is found there, especially relative to what can be learned about female students composing from Emig's original work and from writing in women's studies at Aspen Grove. Instead, compositionists should recover constructivist characteristics of process-orientations and accomplish the democratic ideals upon which the "subject" of composition is grounded.

The tentative and momentary exuberance of processes that have been named in expressive and cognitive work can lead to historical, social, and political analyses. Without them, writing cannot accomplish its democratic and egalitarian aims of mitigating against multiple illiteracies. Indeed, exciting recent analyses by Hephzibah Roskelly and Kate Ronald of the connections among romantic views of the writer and pragmatic approaches to teaching writing demonstrate the power held in reexamining process approaches to teaching writing. Roskelly and Ronald encourage mediation between the romantic and the practical and suggest that privileging public argumentation over the work of the individual writer writing in community with other writers stalls progressive pedagogy. For example, inviting students to write about portrayals of women in the media is profoundly different from inviting a student to explore her relationship with bulimia in light of what she is learning about portrayals of women in the media. She emerges with strategies for (re)positioning herself not as a single individual but as a constituent of culture—writing herself from the margins to the center, possessing a confident voice, proposing a transformative course of action, and arguing a politicized/feminist stance.

The girls in this study engage in a variety of *reflexive* and *extensive* writing activities, which mime the types of invitations Emig recommends in her study of 12th graders. In the early years of the discipline, compositionists did not take exception among writing done in public school settings and writing done in higher education. A fissure between K-12 teachers of writing and college compositionists weakens the potential for social transformation. The institutional and intellectual boundaries that separate the teaching of writing in the public schools from the teaching of writing in postsecondary schools troubles efficacy and ignores the needs of young women (and others) in both arenas.

Composition scholars might begin to think about ways to reconnect with those who teach writing in secondary schools and in the university. As postmodern theories of whatever origin have become an integral part of thinking in scholarly circles, the complexity of postmodern writing has become accessible to fewer and fewer people. Those engaged in the teaching of writing are rarely considered in "post" and "neo" discussions. For example, secondary teachers of writing are currently concerned with meeting the various social and academic needs of students in widely diverse classrooms at the same time students are being expected to perform better on standardized forms of assessment and other high-stakes testing. How might scholarship in composition and rhetoric help strengthen teaching and learning in classrooms in ways that will help teachers deal with the realities and pressures of high-stakes testing? How might scholarship in composition and rhetoric help teachers create supportive, multicultural classrooms where difference is valued, not feared? How might scholarship in composition and rhetoric cross levels of instruction in ways that will help illuminate skills and attitudes that are important in all classrooms? It seems imminently vital that those engaged in composition and rhetoric scholarship begin to imagine the kinds of links we can make between instructional levels to improve the teaching and learning of writing for all in both public school and university classrooms.

Implications for Feminist Research in Composition Studies

So much remains unexamined regarding the effects of composing among adolescent female writers in the women's studies class at Aspen

Grove, not to mention how infinitesimally small may be the connective links between this work and the still relatively unexamined world of writing among adolescent females in public schools in general. To catalogue all potential research questions arising from this study could fill several more chapters. Therefore, I will only present questions pertaining in some direct way to this study.

First, investigation of the writing processes and products of case study students might also include examining these students' ways of writing and texts in comparison with their ways of writing and texts produced in their other classes. Such investigations might lead to broader generalizations about the effects of writing among adolescent girls in public schools. Similarly, compose aloud protocol analyses, such as those conducted by Janet Emig, and those in several studies conducted by Linda Flower and John R. Hayes, would provide more objective insight into the writing processes of these students than that which can be gathered from the self-report data that I have collected here.

Additionally, findings from context-sensitive analyses of the students' written products might be more widely generalizable if students were to be studied in greater ethnographic depth. For example, more in-depth case histories of the women's studies students might be conducted by shadowing several students throughout the course of their school day. Investigations of before- and after-school and weekend activities would contribute to a fuller cultural understanding of the typical women's studies student. Interviews with the students' other teachers and family members might also contribute to greater understanding of these students as writers. A fuller cultural understanding of the students, in turn, would enhance context-sensitive analyses of the writing these students complete. Context-sensitive analyses of writing completed by these students in other classes could be compared to writing completed in women's studies, which might enrich the information base in untold ways. Additionally, in-depth critical discourse analyses of one student's writing across a range of writing invitations both in women's studies and in other classes could help to develop a deeply textualized portrait of the writer as a young woman.

Another interesting approach would be to conduct longitudinal studies of a given sample of women's studies students, following them into their postsecondary years and beyond to examine the ongoing effects of both writing and of women's studies in their lives. Such an approach would permit far more direct observations by investigators of how female writers are taught. Such an approach would allow investigators to examine what they learn about themselves as writers, as a result, with much less reliance upon the self-report of the informants and upon the confounding interventions of participant observation. It might also help to sort through the effects of writing from the effects of women's studies in ways that could prove expansive.

Yet another interesting approach would be to conduct a study similar to this one in a more traditional academic high school class, such as an English class, and compare the findings regarding female writers in that class to the findings of this study. Perhaps responses to the following questions could be obtained: Can writing interrupt cultural understandings of gender in a class that does not consciously politicize a gendered agenda? What do female students have to say about their writing processes and the value of school-sponsored writing in more traditional academic classes? Can writing serve a contextually meaningful purpose for female students in a variety of scholastic settings? Can writing serve to help female students build relational connections among their peers and teachers in other classes? Can writing serve female students as a tool for critical and analytical thinking and learning in other academic classes? Can writing provide young women with opportunities to "speak" with authority, to construct and argue credibly supportable positions, to express emotions and find therapeutic solace, to script transformative performatives, which propose altered courses of life action outside the arena of women's studies?

Additionally, implications for collaborative teacher research gained in this study might be much more fully investigated. Whereas Walker helped me to understand women's historical development and a host of content issues with which I was unfamiliar, I helped her to imagine ways to incorporate writing as a tool for learning in her classes. Because Walker is not trained as a composition teacher, she did not imagine that pedagogical adjustments might be made when the students were unable to engage writing at any meaningful level when she first attempted to incorporate journal writing in class. Because of my expertise as a writing teacher, I was able to model other possible approaches for Walker throughout the course of the study. As a result, she was able to see new possibilities for incorporating writing as a tool to accomplish her educational and pedagogical goals:

It's important enough now. I mean, I was stuck because before when I tried to do journal writing, I ended up with diaries, you know, that had nothing to do with the class. And by having you come and demonstrate—this is what a journal is and this is the way to do it to get them to react the way you want. And, of course, it is a reading response log—is what it's called—is really a journal in the class, but you can call it that and not get a diary. By doing it—by presenting it in that fashion, showing me and them how to do it, really helped the class across the board. And it helps the students with their writing in their other classes. (Walker, personal interview, June 26, 1995)

Walker realizes that it was not that writing was not useful, but that there were other ways to teach writing to the students that might better enable her goals—ideas I had gained from expressive and cognitive process models of writing processes. Now that she understands different ways to go about writing with students, she believes the class is better as a result: "The highlights of the three years is that I think the class is better. I think writing obviously is the big benefit" (Walker, personal interview, June 26, 1995). One pedagogical benefit that has occurred as a result of the study is that the teaming efforts of the classroom teacher and me reveal alternative strategies for providing quality educational experiences for students. This phenomena might provide the central focus in studies of composition reseacher/disciplinary teacher collaborations similar to those completed at the college level by philosopher Fishman and compositionist McCarthey (*John Dewey*, "Teaching for Change," *Unplayed Tapes*).

Perhaps the most promising aspect of this study for further research would be to investigate what it would take to construct and implement in public schools all across the nation women's studies classes that incorporate uses for writing in ways similar to those developing in Emma Walker's class at Aspen Grove High School. Much could be gained from such an investigation to enable the construction of institutionally authorized locations for the female "subject" of composition, the writer and her writing to emerge more publicly.

Implications for Feminist Teaching in Composition Studies

This investigation strongly suggests that not enough has changed for (female) writers in public schools since Janet Emig (*Composing Processes*) berated secondary English teachers for teaching writing in a neurotic and trivializing fashion. The grassroots efforts of the National Writing Project (Gray) and its satellites have accomplished much in the way of teacher training in ways responsive to Emig's recommendations that teachers learn to teach writing by writing themselves and by sharing teaching ideas with other teachers of writing. However, the effects of National Writing Project efforts are not unilaterally influential in ways that Emig might have hoped. Students in secondary schools still do far too little writing in school (Applebee and Langer; Myers) and the writing they currently do is still far removed from their day-to-day lives.

Emig's (*Composing Processes*) hope that teachers would "abandon the unimodal approach to writing and show far greater generosity in the width of writing invitations they extend to all students" (100) has not occurred with any degree of regularity. The teacher-centered presentation of composition and the retention of the "Fifty-Star Theme" as the form of greatest focus in public secondary schools is still "pedagogically, developmentally, and politically an anachronism" (100).

Additionally, this study again confirms what Emig (*Composing Processes*) supposed about interactions between teachers and (female) writing students. The effects of writing are circumspectly dependent on relational connections built between (female) teachers and their (female) students. Students conclude that in order for school-sponsored writing to provide any meaningful effect, the teachers authorized to teach it need to listen to them, to accept and respect their ideas, and to challenge them to think differently about the issues raised in textual exchange. The rhetorical relationship established between teacher and students should be one constructed in the spirit of educative exchange of ideas rather than in overly critical attention to surface features of writing.

However, the types of relational connections defined in this study should not be confused with those suggested by liberal and cultural feminists. Relational connection in female-friendly teaching is not defined by these students as a matter of maternalistic nurturance, cooperation, female friendship, or compromise. It is not a matter of writing narratives instead of arguments. The female students in women's studies at Aspen Grove High School value relational, not personal, outreach from their teacher. They do not want in their teacher a mother or someone who will coddle them or shelter them from the tough issues they must and expect to face. They do not want their teacher as a companion, friend, or confidante.

They want an expendable adult who will take them and their ideas seriously, who, as Gilligan suggests ("Teaching Shakespeare's Sister"), will "listen and will not leave in the face of conflict or disagreement" (24). In fact, they demand that their ideas and their writing be treated with the respect it deserves. Only when they are certain that their teacher(s) will meet them on equal ground are they willing to relinquish the stilted vapid prose that Ken Macrorie referred to as "Engfish" so many years ago. Theirs is not so much a matter of "finding a voice" but rather of "opening their mouths" in a space that allows their voices to be heard. For the writing teacher, helping female students to write texts that best fit the rhetorical situation might be a matter, as Adrienne Rich suggests, of taking seriously both them and the enormity of the conditions out of which they are attempting to write.

Taking female students seriously also means making them visible at the center of the writing curriculum. The women's studies students at Aspen Grove report that issues of relevant concern to females are sidelined or invisible in the mainstream curriculum. Sexism is still a problem in the American secondary school. Writing invitations might explicitly take into account issues of relevant concern to adolescent girls. This is best accomplished by incorporating textual materials in the curriculum that focus on the lives, accomplishments, situations, and predicaments of women and girls without trivializing, sensationalizing, or pathologizing them. Women's studies classes at the high school are unlikely the only possible answer, although they provide a space where coalitions (Ellsworth) or affinity groups (Pratt) can be formed that help students build the confidence, which might enable them to meet the "outside world" head-on. Both the mainstream high school and the mainstream writing curriculum need to be revised so that issues of concern to females receive equal representation as issues of concern to males, but until that reconstruction occurs, women's studies classes may provide a good starting place.

Demonstrating and modeling techniques for using personal experience as evidence in support of an argument helps girls make the personal, intellectual, and political connections that the girls in women's studies at Aspen Grove find so meaningful. These include (a) developing a thesis that generalizes a position taken; (b) searching for and writing about only the most relevant details, which are needed to communicate the experience clearly and succinctly; (c) explaining why the writer finds this to be a significant experience; (d) demonstrating how the experience is an example of the thesis or position argued; and (e) drawing generalizations from the experience to support the position argued. These techniques help girls move across the extensive, reflexive spectrum because they learn the rhetorical techniques for invoking the meaningfulness of personal experience in support of a political and intellectual purpose, or both.

Additionally, demonstrating how young women might proactively approach assignments in their other classes so that they are able to engage them more meaningfully can be helpful. Several of the students in women's studies pursued topics that they had uncovered in women's studies in their other classes. For example, as a result of what she was learning in women's studies, when Trisha was assigned to do a biographical research report in her world history class, she asked her teacher for permission to research the life of Anne Boleyn, even though there were no female names on the list the teacher had distributed in class. Trisha wrote a great paper because she knew how to negotiate a proactive approach with her teacher and could meaningfully engage with a topic of her choice. Feminist compositionists can teach their female students how to ask textual questions that urge attention to issues of female and feminist concern and how to negotiate the pursuit of these topics through writing in their other classes.

Finally, if as Gilligan suggests, women writing teachers, and most of us are women, "can sustain girls' gaze and respond to girls' voices" ("Teaching Shakespeare's Sister" 26) with the seriousness and the respect that their voices deserve, in full recognition of what they have covered over, of what has been silenced, then perhaps girls truly can find the "habit of freedom and the courage to write and say exactly what we think" (Gilligan "Teaching Shakespeare's Sister" 27)

The findings of this study provoke me to redescribe process-oriented strategies, which have been calculated and dismissed as romantic and modernist in orientation, in postmodern terms by using Judith Butler's translation of the expressive into the performative. I recuperate the value of process strategies for their usefulness in giving voice to (female) diversity; by exploding the belief in a stable, unified self; and by offering means for exploring how (gender) identity is multiply constructed and how agency resides in the power of connecting with others and in building alliances. When adults who will "listen and will not leave in the face of conflict or disagreement" (Gilligan "Teaching Shakespeare's Sister" 24) extend invitations at school to write across multiple theoretical perspectives and modes of discourse identified in the last three decades of composing research, writing might yet be considered part of a process that subverts and (ideally) transforms, at least partially, locally, and temporarily, the punitive and oppressive mechanisms of a system that genders sexes by binary oppositions, which privilege one member of the pair over other(s). The wavelike, ebbing and flowing movement of written discourse (Faigley, *Fragments*) in these literacy episodes intermingles with the many crosscurrents of gendered constructions discussed in a women's studies class. Students are helped to construct alternate subjectivities and to become aware of the ways in which their writing might participate fully in the discourses that shape their lives.

The findings of this study suggest that Susan Miller's call in *Textual Carnivals* to move us forward in achieving composition studies' goals for student empowerment and widespread written literacy by turning us back to the processes of students writing makes empirical as well as theoretical sense. The writing of Aspen Grove's women's studies students are viewed as performative scripts enacted in specifically located writing situations. Writing in women's studies discursively erupts from struggles that form the lives of (female) students. The sentences and silences these students construct as representative of supposedly coherent mental or disciplinary biographies explode meaning. I conclude that writing may allow student writers to think and rethink gendered behavior beyond the constraints of ordinary social experience—to "imagine alternate, possible, and resistant worlds" (Brandt 3).

Note

1. I am grateful both to Michelle and Mona for reading earlier drafts of this section. Much of Mormon mores are tacit, not explicit. In order for outsiders, like myself, to understand the sex role expectations upheld in Mormon culture, the cooperation of insiders is necessary. These are secret ideals known only to those who uphold the faith. Insiders reveal them at risk of excommunication.

Bibliography

Abrams, M.H. (Meyer Howard). *The Mirror and the Lamp: Romantic Theory and the Critical Tradition*. New York: Oxford University Press, 1953.

Ackerman, John M. "The Promise of Writing to Learn." *Written Communication* 10 (1993): 334–370.

Agar, Michael. *The Professional Stranger: An Informal Introduction to Ethnography*. New York: Academic Press, 1980.

———. *Speaking of Ethnography*. Beverly Hills, CA: Sage Publications, 1986.

Alvine, Lynne, and Linda Cullum. (Eds.). *Breaking the Cycle: Gender, Literacy, and Learning*. Portsmouth, NH: Boynton/Cook Heinemann, 1999.

American Association of University Women (AAUW). *Hostile Hallways: The AAUW Survey on Sexual Harassment in America's Schools*. (Commissioned by the AAUW Education Foundation and conducted by Louis Harris and Associates.) Wellesley, MA: Wellesley College Center for Research on Women, 1993.

———. *Out of the Classroom: A Chilly Campus Climate for Women*. Washington, DC: Association of American Colleges Project on the Status and Education of Women, 1984.

———. *The Campus Climate Revisited: Chilly for Women Faculty, Administrators, and Graduate Students*. Washington, DC: Association of American Colleges Project on the Status and Education of Women, 1986: 278–283.

Applebee, Arthur. "Writing and Reasoning." *Review of Educational Research* 54 (1984): 577–596.

Applebee, Arthur N., Judith A. Langer, and Ina V.S. Mullis. *NAEP 1992 Writing Report Card*. Washington, DC: U.S. Department of Education, 1994.

Atwell, Nancie. *In the Middle: Writing, Reading and Learning with Adolescents*. Portsmouth, NH: Heinemann, 1997.

Austin, J. L. *How to Do Things with Words: The William James Lectures Delivered at Harvard University in 1955*. New York: Oxford University Press, 1962.

Barbieri, Maureen. *Sounds from the Heart: Learning to Listen to Girls.* Portsmouth, NH: Heinemann, 1995.

Barlowe, Jamie. "Daring to Dialogue: Mary Wollstonecraft's Rhetoric of Feminist Dialogics." In *Reclaiming Rhetorica: Women in the Rhetorical Tradition.* Pittsburgh: University of Pittsburgh Press, 1995. 117–136.

Barritt, L. S., and Kroll, Barry M. "Some Implications of Cognitive-developmental Psychology for Research in Composing." In *Research on Composing: Points of Departure.* Eds. Charles Cooper and Lee O'Dell. Urbana, IL: National Council of Teachers of English, 1978. 49–57.

Bartholomae, David. "Inventing the University." *Journal of Basic Writing* 5 (1986): 4–23.

Beck, Joan. 27 January 1998. "Scandal Embarrasses Nation As Well As Clinton." *The Chicago Tribune.*

Belanoff, Pat. "Silence: Reflection, Literacy, Learning, and Teaching." *College Composition and Communication* 52.3 (2001): 399–428.

Belenky, Mary Field, Blythe McVicker Clinchy, Nancy Rule Goldberger, and Jill Mattuck Tarule. *Women's Ways of Knowing: The Development of Self, Voice, and Mind.* New York: Basic Books, 1986.

Berlin, James. "Rhetoric and Ideology in the Writing Class." *College English* 50 (1988): 477–494.

———. *Rhetoric and Reality: Writing Instruction in American Colleges, 1900–1985.* Carbondale: Southern Illinois University Press, 1987.

———. *Writing Instruction in Nineteenth-Century American Colleges.* Carbondale, IL: Southern Illinois University Press, 1984.

Bizzell, Patricia. *Academic Discourse and Critical Consciousness.* Pittsburgh: University of Pittsburgh Press, 1993.

Bordo, Susan. "Feminism, Postmodernism, and Gender-skepticism." *Feminism/Postmodernism.* Ed. Linda J. Nicholson. New York: Routledge, 1990. 133–156.

Brady, Laura. "The Reproduction of Othering." In *Feminism and Composition Studies: In Other Words.* Eds. Susan Jarratt and Lynn Worsham. New York: Modern Language

Association, 1998. 21–44.

Brandt, Deborah. *Literacy as Involvement: The Acts of Writers, Readers and Texts*. Carbondale: Southern Illinois University Press, 1990.

Bridwell-Bowles, Lillian. "Freedom, Form, Function: Varieties of Academic Discourse." *College Composition and Communication* 46 (1995): 46–61.

Britton, James, Tony Burgess, Nancy Martin, A. McLeod, and Harold Rosen. *The Development of Writing Abilities, 11–18*. (Schools Council Research Studies). London, UK: Macmillan Education, 1975.

Brody, Miriam. *Manly Writing: Gender, Rhetoric, and the Rise of Composition*. Carbondale: Southern Illinois University Press, 1993.

Broe, Mary Lynn, and Angela Ingram. *Women's Writing in Exile*. Chapel Hill: University of North Carolina Press, 1989.

Broverman, I. K., D. M. Broverman, and P. Rosenkrantz. "Sex-role Stereotypes: A Current Appraisal." *Journal of Social Issues* 28 (1972): 59-79.

Brown, Lyn Mikel, and Carol Gilligan. *Meeting at the Crossroads: Women's Psychology and Girls' Development*. Cambridge, MA: Harvard University Press, 1992.

Bruce, Heather E. *Writing in the Margins: Revising the Scripts of Gendered Constructions in a High School Women's Studies Class*. Diss. University of Utah, 1997.

Brumberg, Joan Jacobs. *The Body Project: An Intimate History of American Girls*. New York: Random House, 1997.

Burraston-Wood, Arlene. "The Feminization of Poverty." *Ladies Home Journal*. January 1993: 127–132.

Butler, Judith. *Bodies that Matter: On the Discursive Limits of Sex*. New York: Routledge, 1993.

———. "Contingent Foundations: Feminism and the Question of 'Postmodernism.'" In Butler and Scott. 3–21.

———. *Excitable Speech: A Politics of the Performative*. New York: Routledge, 1997.

———. *Gender Trouble: Feminism and the Subversion of Identity*. New York: Routledge, 1990.

————. "Gender Trouble, Feminist Theory, and Psychoanalytic Discourse." In *Feminism/postmodernism*. Ed. Linda J. Nicholson. New York: Routledge, 1990. 324–340.

————. "Imitation and Gender Insubordination." In *Inside/Out: Lesbian Theories, Gay Theories*. Ed. Diana Fuss. New York: Routledge, 1991. 13–31.

————. "Performative Acts and Gender Constitution: An Essay in Phenomenology and Feminist Theory." In *Performing Feminisms: Feminist Critical Theory and Theatre*. Ed. Sue Ellen Case. Baltimore, MD: Johns Hopkins University Press, 1990. 270–282.

Butler, Judith, and Joan W. Scott (Eds). *Feminists Theorize the Political*. New York: Routledge, 1992.

Calkins, Lucy McCormick. *The Art of Teaching Writing*. Portsmouth, NH: Heinemann, 1986.

Carlip, Hillary. *Girl Power: Young Women Speak Out!* New York: Warner Books, 1995.

Carlton, Susan Brown. "Composition as a Postdisciplinary Formation." *Rhetoric Review* 14 (1995): 79–87.

Caywood, Cynthia, and Gillian R. Overing (Eds). *Teaching Writing: Pedagogy, Gender, and Equity*. Albany: State University of New York Press, 1987.

Chodorow, Nancy. *The Reproduction of Mothering: Psycholanalysis and the Sociology of Gender*. Berkeley: University of California Press, 1978.

Cixous, Helene. "The Laugh of the Medusa." Trans. Keith Cohen and Paula Cohen. *Signs* I (1976): 875–893.

Clark, Suzanne. "Argument and Composition." In *Feminism and Composition Studies: In Other Words*. Eds. Susan Jarratt and Lynn Worsham. New York: Modern Language Association, 1998. 94–99.

————. "Julia Kristeva: Rhetoric and the Woman as Strange." In *Reclaiming Rhetorica: Women in the Rhetorical Tradition*. Pittsburgh: University of Pittsburgh Press, 1995. 305–318.

Collins, Patricia Hill. *Black Feminist Thought: Knowledge, Consciousness, and the Politics of Empowerment*. New York: Routledge, 1990.

Crowley, Sharon. "Composition's Ethic of Service, the Universal Requirement, and the Discourse of Student Need." *JAC: A Journal of Composition Theory*. Spring 1995. 227–239.

Culley, Margo, and Catherine Portuges (Eds.). *Gendered Subjects: The Dynamics of Feminist Teaching.* London: Routledge and Kegan Paul, 1985.

Daly, Mary. *Gyn/Ecology: The Metaethics of Radical Feminism.* Boston: Beacon Press, 1978.

De Beauvoir, Simone. *The Second Sex.* (1949). Trans. H.M. Parshley. New York, NY: Knopf, 1953.

DeCerteau, Michel. *The Practice of Everyday Life.* Trans. Stephen Rendall. Berkeley: University of California Press, 1988.

Deyhle, Donna, and Frank Margonis. "Navajo Mothers and Daughters: Schools, Jobs, and the Family." *Anthropology and Education Quarterly.* Vol. 26, June 1995: 135–167.

Doane, Mary Ann. *The Desire to Desire.* Bloomington: Indiana University Press, 1987.

Ebert, Teresa. "The 'Difference' of Postmodern Feminism." *College English* 53 (1991): 886–904.

Elbow, Peter. *Writing without Teachers.* New York: Oxford University Press, 1973.

———. *Writing with Power.* New York: Oxford University Press, 1981.

Ellsworth, Elizabeth. "Why Doesn't This Feel Empowering?" In *Feminisms and Critical Pedagogy?"* Eds. Carmen Luke and Jennifer Gore. New York: Routledge, 1992. 90–119.

Emig, Janet. *The Composing Processes of Twelfth Graders.* Urbana, IL: National Council of Teachers of English, 1971.

———. "The Uses of the Unconscious in Composing." *College Composition and Communication,* 16 (1964): 6–11.

———. *The Web of Meaning: Essays on Writing, Teaching, Learning, and Thinking.* Portsmouth, NH: Boynton/Cook, 1983.

———. "Writing as a Mode of Learning." *College Composition and Communication,* 28 (1977): 122–127.

Emig, Janet, with Louise Weatherbee Phelps. "Introduction: Context and Commitment." In *Feminine Principles and Women's Experience in American Composition and Rhetoric.* Eds. Louise Weatherbee Phelps and Janet Emig. Pittsburgh: University of Pittsburgh Press, 1995. xi–xviii.

Enos, Richard Leo. Preface. *Rhetoric Review* 12 (1994): 237–239.

Faigley, Lester. "Competing Theories of Process: A Critique and a Proposal." *College English* 48 (1986): 527–542.

————. *Fragments of Rationality: Postmodernity and the Subject of Composition.* Pittsburgh: University of Pittsburgh Press, 1992.

Fairclough, Norman. *Discourse and Social Change.* Cambridge, UK: Blackwell, 1992.

Ferganchick, Julia K. "Challenging the Myths of Contrapower Harassment in the Writing Classroom." *Dialogue: A Journal for Writing Specialists* (Spring 1999): 6–11.

Finders, Margaret J. *Just Girls: Hidden Literacies and Life in Junior High.* New York: Teachers College Press, 1997.

Fine, Michelle. *Disruptive Voices: The Possibilities of Feminist Research.* Ann Arbor: University of Michigan Press, 1992.

————. "Sexuality, Schooling, and Adolescent Females: The Missing Discourse of Desire." In *Beyond Silenced Voices: Class Race and Gender in United States Schools.* Eds. Lois Weis and Michelle Fine. Albany, NY: State University of New York Press, 1993. 75–100.

Fishman, Stephen and Lucille McCarthy. *John Dewey and the Challenge of Classroom Practice.* New York: Teachers College Press, 1998.

————. "Teaching for Student Change: A Deweyan Alternative to Radical Pedagogy." *College Composition and Communication* 47.3 (1996): 342–366.

————. *Unplayed Tapes: A Personal History of Collaborative Teacher Research.* New York: Teachers College Press, 2000.

Fiske, John. "Madonna." In *Ways of Reading: An Anthology for Writers.* Eds. David Bartholomae and Anthony Petrosky. Boston: Bedford Books, 1989. 156–173.

Fleckenstein, Kristie S. "Writing Bodies: Somatic Mind in Composition Studies." *College English* 58 (1999): 281–306.

Flower, Linda. "Writer-based Prose: A Cognitive Basis for Problems in Writing." *College English* 41 (1979): 19–37.

Flower, Linda, and John R. Hayes. "A Cognitive Process Theory of Writing." *College Composition and Communication* 32 (1981): 365–387.

Flynn, Elizabeth A. "Composing as a Woman." *College Composition and Communication* 39 (1988): 423–435.

———. "Composition Studies from a Feminist Perspective." In *The Politics of Writing Instruction: Postsecondary.* Eds. Richard H. Bullock and John Trimbur. Portsmouth, NH: Boynton/Cook, 1991. 137–154.

———. "Feminism and Scientism." *College Composition and Communication* 46 (1995): 353–368.

———. "Review: Feminist Theories/Feminist Composition." *College English* 57 (1995): 201–212.

Flynn, Elizabeth A., Catherine Lamb, and Louise Smith. *Responding to Essentialism in Feminist Theory and Practice.* Panel presentation given at the Conference on College Composition and Communication Convention. Convention Center, Cincinnati, OH. 19–21 March 1992.

Foster, David. *A Primer for Writing Teachers: Theories, Theorists, Issues, Problems.* (second edition). Portsmouth, NH: Boynton/Cook-Heinemann, 1992.

Fowler, Roger. "Power." In *Handbook of Discourse Analysis, Vol. 4, Discourse Analysis in Society.* London, UK: Academic Press, 1985.

Frymer, Murray. "For Sexes, Early Communication Helps." *San Jose Mercury News.* 249.4.

Fuss, Diana. *Essentially Speaking: Feminism, Nature and Difference.* New York: Routledge, 1989.

Gabriel, Susan, and Isaiah Smithson (Eds.). *Gender in the Classroom: Power and Pedagogy.* Urbana: University of Illinois Press, 1990.

Gallop, Jane. (Ed.). *Pedagogy: The Question of Impersonation.* Bloomington and Indianapolis: University of Indiana Press, 1995.

Gannett, Cinthia. *Gender and the Journal: Diaries and Academic Discourse.* Albany: State University of New York Press, 1992.

Gee, James Paul. *Social Linguistics and Literacies: Ideology in Discourses.* London, UK: Taylor and Francis, 1996.

Gere, Anne Ruggles. "Revealing Silence: Rethinking Personal Writing." *College Composition and Communication* 53.2 (2001): 203–223.

Gilbert, Sandra M., and Susan Gubar. *The Mandwoman in the Attic.* New Haven, CT: Yale University Press, 1984.

Gilligan, Carol. *In a Different Voice: Psychological Theory and Women's Development.* Cambridge, MA: Harvard University Press, 1982.

———. "Teaching Shakespeare's Sister." *Making Connections: The Relational Worlds of Adolescent Girls at Emma Willard School.* Eds. Carol Gilligan, Nona P. Lyons, and Trudy J. Hanmer. Cambridge, MA: Harvard University Press, 1990. 1–32.

Gilligan, Carol, Nona P. Lyons, and Trudy J. Hanmer. *Making Connections: The Relational Worlds of Adolescent Girls at Emma Willard School.* Cambridge, MA: Harvard University Press, 1990.

Gilyard, Keith. "Literacy, Identity, Imagination, Flight." *College Composition and Communication* 52.2 (2000): 260–272.

———. "African American Contributions to Composition Studies." *College Composition and Communication* 50.4 (1999): 626–644.

Glenn, Cheryl. "Sex, Lies, and Manuscript: Refiguring Aspasia in the History of Rhetoric." *College Composition and Communication* 45 (1994): 180–199.

Gore, Jennifer. *The Struggle for Pedagogies. Critical and Feminist Discourses as Regimes of Truth.* New York: Routledge, 1993.

Gradin, Sherrie L. *Romancing Rhetorics: Social Expressivist Perspectives on the Teaching of Writing.* Portsmouth, NH: Boynton/Cook-Heinemann, 1995.

Graff, Gerald. "Teach the Conflicts." *South Atlantic Quarterly* 89 (1991): 53–67.

Graves, Donald. *Writing: Teachers and Children at Work.* Portsmouth, NH: Heinemann, 1983.

Graves, Heather Brodie. "Regrinding the Lens of Gender: Problematizing 'Writing as a Woman.'" *Written Communication* 10 (1993): 139–163.

Gray, James. "New Ideas about English and Departments of English." *English Education* 18.3 (1986): 147–152.

Griffin, Susan. "Matter." *Woman and Nature: The Roaring Inside Her.* New York: Harper and Row, 1978. 5–46.

Grumet, Madeline. *Bitter Milk: Women and Teaching.* Amherst: University of Massachusetts Press, 1988.
———. *"Scholae Personae*: Masks for Meaning" *Pedagogy: The Question of Impersonaltion* Ed. Jane Gallup. Bloomington: Indiana University Press, 1995. 36–45.

Hall, G. Stanley. *Adolescence: Its Psychology and Its Relations to Physiology, Anthropology, Sociology, Sex, Crime, Religion and Education.* 2 v. illus. New York: D. Appleton and Company, 1904, 1969.

Hall, Roberta M., and Bernice R. Sandler. *Out of the Classroom: A Chilly Climate for Women.* Washington, DC: Association of American Colleges Project on the Status and Education of Women, 1982.

Hallin, Annika. "A Rhetoric for Audiences: Louise Rosenblatt on Reading and Action." *Reclaiming Rhetorica: Women in the Rhetorical Tradition.* Pittsburgh: University of Pittsburgh Press, 1995. 285–304.

Harkin, Patricia. "The Post-Disciplinary Politics of Lore." In *Contending with Words: Composition and Rhetoric in a Postmodern Age.* Eds. Patricia Harkin and John Schilb. New York: Modern Language Association, 1991. 124–138.

Heath, Shirley Brice. "Critical Factors in Literacy Development." In *Literacy, Society, and Schooling: A Reader.* Eds. Suzanne de Castell, Alan Luke, and Kieran Egan. Cambridge, UK: Cambridge University Press, 1986: 209–229.

———. *Ways with Words.* New York: Cambridge University Press, 1983.

Heilbrun, Carolyn. *Writing a Woman's Life.* New York: W.W. Norton, 1988.

Holland, Dorothy C., and Margaret A. Eisenhart. *Educated in Romance: Women, Achievement, and College Culture.* Chicago: University of Chicago Press, 1990.

hooks, bell. *Talking Back: Thinking Feminist, Thinking Black.* Boston: South End Press, 1989.

———. *Teaching to Transgress: Education as the Practice of Freedom.* New York: Routledge, 1994.

———. *Yearning: Race, Gender, and Cultural Politics.* Boston: South End Press, 1990.

Huckin, Thomas N. "Context-sensitive Text Analysis." In *Methods and Methodology in Composition Research*. Eds. Gesa Kirsch and Patricia A. Sullivan. Carbondale: Southern Illinois University Press, 1992. 84–104.

———. "Critical Discourse Analysis." *The Journal of TESOL-France* 2.2. (1995): 95–111.

Irigaray, Luce. *Speculum of the Other Woman*. Trans. Gillian C. Gill. Ithaca, NY: Cornell University Press, 1985.

———. *This Sex Which Is Not One*. Trans. Catherine Porter. Ithaca, NY: Cornell University Press, 1985.

Jacobus, Mary (Ed.). *Women Writing and Writing about Women*. New York: Harper and Row, 1979.

Jarratt, Susan. "Feminism and Composition: The Case for Conflict." In *Contending with Words*. Eds. Patricia Harkin and John Schilb. New York: Modern Language Association, 1991. 105–123.

———. *Rereading the Sophists: Classical Rhetoric Refigured*. Carbondale: Southern Illinois University Press, 1991.

Jarratt, Susan, and Lynn Worsham (Eds.). *Feminism and Composition Studies: In Other Words*. New York: Modern Language Association, 1998.

Jay, Gerald. "The End of 'American' Literature: Towards a Multicultural Practice." *College English* 53 (1991): 264–281.

Jonsberg, Sara Dalmas, with Maria Salgado and the Women of The Next Step. "Composing the Multiple Self: Teen Mothers Rewrite Their Roles." In *Feminine Principles and Women's Experience in American Composition and Rhetoric*. Eds. Louise Weatherbee Phelps and Janet Emig. Pittsburgh: University of Pittsburgh Press, 1995. 211–230.

Joreen. "The BITCH Manifesto." In *Notes from the Second Year: 1970*. Documents from the Women's Liberation Movement: An On-line Archival Collection, Special Collections Library, Duke University: http://scriptorium.lib.edu/wlm/bitch/.

Kirby, Dan, and Tom Liner. *Inside Out*. Portsmouth, NH: Boynton/Cook-Heinemann, 1988.

Kirsch, Gesa. *Women Writing the Academy*. Carbondale: Southern Illinois University Press, 1993.

Kirsch, Gesa, and Joy Ritchie. "Beyond the Personal." *College Composition and Communication* 46 (1995): 7–29.

Kohlberg, Lawrence. *The Philosophy of Moral Development: Moral Stages and the Idea of Justice*. San Francisco: Harper and Row, 1981.

Kramarae, Cheris. *Women and Men Speaking: Frameworks for Analysis*. Rowley, NJ: Newbury House, 1981.

Kress, Gunther. *Linguistic Processes in Sociocultural Practice*. Oxford, UK: Oxford University Press, 1989.

Kristeva, Julia. *The Kristeva Reader*. Ed. Toril Moi. New York: Columbia University Press, 1987.

Kroll, Barry M. "Cognitive Egocentrism and the Problem of Audience Awareness in Written Discourse." *Research in the Teaching of English* 12 (1978): 269–281.

Kutz, Eleanor, and Hephzibah Roskelly. *An Unquiet Pedagogy: Transforming Practice in the English Classroom*. Portsmouth, NH: Boynton/Cook-Heinemann, 1991.

Lacan, Jacques. *Feminine Sexuality*. Trans. Juliet Mitchell and Jacqueline Rose. New York: W. W. Norton, 1982.

Lakoff, Robyn. *Language and Women's Place*. New York: Harper and Row, 1975.

Lamb, Catherine. "Beyond Argument in Feminist Composition." *College Composition and Communication* 42 (1991): 11–24.

Lauer, Janice M. "Issues and Discursive Practices." In *Feminine Principles and Women's Experience in American Composition and Rhetoric*. Ed. Louise Weatherbee Phelps and Janet Emig. Pittsburgh: University of Pittsburgh Press, 1995. 353–360.

Lauer, Janice M., and J. William Asher. *Composition Research: Empirical Designs*. New York: Oxford University Press, 1988.

Lay, Mary M. "Feminist Theory and the Redefinition of Technical Communication." *Journal of Business and Technical Communication* 5 (1991): 348–370.

LeCompte, Margaret, Wendy Millroy, and Judith Preissle (Eds.). *The Handbook of Qualitative Research in Education*. San Diego: Academic Press, 1992.

Lerner, Gerda. *The Grimke Sisters from South Carolina: Rebels against Slavery*. New York:

Houghton Mifflin, 1967.

Lewis, Magda. "Interrupting Patriarchy: Politics, Resistance and Transformation in the Feminist Classroom." In *Feminisms and Critical Pedagogy*. Eds. Carmen Luke and Jennifer Gore. New York: Routledge, 1992. 167–191.

Lincoln, Yvonne, and Egon Guba. *Naturalistic Inquiry*. Newbury Park, CA: Sage, 1985.

Lipscomb, Drema R. "Sojourner Truth: A Practical Public Discourse." *Reclaiming Rhetorica: Women in the Rhetorical Tradition*. Pittsburgh: University of Pittsburgh Press, 1995. 227–246.

Lorber, Judith. *Paradoxes of Gender*. New Haven, CT: Yale University Press, 1994.

Luke, Carmen, and Jennifer Gore (Eds.). *Feminisms and Critical Pedagogy*. New York: Routledge, 1992.

Macrorie, Ken. *Telling Writing*. Rochelle Park, NJ: Hayden, 1970.

————. *Writing to Be Read*. Rochelle Park, NJ: Hayden, 1968.

Malinowitz, Harriet. *Textual Orientations: Lesbian and Gay Students and the Making of Discourse Communities*. Portsmouth, NH: Boynton/Cook-Heinemann, 1995.

Martin, Jane Roland. *Reclaiming a Conversation: The Ideal of the Educated Woman*. New Haven, CT: Yale University Press, 1985.

————. "Becoming Educated: A Journey of Alienation or Integration?" *Journal of Education* 79 (1987): 204–213.

McCracken, Nancy, and Bruce Appleby (Eds.). *Gender Issues in the Teaching of English*. Portsmouth, NH: Boynton/Cook-Heinemann, 1992.

McIntosh, Peggy. *Interactive Phases of Curricular Re-Vision: A Feminist Perspective. Working Paper No. 124*. Wellesley: Wellesley College Center for Research on Women, 1983.

McLaren, Peter. *Schooling as a Ritual Performance: Towards a Political Economy of Educational Symbols and Gestures*. New York: Routledge, 1993.

Miller, Susan. "*In Loco Parentis*: Addressing (the) Class." In *Pedagogy: The Question of Impersonation*. Ed. Jane Gallup. Bloomington: Indiana University Press, 1995: 155–164.

_____. *Rescuing the Subject: A Critical Introduction to Rhetoric and the Writer.* Carbondale: Southern Illinois University Press, 1989.

————. *Textual Carnivals: The Politics of Composition.* Carbondale: Southern Illinois University Press, 1991.

Modleski, Tania. *Feminism without Women.* New York: Routledge, 1991.

Mortensen, Peter. "Going Public." *College Composition and Communication* 50 (1998): 182–205.

Moss, Beverly J. "Ethnography and Composition." In *Methods and Methodology in Composition Research.* Eds. Gesa Kirsch and Patricia A. Sullivan. Carbondale: Southern Illinois University Press, 1992. 153–171.

Murphy, James J. "Foreword." In *Reclaiming Rhetorica: Women in the Rhetorical Tradition.* Ed. Andrea A. Lunsford. Pittsburgh: University of Pittsburgh Press, 1995. ix–xi.

Murray, Donald M. *A Writer Teaches Writing,* second edition. Portsmouth, NH: Boynton/Cook-Heinemann, 1985.

Myers, Miles. *Changing Our Minds: Negotiating English and Literacy.* Champaign-Urbana: National Council of Teachers of English, 1996.

Nelms, Gerald. "Reassessing Janet Emig's *The Composing Processes of Twelfth Graders.*" *Rhetoric Review* 13 (1994): 108–130.

Newkirk, Thomas (Ed.). *To Compose: Teaching Writing in High School and College,* second edition. Portsmouth, NH: Boynton/Cook-Heinemann, 1990.

Nicholson, Linda J. (Ed.). *Feminism/postmodernism.* New York: Routledge, 1990.

North, Stephen. *The Making of Knowledge in Composition.* Portsmouth, NH: Boynton/Cook-Heinemann, 1987.

Olson, Tillie. *Silences.* New York: Delacorte, 1965.

Orenstein, Peggy. *School Girls: Young Women, Self-Esteem, and the Confidence Gap.* New York: Doubleday, 1994.

Penelope, Julia. *Speaking Freely: Unlearning the Lies of the Fathers' Tongues.* New York: Teachers College Press, 1990.

Perl, Sondra. "Reading, Writing, and Feminism: Approaches to an Emancipatory Classroom." Paper presented at the Conference on College Composition and Communication, Cincinnati, OH. March 1992.

Peterson, L. H. "Gender and the Autobiographical Essay." *College Composition and Communication* 42 (1991): 170–181.

Phillips, Susan. "Participant Structures and Communicative Competence: Warm Springs Children in Community and Classroom." In *Functions of Language in the Classroom.* Eds. Courtney Cazden, V. Johns, and Dell Hymes. New York: Teachers College Press, 1972. 370–394.

Pipher, Mary. *Reviving Ophelia: Saving the Selves of Adolescent Girls.* New York: Ballantine Books, 1994.

Pratt, Mary Louise. "Arts of the Contact Zone." *Profession '91.* New York: Modern Language Association, 1991. 55–72.

Probyn, Elsbeth. *Sexing the Self: Gendered Positions in Cultural Studies.* London: Routledge, 1993.

Project on the Status and Education of Women. *Classroom Climate: A Chilly One for Women?* Washington, DC: American Association of University Women, 1982.

Rief, Linda. *Seeking Diversity: Language Arts with Adolescents.* Portsmouth, NH: Heinemann, 1992.

Reynolds, Nedra. "Interrupting Our Way to Agency: Feminist Cultural Studies and Composition." In *Feminism and Composition Studies: In Other Words.* Eds. Susan Jarratt and Lynn Worsham. New York: Modern Language Association, 1998. 58–73.

Rich, Adrienne. *On Lies, Secrets, and Silence.* New York: W.W. Norton, 1979.

———. "Taking Women Students Seriously." In *On Lies, Secrets, and Silence.* New York: W.W. Norton, 1979. 237–246.

Ritchie, Joy. "Confronting the 'Essential' Problem: Reconnecting Feminist Theory and Pedagogy." *Journal of Advanced Composition* 10 (1990): 249–271.

Rohman, D. Gordan, and A. Wlecke. *Pre-Writing: The Construction and Application of Models for Concept Formation in Writing.* U.S. Office of Education Cooperative Research project no. 2174. East Lansing: Michigan State University Press, 1964.

Romano, Thomas. *Clearing the Way: Working with Teenage Writers.* Portsmouth, NH: Boynton/Cook-Heinemann, 1987.

Roskelly, Hephzibah, and Kate Ronald. *Reason to Believe: Romanticism, Pragmatism, and the Teaching of Writing.* Albany: State University of New York, 1998.

Rossi, Alice S. *The Feminist Papers: From Adams to De Beauvoir.* New York: Bantam Books, 1974.

Royster, Jacqueline Jones. "To Call a Thing by Its True Name: The Rhetoric of Ida B. Wells." In *Reclaiming Rhetorica: Women in the Rhetorical Tradition.* Ed. Andrea A Lunsford. Pittsburgh: University of Pittsburgh Press, 1995. 167–184.

Royster, Jacqueline Jones, and Jean C. Williams. "History in the Spaces Left: African American Presence and Narratives of Composition Studies." *College Composition and Communication* 50.4 (1999): 563–584.

Rubin, Donnalee. *Gender Influences: Reading Student Texts.* Carbondale: Southern Illinois University Press, 1993.

Rubin, Donnalee, and Kenneth Greene. "Gender-typical Style in Written Language." *Research in the Teaching of English* 26 (1992): 7–40.

Sacks, Oliver. *The Man Who Mistook His Wife for a Hat and Other Clinical Tales.* New York: Harper and Row, 1970.

Sadker, Myra, and David Sadker. *Failing at Fairness: How America's Schools Cheat Girls.* New York: Scribner, 1994.

St. Pierre, Elizabeth A. "A Historical Perspective on Gender." *English Journal* 88 (1999): 29–34.

Saville-Troike, Marilyn. *The Ethnography of Communication.* Oxford, UK: Basil Blackwell, 1982.

Scardemalia, Marlene, Carl Bereiter, and H. Goelman. "The Role of Production Factors in Writing Ability." In *What Writers Know: The Language, Process, and Structure of Written Discourse.* Ed. Martin Nystrand. New York: Academic Press, 1982. 173–210.

Schell, Eileen E. "With Friends Like These Who Needs Enemies?: Reading the Rhetorics of Feminism's Internal Critics." In *Anti-Feminist, Anti-Gay, Anti-Affirmative Action Rhetorics: Analysis and Response (Sponsored by the CCC Committee on the Status of Women in the Profession).* Paper presented at the Conference on College Composition and

Communication, Minneapolis Hilton and Towers, Minneapolis, MN, April 13, 2000.

Schilb, John. "Getting Disciplined?" *Rhetoric Review* 12 (1994): 398–405.

Schreiner, Steven. "A Portrait of the Student as a Young Writer: Re-evaluating Emig and the Process Movement." *College Composition and Communication* 48 (1997): 86–104.

Sedgwick, Eve. *Epistemology of the Closet*. Berkeley: University of California Press, 1990.

Smith, Dorothy. *Texts, Facts, and Femininity: Exploring the Relations of Ruling*. London: Routledge, 1990.
———.*The Everyday World as Problematic*. Boston: Northeastern University Press, 1987.

Spender, Dale. *Man-Made Language*. London: Routledge and Kegan Paul, 1980.

———. *Women of Ideas and What Men Have Done to Them*. London: Routledge and Kegan Paul, 1982.

Spivak, Gayatri Chakravorty. "Imperialism and Sexual Difference." *Oxford Literary Review* 8: 1–2, 225–240.

———. *In Other Worlds: Essays in Cultural Politics*. New York, NY: Methuen, 1987.

Spradley, James. *Participant Observation*. Fort Worth, TX: Holt, Rinehart, and Winston, 1980.

———. *The Ethnographic Interview*. Fort Worth, TX: Harcourt Brace Jovanovich, 1979.

Stein, Nan, Nancy L. Marshall, and Linda Tropp. *Secrets in Public: Sexual Harassment in Our Schools*. Wellesley, MA: A joint project of NOW Legal Defense and Education Fund and the Wellesley College Center for Research on Women, 1993.

Stewart, Donald C. "Collaborative Learning and Composition: Boon or Bane?" *Rhetoric Review* 7 (1988): 58–83.

———. "Prose with Integrity: A Primary Objective." *College Composition and Communication* 20 (1969): 223–227.

———. *The Authentic Voice: A Pre-Writing Approach to Student Writing*. Dubuque, IA: Brown, 1972.

Sullivan, Patricia A. "Feminism and Methodology in Composition Studies." In *Methods and Methodology in Composition Research*. Eds. Gesa Kirsch and Patricia A. Sullivan.

Carbondale: Southern Illinois University Press, 1992. 37–61.

Sullivan, Patricia A., and Donna Qualley (Eds.). *Pedagogy in the Age of Politics: Writing and Reading (in) the Academy.* Urbana: National Council of Teachers of English, 1994.

Tannen, Deborah. *Gender and Discourse.* Oxford, UK: Oxford University Press, 1996.

_____. *You Just Don't Understand: Women and Men in Conversation.* New York: Quill, 2001.

Thompson, Audrey. "A Review of Between Voice and Silence: Women and Girls, Race and Relationship by Jill M. Taylor, Carol Gilligan, and Amy M. Sullivan." *Educational Studies* 27 (1996): 253–261.

Thompson, Sharon. *Going All the Way: Teenage Girls' Tales of Sex, Romance, and Pregnancy.* New York: Hill and Wang, 1995.

Tong, Rosemarie. *Feminist Thought: A Comprehensive Introduction.* Boulder, CO: Westview, 1989.

Tyack, David, and Elizabeth Hansot. *Learning Together: A History of Coeducation in American Schools.* New Haven, CT: Yale University Press, 1990.

Van Slyck, Patricia. "Repositioning Ourselves in the Contact Zone. *College English* 59 (1997): 149–170.

Villanueva, Victor. "On Rhetoric and Precedents of Racism." *College Composition and Communication* 50.4 (1999): 645–662.

Voss, Ralph. "Janet Emig's *The Composing Processes of Twelfth Graders:* A Reassessment." *College Composition and Communication* 34 (1983): 278–283.

Walker, Alice. "Afterword: Looking for Zora." In *I Love Myself When I Am Laughing....And Then Again When I Am Looking Mean and Impressive: A Zora Neale Hurston Reader.* Ed. Alice Walker. Boston: Feminist Press, 1989. 297–305.

_____. "On Refusing to Be Humbled by Second Place in a Contest You Did Not Design: A Tradition by Now." In *I Love Myself When I Am Laughing....And Then Again When I Am Looking Mean and Impressive: A Zora Neale Hurston Reader.* Ed. Alice Walker. Boston: Feminist Press, 1989. 1–6.

Walkerdine, Valerie. *Schoolgirl Fictions.* London: Verso, 1990.

Walkerdine, Valerie, and the Girls and Mathematics Unit. *Counting Girls Out.* London, UK:

Virago, 1989.

Washington, Mary Helen. "Zora Neale Hurston: A Woman Half in Shadow." In *I Love Myself When I Am Laughing...And Then Again When I Am Looking Mean and Impressive: A Zora Neale Hurston Reader*. Ed. Alice Walker. Boston: Feminist Press, 1989. 7–25.

Weiler, Kathleen. "Freire and a Feminist Pedagogy of Difference." *Harvard Educational Review* 61.4 (1991): 449–474.

———. *Women Teaching for Change*. New York: Bergin and Garvey, 1988.

Weis, Lois, and Michelle Fine (Eds.). *Beyond Silenced Voices: Class, Race, and Gender in United States Schools*. Albany: State University of New York Press, 1993.

Wells, Susan. "Rogue Cops and Health Care: What Do We Want from Public Writing? *College Composition and Communication* 47.3 (1996): 323–341.

Whaley, Liz, and Liz Dodge. *Weaving in the Women: Transforming the High School English Curriculum*. Portsmouth, NH: Boynton/Cook-Heinemann, 1993.

Winterowd, Ross. "I. A. Richards and Romantic Composition." Paper presented at the Conference on College Composition and Communication. Cincinnati, OH. March 20, 1992.

Winterson, Jeannette. *Written on the Body*. New York: Vintage Books, 1992.

Witherell, Carol, and Nel Noddings. (Eds.). *Stories Lives Tell: Narrative and Dialogue in Education*. New York: Teachers College Press, 1991.

Wolf, Naomi. *Promiscuities: The Secret Struggle for Womanhood*. New York: Fawcett Columbine, 1997.

Woolf, Virginia. *A Room of One's Own*. New York: Harcourt Brace Jovanovich, 1929.

Zawicki, Teresa. "Recomposing as a Woman—An Essay in Different Voices." *College Composition and Communication* 43 (1992): 33–40.

Index

W

AC SS | Adolescent Cultures, School & Society

Joseph L. DeVitis & Linda Irwin-DeVitis
GENERAL EDITORS

As schools struggle to redefine and restructure themselves, they need to be cognizant of the new realities of adolescents. Thus, this series of monographs and textbooks is committed to depicting the variety of adolescent cultures that exist in today's post-industrial societies. It is intended to be a primarily qualitative research, practice, and policy series devoted to contextual interpretation and analysis that encompasses a broad range of interdisciplinary critique. In addition, this series will seek to provide a pragmatic, pro-active response to the current backlash of conservatism that continues to dominate political discourse, practice, and policy. This series seeks to address issues of curriculum theory and practice; multicultural education; aggression and violence; the media and arts; school dropouts; homeless and runaway youth; alienated youth; at-risk adolescent populations; family structures and parental involvement; and race, ethnicity, class, and gender studies.

Send proposals and manuscripts to the general editors at:

Joseph L. DeVitis & Linda Irwin-DeVitis
College of Education and Human Development
University of Louisville
Louisville, KY 40292-0001

To order other books in this series, please contact our Customer Service Department at:

(800) 770-LANG (within the U.S.)
(212) 647-7706 (outside the U.S.)
(212) 647-7707 FAX

or browse online by series at:

WWW.PETERLANGUSA.COM